Prefaces to Shakespeare

Prefaces to
SHAKESPEARE

By Harley Granville-Barker

VOLUME III

Antony and Cleopatra
Coriolanus

WITH NOTES AND ILLUSTRATIONS BY
M . ST. CLARE BYRNE

PRINCETON, NEW JERSEY
PRINCETON UNIVERSITY PRESS

Publisher's Foreword

Because of the death of Harley Granville-Barker in Paris in August 1946, proof of this volume was not read by the author. The Preface to *Othello* was set from galley proof of the British edition, proofread by Mr. Granville-Barker before his death. The Preface to *Coriolanus* was set from the author's manuscript. The Prefaces to *Romeo and Juliet, Julius Cæsar* and *Love's Labour's Lost* are taken from the previously published British editions, with the exception of the analysis of the character of Cassius in *Julius Cæsar*, which the author reworked for this edition.

The manuscript of the Preface to *Coriolanus* was accompanied by the following note by Mr. Granville-Barker, dated March 1946:

"This Preface was first outlined in the form of lectures— the Alexander Lectures—given at University College, Toronto, in 1942. Let me thank Principal Wallace for his unbounded kindness to me on that occasion, his colleagues too. Professor Alexander himself was then still alive, and I found him among my audience; that also something not easily to be forgotten.

"For text I have used the (English) Arden edition, noting any departures from it and my reasons for them."

About the Author

THE unique appeal of Harley Granville-Barker's *Prefaces to Shakespeare* lies in his position as a great figure of the English theater in his own right. As a dramatist, actor and producer, he was keenly aware of the problems faced by the playwright Shakespeare.

Born in London in 1877, Granville-Barker began his stage career touring with Ben Greet and Mrs. Patrick Campbell before he made his first London appearance in 1892. A list of his engagements at the turn of the century contains plays which made theatrical history: *Under the Red Robe, Mrs. Warren's Profession, Man and Superman.* In 1904 he joined with J. E. Vedrenne in management, an event which has been called one of the most notable theatrical enterprises of the modern stage. They produced a distinguished series of plays—revivals of Euripides, Shakespeare and Ibsen, and the work of the rising young dramatists Shaw and Galsworthy. In 1915 his company made its first New York appearance, bringing American playgoers *Androcles and the Lion.*

As a playwright Granville-Barker added to his reputation in the theater. Perhaps his best-known works are *The Voysey Inheritance, Waste,* and *Madras House. Prunella* he wrote with Laurence Housman, and he adapted a number of plays from French, Spanish and German for the English stage. He was one of the foremost champions of a national theater for Great Britain, and was co-author with William Archer of *Scheme and Estimates for a National Theatre.* In 1934 he wrote with G. B. Harrison *A Companion to Shakespeare Studies.* The Prefaces, originally commissioned for an edition of *The Players' Shakespeare,* which was never completed, appeared over a period of twenty years. The Preface to *Coriolanus* was finished in 1946 shortly before his death.

Contents

The Illustrations

IN Volume I the first sixteen pages of plates provided a pictorial commentary for some of the ideas expounded by Granville-Barker in his *Introduction*. In this volume the first eight pages give a visual account of classical costume as seen through the Renaissance imagination, as this, Barker believed, was the way the Roman plays were dressed in Shakespeare's theatre; and in the *Preface* to *Antony and Cleopatra* he states that although the players may not have been able to indulge in equal splendour, "we can guess at the sort of figures they made by turning to extant designs for the Court Masks" (p. 42). It was the method he advocated for modern productions, and it has behind it a long theatrical tradition, which, as these preliminary illustrations show, was not abandoned in favour of archaeology and accuracy until the nineteenth century. Barker discusses the subject in his *Introduction* (Vol. I, pp. 18-21), in the *Julius Caesar* Preface (Vol. II, pp. 217-219), and in this *Antony and Cleopatra* Preface (pp. 41-44). After reading these passages, the illustrations should prove largely self-explanatory. Two of Ernst Stern's costume designs for *Julius Caesar* in *The Players' Shakespeare* are included, as I cannot think the resemblance between Barker's ideas and Stern's drawings was fortuitous.

THE PLATES

1-18 RENAISSANCE-ROMANISM

LINE ILLUSTRATION

Acknowledgments

MY thanks are due, as in the former volumes, to the Arts Council of Great Britain for permission to use the material I collected for their 1947 exhibition, *The History of Shakespearian Production in England*; and I am again indebted to Common Ground (1951) Ltd. and Miss Joan Beard for photographic work. I gratefully acknowledge the courtesy of the owners in permitting reproduction of the following items: the Trustees of the National Gallery, London, No. 1; the Most Honourable the Marquess of Bath, No. 2; His Grace the Duke of Devonshire and the Trustees of the Chatsworth Settlement, No. 4; the Trustees of the London Museum, Nos. 11, 12, 37, 38, 49; the Vic-Wells Association, Nos. 17, 18, and the *Daily Sketch*, No. 18; the *Daily Mirror*, Nos. 19-22; the Birmingham Public Library, No. 36; Mr. W. Bridges-Adams and Mr. J. B. Charlesworth, Nos. 40, 41; the British Theatre Museum Association, (photos, the late J. W. Debenham), Nos. 44 and 46; Mr. C. Walter Hodges and Messrs. Ernest Benn for Fig. A; and the Old Vic and the Royal Shakespeare Theatre, Stratford-upon-Avon for all photographs of their productions. Acknowledgments are also due to the following for the use of copyright photographs: Peter Norris, No. 23; Houston Rogers, Nos. 24-27; Angus McBean, Nos. 28, 29, 31-34, 47; Cecil Beaton, No. 30; John Vickers, Nos. 42, 43. The following authors, editors, representatives and publishers have kindly given permission for the use of extracts: Mr. George Rylands and *Shakespeare Survey*; Mr. Richard Findlater and William Heinemann Ltd., *Michael Redgrave, Actor; Shakespeare Quarterly*; Jonathan Cape Ltd., *Brief Chronicles* by James Agate; Mr. Laurence Kitchin and Faber and Faber Ltd., *Mid-Century Drama*; Miss Audrey Williamson and Barrie and Rockliff (Barrie Books Ltd.) *Old Vic Drama*; Mr. Kenneth Tynan and Longmans, Green and Co. Ltd., *Curtains*. My personal thanks for help, information and loans are due to the following: Sir Michael Redgrave, Mr. Glen Byam Shaw, Mr. Anthony Quayle, Mr. Alec Clunes, Mr. J. C. Trewin; Mr. Martin Holmes of the London Museum; Mr. George Nash of the Enthoven Collection and his assistants, Miss M. Johnson and Mr. E. Lovelock; Miss Ranken of the Vic-Wells Association; Miss Eileen Robinson, Librarian of the Royal Shakespeare Theatre; Miss Mary Garnham, Librarian of the British Drama League; and Miss Anne Bolton of the Old Vic and Mr. Vincent Pearmain of the Royal Shakespeare Theatre.   M.S.B.

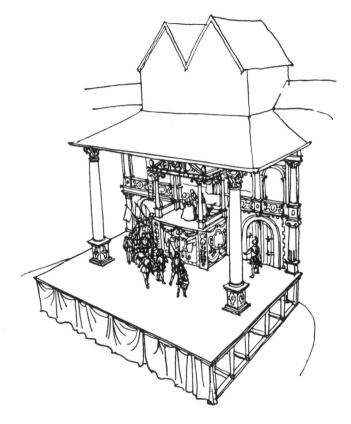

(A) ANTONY AND CLEOPATRA

A conjectural arrangement of the monument scene on the Shakespearian
stage, by C. Walter Hodges

Antony and Cleopatra

HERE is the most spacious of the plays. It may lack the spiritual intimacy of *Hamlet*, the mysterious power of *Macbeth*, the nobilities of *Othello*, may reach neither to the heights nor depths of *King Lear*; but it has a magnificence and a magic all its own, and Shakespeare's eyes swept no wider horizon.

Eight years or so earlier he had written *Julius Cæsar*. There already are these rivals Antony and Octavius, comrades then; and the main clash of fortune and character is between Antony and Brutus, between the man of action and the idealist. Antony comes from it victorious; the tragedy is the soul's tragedy of Brutus. Thereafter Shakespeare gives us play after play upon this theme of the self-torturing soul. Hamlet (its chief exemplar), Othello, Macbeth, Lear are all concerned with the world within themselves. Now he returns to the world of great affairs, and, almost as if for emphasis, to the very pair that he left standing over the dead body of the idealist in defeat.[1]

We have a play of action, then, not of spiritual insight; that is the first thing to mark. Of a large field of action too. For if with *Julius Cæsar* the insularity of the earlier Histories was left behind, we are shown now not Rome in her might only, but the whole range of the Empire, eastward to Athens, Egypt and the Parthian bounds. Antony, the once-triumphant man of action, is hero; we are to watch his defeat by his subtler sometime pupil. Truly it is his passion for Cleopatra that is his ruin, and the action pulses to this; but the wider issue dictates form, method and the bulk of the play's content.

---

[1] And a little later he took Coriolanus, another Roman, another man of action, for tragic hero.

A tragedy of disillusion, we might call it. As to the lovers, from the beginning they have little to learn about each other.

> She is cunning past man's thought.

says Antony; and Cleopatra is very soon lashing at him with

> O most false love!
> Where be the sacred vials thou shouldst fill
> With sorrowful water? Now I see, I see,
> In Fulvia's death, how mine received shall be.

(though the event belies her). But the whole picture is shaded to this sere hue. "My son," said Oxenstierne, "you will be amazed to discover with how little wisdom the world is governed." We may sit through this play and add, "With how little honor or honesty or decency either!" Shakespeare had not idealized the earlier Antony, nor—though the sketch of him is so slight— underrated Octavius.[2] But the dead Cæsar's champion was at least a gallant fellow, able and alert. In his stead we now see

> The triple pillar of the world transformed
> Into a strumpet's fool.

And that industrious apprentice Octavius, as he nears his reward, grows under our eyes ever colder of heart, more meanly calculating, more deliberately false. We meet Lepidus again, the "barren-spirited fellow," as barren still of everything but efforts to keep the peace somehow, since only so can he hope to keep his own weak head above water; and we see Octavius belatedly following Antony's politic advice to

> turn him off,
> Like to the empty ass, to shake his ears
> And graze in commons.

We meet Pompey, the foolish optimist, the lucky fighter cajoled to an unstable peace, standing on his honor, but as willing to profit by the vilest treachery. Ventidius is the one Roman to be found fighting Rome's enemies instead of his fellow Romans; and he dare not push victory home for fear of Antony's jealousy. We have Enobarbus; a man (the bitter paradox!) corrupted most by fidelity to his friend, then turning traitor—too late! Towards the

---

[2] And we may even read into passages of *Julius Cæsar* a foreshadowing of the breach between the two.

play's end comes a very procession of generals, soldiers and dutiful servants, their fidelity abused, their valor wasted. Some desert while they can and some are caught in their leader's insensate ruin. While as to the Roman people themselves, the republic for which Brutus and Cassius died, the Friends, Romans, Countrymen who were Antony's "good friends, sweet friends," what have their saviors and masters to say of them now? For Antony they are

> our slippery people,
> Whose love is never linked to the deserver
> Till his deserts are past . . .

and Cæsar, a scene or so later (it cannot be fortuitously), is made to speak of

> The ebb'd man, ne'er loved till ne'er worth love . . .

and, with what contempt, of how

> This common body,
> Like to a vagabond flag upon the stream,
> Goes to and fro, lackeying the varying tide,
> To rot itself with motion.

Not, on the whole then, a hopeful picture of the Roman world. And it is, in the main, Shakespeare's own picture; if he pillages Plutarch for facts, even for phrases, their interpretation and emphasis—all that makes a picture—are his.

Bradley will not place the play with the four great tragedies, because, he says, Antony and Cleopatra themselves do not kindle pity and admiration to the full. He admits, though, that their passion and its ending is by no means the whole of the story. Certainly it is not. What are we shown to begin with? Far less a pair of tragic lovers in the making than—through the indignant Roman eyes of Philo and Demetrius—a doting general, effeminate in Egyptian finery,[3] ignoring Cæsar's messengers, capable of a

> Let Rome in Tiber melt, and the wide arch
> Of the ranged empire fall! . . .

(whoever will may hear it!), and a debauched Eastern queen, mocking at things Roman, battening on his apostasy. Here at once

---

[3] The "strumpet's fool" is some warrant for this; Cæsar's reference to Cleopatra not being "more womanly than he" is more.

is the larger theme emphasized, the discord which is to be resolved at last to a full close in the elaborate confusions of their defeat and death. The love-tragedy, we might almost say, is not made the main question till no other question is left, till the ruin wreaked by Triumvir and Queen is accomplished. And the action of the play is schemed throughout for the picturing of this wider ruin. Hence its diffuseness; and hence, if this is not understood, much misunderstanding of its artistry.

"*Feliciter audax*," says Coleridge of the style, and the label has stuck. Dr. Johnson, however, is stern. "The events, of which the principal are described according to history, are produced without any art of connection or care of disposition." It never does to neglect Johnson. His plain-sailing sanity will cut a clear way for us through many a metaphysical fog of nineteenth century criticism. Even if at last we must disagree with him, he takes answering. But he owns besides that "this play keeps curiosity always busy and the passions always interested" and that "the continual hurry of the action, the variety of incidents, and the quick succession of one personage to another call the mind forward without intermission from the first Act to the last." So in the end—Johnson exhibiting, perhaps, less consistency than usual—he and Coleridge are found not so far apart.

Feliciter audax! Shakespeare does seem to be amazingly at his ease. He brings in characters lavishly, flings Plutarch into dialogue; his verse is at its supplest, we are hardly conscious of the convention, and he shifts it to prose and back again without a jar. The action moves forthright and unchecked. Yet little or nothing in it shows superfluous; and, though endowed with but a line or two, the characters never fail to come to life. And if all this comes about "without any art of connection or care of disposition," if it all seems haphazard, is it not just possible Shakespeare may mean it to, may at least be content that it should? There is little luck in these matters, as the inexpert playwright who tries his along these lines will find. Do we perhaps pay a tribute to this art in so condemning it? Critics have found themselves performing this feat before now. But, in fact, the play's scheme is plain and ordered enough once we grasp its purpose, and—the essential thing—once we relate it to the theater of its nativity.

The Play's Construction

THE MAIN PROBLEM AND SOME MINOR ONES

WE should never, probably, think of Shakespeare as sitting down to construct a play as an architect must design a house, in the three dimensions of its building. His theater did not call for this, as the more rigorous economics of modern staging may be said to do. He was liker to a musician, master of an instrument, who takes a theme and, by generally recognized rules, improvises on it; or even to an orator, so accomplished that he can carry a complex subject through a two-hour speech, split it up, run it by divers channels, digress, but never for too long, and at last bring the streams abreast again to blend them in his peroration. Clarity of statement, a sense of proportion, of the value of contrast, justness of emphasis—in these lie the technique involved; and these, it will be found, are the dominant qualities of Shakespeare's stagecraft—of the craft merely, be it understood.

He is apt to lay the main lines of his story very firmly and simply, and to let us see where we are going from the start, to cut the complexities from borrowed plots, and if any side issue later promises distraction, to make (literally) short work of it. Here he reduces the actual story to simplicity itself. Antony breaks from Cleopatra to patch up an insincere peace with Cæsar, since Pompey threatens them both; he marries Octavia, and deserts her to return to Cleopatra; war breaks out, Cæsar defeats them and they kill themselves. That is the plot; every character is concerned with it, hardly a line is spoken that does not relate to it; and much strength lies in this concentration of interest. There is no underplot, nor any such obvious relief (which must, however, bring dissipation of interest too) as Falstaff, Nym, Bardolph, Pistol and Fluellen give to the heroics of the Henriad.

But, for a broad picturesque contrast, Roman and Egyptian are set against each other; and this opposition braces the whole body of the play, even as conflict between character and character will sustain each scene. He asserts the contrast at once; for we assemble expectant in a theater, therefore first impressions cut deep and a first stretch of action will be of prime importance. We have the two indignant, hard-bitten Roman campaigners, who must stand aside while the procession passes—

Cleopatra, her ladies, the train, with Eunuchs fanning her.

—and see Antony in the toils. Their bitter comments follow it. Next, we have a taste of the chattering, shiftless, sensual, credulous Court, with its trulls and wizards and effeminates.[4] Then we see Antony, with Rome, the "garboils" of his wife's making and the threats of Pompey calling him, breaking his toils for a time; and the statement of the theme is complete.

Do events now proceed (we ask Dr. Johnson) "without any art of connection or care of disposition"? We are shown Cæsar, the passionate Antony's passionless rival, correct and charmless, in conference with Lepidus—that third and very feeble pillar of the world!—upon their poor prospects, while Antony's "lascivious wassails" hold him in Egypt. The action then swings back to a Cleopatra sighing after an Antony, who is already travelling Romeward; then to Pompey, questionably confident in his rising star.

> If the great gods be just, they shall assist
> The deeds of justest men.

Much virtue—and some risk—in such an if! And we pass at once to the knitting-up of the alliance that is to eclipse him.

Cæsar and Antony (when he is in his senses) are realists both, and there is neat wary work all round before their bargain is made, with the marriage to Octavia for a seal to it. A long passage, comparatively; but how artfully it is proportioned and modulated! First comes the straight dispute between the rivals. This must, of course, be given full importance, for here is the play's main clash. But it is salted by the ironies of Enobarbus, lightened by Lepidus and his fussiness, eased by Mæcenas and Agricola and their tact. Now, the dispute over and the alliance made, the worth of it will be shown us. The great men depart to the sound of

---

[4] There was possibly more matter in the scene at one time. Lamprius, Rannius and Lucillius, whose entrance survives, will hardly have been brought on, this first and last time, for nothing. Was there chaffing between Romans and Egyptians? Nothing is left of it, if so, but Enobarbus'

> Mine, and most of our fortunes to-night shall be—drunk to bed.

Or did Shakespeare, having written the stage directions, discover he could make enough effect without them?

trumpets; the three pillars of the world, mutual in its support
again. And while Antony, absent from our sight, does his brisk
wooing, Enobarbus talks to the gloating Agrippa, and the somewhat shocked Mæcenas—of Cleopatra! Note that the famous
panegyric comes from a coarse-mouthed cynic; he, too, can feel
her witchery.

> MÆCENAS. Now Antony must leave her utterly.
> ENOBARBUS. Never! He will not.
> Age cannot wither her, nor custom stale
> Her infinite variety. Other women cloy
> The appetites they feed: but she makes hungry
> Where most she satisfies; for vilest things
> Become themselves in her, that the holy priests
> Bless her when she is riggish.

With this in our ears,

> *Enter Antony, Cæsar, Octavia between them.*

and we hear Octavia (the difference!) with her gentle gravity,
saying

> Before the gods my knee shall bow my prayers
> To them for you.

So Shakespeare weaves his pattern—for another simile—as he
goes along, setting color against color, coarse thread by fine. And
certainly the thing is done with such seeming ease and natural
subtlety that we hardly note the artistry involved. We should feel
the flat poverty of its absence soon enough.

Now another thread is woven in. The Soothsayer, symbol of the
East, comes shadowing Antony, warping and weakening his
will.[5] Then follows (contrast again) a touch of Roman energy;
Ventidius is dispatched to Parthia. Then we are flung back to
Egypt and to Cleopatra; and in redoubled contrast—for Shake-
speare has now begun to bite upon the ironies of his theme—to a
Cleopatra most unlike the golden vision of Cydnus, a spitting

[5] The Romans had their soothsayers too; but this one, by costume and association, would recall us to Cleopatra's Court. What modern playwright would so
opulently employ him—bring him from Egypt, even by Plutarch's permission
—to such seemingly small purpose? Here we see the extravagant ease of Shakespeare's maturest stagecraft. But the episode yields the exact effect needed, not an
iota more.

fury that hales the messenger of Antony's faithlessness up and
down by the hair of his head. Truly

> Age cannot wither her, nor custom stale
> Her infinite variety.

Now we return to Cæsar and his policies, to the successful
maneuvering of Pompey to a peace, thanks to Antony and his
prestige. What the worth of this also will be we learn as before
when the great men have done and their followers talk things
over (harsh truths are heard in anterooms). Or we might judge
it for ourselves by its crowning in a drinking bout. The wretched
Lepidus cannot last this out; and that first bitter outbreak at the
sight of the "strumpet's fool" has its derisive echo in Enobarbus'

> There's a strong fellow, Menas . . . . 'A bears the third part of
> the world, man: see'st not?

And the chivalrous Pompey, we find, would be glad to have his
guests' throats cut—by someone less chivalrous than he! Cæsar
alone keeps his head; but we hardly like him the better for that.
Then, sharp upon the crapulous business, Shakespeare shows us

> *Ventidius, as it were in triumph, . . the dead body of Pacorus*
> *borne before him.*

He has beaten back the Parthians. But now he dare not, for his
own safety's sake, do Rome better service still, with such masters
—hers and his—jealously watching him.

> Oh Silius, Silius,
> I have done enough; a lower place, note well,
> May make too great an act: for learn this, Silius;
> Better to leave undone, than by our deed
> Acquire too high a fame when him we serve's away.

Here is so notable and typical a piece of stagecraft that it is
worth while to try and see the full effect of it. There is, of course,
the aspect, which any alert reader discovers: the contrasting of
the soldiers at their duty with the rulers at their drinking bout.[6]
But we must keep Shakespeare's stage well in mind if we are to
realize the dramatic value to the spectator of the quick shift from

---

[6] The Folio page displays the relation between the two scenes. But Rowe made
an act-division between them, and later editors have copied him (of which more
on p. 12), so that even this much of the effect may pass unnoticed.

singing and dancing and the confusion of tipsy embracings to the strict military march that brings Ventidius *as in triumph* upon the stage. There was no pause at all; Enobarbus and Menas would hardly have vanished, their drunken halloos would still be echoing when Ventidius and his procession appeared. This set the contrast at its sharpest; yet, since change of scene did not mean change of scenery, there was no distracting of mind or eye, a unity of effect was kept, and the action flowed on unchecked.

With one more interweaving of themes we shall be halfway through the play. Enobarbus' and Agrippa's mockeries give an acrid aftertaste to feast, treaty and marriage, all three; and we are to guess that poor Lepidus—so spendthrift of good nature!—will be made bankrupt soon. Antony and Octavia take their loving farewell of Cæsar and lovingly depart. An instant after we see Cleopatra, recovered from her fury, having Octavia's attractions picked to pieces for her comfort by the much repentant messenger.

> Dull of tongue and dwarfish! . . .
> Widow! Charmian, hark! . . .
>   Why, methinks by him
> This creature's no such thing. . . .
> The man hath seen some majesty, and should know. . . .
> All may be well enough.

And, watching her smile, we need have little doubt but that it will be. Very little; for as she leaves the stage (yet again only upon an Elizabethan stage will the effect fully count),

> *Enter Antony and Octavia.*

with the rift that is to part them already showing.

Thus (if Johnson still needs answering, we can turn his own words against him now) curiosity has been kept busy and the passions interested, and the continual hurry of the action, the variety of incidents and the quick succession of one personage to another have called the mind forward without intermission . . . which is what Shakespeare has set out to do. He has told his story, woven his pattern, kept conflict alive and balance true, character prompting action, and action elucidating character, neither made to halt for the other. This really is the be-all and end-all of his stagecraft—and might well be said to be of any stagecraft; it is only the application of the method that will differ from stage to stage.

We may note in passing how he turns one small technical difficulty that he stumbles on to his profit (he has always had the faculty of doing this), and thereafter how he cuts his way out of another. Throughout this first part of the play he has more Roman than Egyptian material to deal with. Somehow he must keep the balance true and Cleopatra pretty constantly in our minds; but all the story asks is that she should be left by Antony and then sit waiting, patiently or impatiently, for his return. A more mechanical minded playwright would have begun, then, with Cæsar and Pompey, and so have accounted for some of the overplus at once; would have made, consequently, a mild beginning, and given a minor interest precedence. With Shakespeare what most matters will have pride of place, nor will he, when he has it, abate a chance; and, as we see, he lets the impulse of his opening carry him to the point of Antony's departure, over a stretch of 365 lines, abundant in life and color (it is actually a tenth of the entire play), till he has his story's master-motive made fertile in our minds. But now he must eke out the rest of the Egyptian material very carefully. The glimpse of Cleopatra pursuing her Antony before he is well away from her with "twenty several messengers" could (if the need were rather for compression) be dispensed with; but it is true and significant Cleopatra, so this may fill up a space. What next? When the news of her lover's treachery has been brought her the material will have run out; so this episode is split up and spread over two scenes. And at once Shakespeare sees and seizes the chance to show us, first the savage and suffering Cleopatra; next, on the rebound, the colder, baser-natured woman, feeding on flattery and deceit—and well aware of their worth. The story is molded to the development of character. Each scene of Cleopatra's, throughout this first part of the play, adds something to our knowledge of her; they accumulate to inform the tragedy of her end.

But now, though the two themes are abreast (Antony's concord with Cæsar seen on the wane, while Cleopatra, spiderlike, sits spinning a new web for him), it is clear, both that the Roman political material still outmeasures the Egyptian and that it may lengthen this part of the play into dangerous monotony. The Antony-Octavia theme might be elaborated for a variation. Shakespeare decides against this; it would still leave Cleopatra in the air. There is no more for her to do, that's evident, till Antony returns to her. Roman politics, then, must in turn suffer heroic compression. The wars upon Pompey and his murder, Cæsar's new quarrel with Antony, the extinction of Lepidus, are reported in a scene or so.

But neither are we shown Antony's return to Cleopatra; Cæsar recounts it to Octavia and his friends. There were other reasons against this. Shakespeare is not, as we have argued, writing a mere love-story, he is transplanting history to the stage; the causes and circumstances of the quarrel and the war that is to end at Actium are, at this juncture, the more important matter to him, and they must be given the widest significance words can give them, a wider if vaguer significance than concrete action will give. He could have shown us effectively enough how

> In Alexandria . . .
> I' the market-place, on a tribunal silvered,
> Cleopatra and himself [Antony] in chairs of gold
> Were publicly enthroned . . . .

But in Cæsar's

> No, my most wronged sister, Cleopatra
> Hath nodded him to her. He hath given his Empire
> Up to a whore; who now are levying
> The kings o' the earth for war. He hath assembled
> Bocchus, the king of Libya; Archelaus,
> Of Cappadocia; Philadelphos, king
> Of Paphlagonia; the Thracian king, Adallas;
> King Manchus of Arabia; King of Pont;
> Herod of Jewry; Mithridates, king
> Of Comagene; Polemon and Amyntas,
> The kings of Mede and Lycaonia,
> With a more larger list of sceptres.

a threat to the whole Roman world seems sounded.

Besides, the play's crisis is to come. These scenes are preparation for it, no more; they must be kept tense, but low in tone. The rivals are still only strengthening themselves for the struggle, with indignation as with arms.

Incidentally, Shakespeare will be glad to avoid a scene of reconciliation if it is to involve his boy-actress in any sort of "amorous transports." The play is dominated by sexual passion, no bones are made about the carnality of it either; yet how carefully he avoids writing any scene which a boy could not act without unpleasantness or in fear of ridicule![7] The fatal reunion is far more significantly marked by Cleopatra's spitfire quarrel with Enobarbus.

> CLEOPATRA. I will be even with thee, doubt it not . . . .
>   Thou hast forspoke my being in these wars,
>   And sayst it is not fit.
> ENOBARBUS. Well, is it, is it? . . .
>   Your presence needs must puzzle Antony,
>   Take from his heart, take from his brain, from 's
>   time,
>   What should not then be spared. He is already
>   Traduced for levity, and 'tis said in Rome,
>   That Photinus an Eunuch, and your maids
>   Manage this war.

For from this it is that disaster springs; this is the beginning of the end.

Yet we are but halfway through the play; and here is another sign that a larger theme than the love-story is being worked out. Would Shakespeare otherwise be giving, against all precedent, half his play's length to its catastrophe? Now, it is the craft and the art of this long ending that have been most distorted by editors, its intention most grievously misunderstood by critics. A producer must not only start afresh from the untouched text, he must read it in the light of a clear understanding of the stage of its origin.[8]

The Question of Act-Division

To begin with he must free the play from act and scene divisions. The Folio gives none. The first five-act division was Rowe's. Johnson thought the first scene of his second act might better be

---

[7] For the further, and important, implication of this, see p. 69 *et seq.*

[8] The Folio text itself may have been edited, I know; but not to the measure of another stage than Shakespeare's.

the last scene of his first, but added ". . . it is of small importance, where these unconnected and desultory scenes are interrupted." Pope made the first scene of Rowe's fifth act into the last scene of Act IV, and after this all the later editors seem to have fallen unquestioningly into line. A five-act division for any play has, of course, its sanctions. The editors of the Folio indulge in it when they think they will. They (they or their printer for them) start out each time with an *Actus Primus, Scæna Prima*; a schoolboy's heading for his copybook. Sometimes they keep this up, once or twice they get halfway through the play and give it up; sometimes, as with *Antony and Cleopatra*, they just leave it at that. Now, whatever other dramatists may have done, whatever Shakespeare may have done in other plays, whatever may have been the custom of the public and private theaters for which he wrote—and it was probably a differing and a changing one—in the matter of making pauses during a performance, and whether those pauses were formal or prolonged, in this play there is no *dramatically* indicated act-division at all. There is, that is to say, (as far as I can discover) no juncture where the play's acting will be made more effective by a pause. On the contrary, each scene has an effective relation to the next, which a pause between them will weaken or destroy. There may have been four pauses in the original performing, or three, two or one; there may have been none at all, though that is hardly likely. But it would always (again, as far as I can discern) be a question of custom or convenience, not of dramatic effect.

Granted five acts, a case can be made for Rowe's choice of them, or Johnson's, or Pope's, or for half a dozen others, doubtless; and as good a one perhaps for a four-act division or a three. And if, pleading weakness of the flesh in actors or audience, a producer thinks it well to split the play into two, he can call a convenient halt, he'll find, at the turn of the action when Antony's drift back to Cleopatra is plainly to be seen. He may pause with some effect after that

> All may be well enough.

or pass on a little further before he pauses and begins again (perhaps with better) with the news that

Cæsar and Lepidus have made wars upon Pompey.

or with Cæsar's own outburst of indignation and the return of
Octavia; or, more forcibly still, with the squabble between Cleopatra and Enobarbus and the launching of the war. But let him
plead convenience merely; for any halt hereabouts must mean
rather the loss of an effect than the making one. And this will be
as true of any other pauses in any other places; and the lengthier
they are the worse it will be.

For the fact is that Shakespeare's work never parcels up very
well. He was not among those writers who industriously gather
material, sort and arrange and rearrange it before they fit it
together. When his mood is operative he creates out of an abun-
dance of vitality, and it is no good service to him to start obstruct-
ing the flow of it. He keeps, however, for all his fervor, a keen
sense of form; it is largely in this marriage of impulse and control
that his genius as pure playwright lies. And when inspiration
flags, he must come to contriving. He is businesslike at that, quite
callously businesslike sometimes. But even to the most workaday
stuff he gives a certain force. And should carelessness—for he can
be wickedly careless—land him in a tight place, there is, to the
practiced observer, a sort of sporting interest in seeing him so
nimbly and recklessly get out of it.

He does not (*pace* Dr. Johnson) write haphazardly; it is not
that. He plans—and more spaciously than those that have need to
plan. He is seldom to be found following a formula, even a proved
one of his own. Incidental devices he'll use again and again, as
we all repeat words and phrases—and the deeper (one notices) the
feelings beneath them the simpler these are apt to be. He is the
last man we should look to find submitting himself to an arbitrary
scheme, whatever its sanction, a five-act scheme or any other. Custom might even be imposing this on a play's performance and
impose it no further on him. And by now he has brought much
to the theater, broken much new ground, has the medium very
plastic in his hands. With such a task as this before him, and his
imagination fired, he will be out to do it as effectively as he can.
There will be no other question. He will have to muster all his
resources, and he will need full freedom for the use of them.

A Digression, Mainly upon the Meaning of the Word "Scene"

But it is hard for us to meet him with a mind as free. The medium that he worked in so spontaneously is alien to us. Even the nomenclature under which we discuss it betrays us to error. Setting disputable act-division aside, what do we mean by scene-division and by "scene"? There are no reliable scene-divisions in the Quartos.[9] The editors of the Folio sometimes run to them, and they customarily draw their dividing lines at each clearance of the stage. But this does not commit them to an imagined change of place, nor connote any check to the action.[10] By Rowe's time, however, "scene" had taken on, though still uncertainly, a new meaning. Painted scenery, of a more or less conventional sort, was in current use. This defined locality; and a change of scene meant a change of place, was a diversion and a check to the action in every sense. The old fluidity of the Elizabethan stage, which really could "call the mind forward without intermission," was gone.

If Rowe finds act-division in the Folio he leaves it, and he cuts the plays with none to a similar pattern. His chief editorial task is to give them geography; but as he leaves scene-division too when he finds it he cannot do this very consistently; his "scene" being no longer the "scene" of the Folio editors. In *As You Like It,* for instance, he must leave some of the old scene-divisions unexplained; there are far too many for him. In *Othello* there are too few; the action will not abide throughout some of these where he has placed it. In *A Midsummer Night's Dream* he announces, to begin with, *Athens, and a wood not far from it,* and troubles no more. He looks at the plays when he can in the light of his own theater, for he is presenting them to readers accustomed to it. He disregards the many signs that they do not really belong there;

---

[9] I insert "reliable," because Q1 of *Romeo and Juliet* does happen to show some uncertain recognition of scenes.

[10] They make their slips, however (see the Preface to *Cymbeline,* Vol. II, p. 99). They followed classic practice, even as today the French, going further, generally begin a fresh scene whenever a fresh character enters or when a character leaves the stage. Scene does not connote place at all, and the "scene" of the play, in the pictorial sense of the word, stays unchanged throughout.

the matter, for one thing, is of no great importance, for another, some memory of the old theater still survives.

Antony and Cleopatra, however, offers Rowe a clean sheet, and he takes trouble. At first he does no more scene-dividing than the sense of place in his own stagecraft compels him to. He is content with a generalized *Alexandria*; *Rome*; *Sicily*; *The coast of Italy near Misenum*; *Athens*. He particularizes the very obvious *Pompey's Galley*, and later rises to the enthusiasm of *A Magnificent Monument*. But the comings and goings of the three days' battle defeat him. *Cæsar's camp* is a clear enough locality. *Cleopatra's Palace* and *Before the walls of Alexandria* will do. But the maneuverings of the armies, and, above all, that tiresome *noise of a sea-fight*, cannot be given exact place; and he is still free enough from realism to let them, with a few more such confusions, take their chance. Nevertheless he has now turned the long, unchecked stretch of action which was Shakespeare's into an Act III and IV of eight localized scenes each.[11] Later editors are to better him. As the theater of their day moves ever further from Elizabethan freedom and is the more committed to integrity of place they, for their part, dissect and define ever more closely; till modern editions give us a third act of thirteen scenes and a fourth of fifteen, with *A Plain near Actium*; *Another part of the Plain*; *Another part of the Plain*, following each other breathlessly. Only that tiresome *noise of a sea-fight* still refuses its pigeonhole.

What of Shakespeare's stagecraft is left? What dramatic purpose of any kind is conveyed by this?

Act III. *Scene viii. A Plain near Actium.*

Enter Cæsar and Taurus with his army, marching.

CÆSAR.   Taurus!
TAURUS. My lord?
CÆSAR.   Strike not by land; keep whole: provoke not battle
    Till we have done at sea. Do not exceed
    The prescript of this scroll: our fortune lies
    Upon this jump.

Exeunt.

Scene ix. Another part of the Plain.
Enter Antony and Enobarbus.

[11] Strictly speaking, Rowe begins his three days' fighting with Act III, Scene vi, *Actium.*

ANTONY. Set we our squadrons on yond' side o' the hill,
 In eye of Cæsar's battle; from which place
 We may the number of the ships behold,
 And so proceed accordingly.

           Exeunt.

  Scene x. Another part of the Plain.
 *Canidius marcheth with his land army one way over
 the stage; and Taurus, the lieutenant of Cæsar, the
 other way. After their going in is heard the noise
 of a sea-fight.*
  Alarum. Enter Enobarbus.

ENOBARBUS. Naught, naught, all naught! I can behold no longer:
 Th' Antoniad, the Egyptian admiral,
 With all their sixty, fly and turn the rudder. . . .

This last so-called "scene" does run on for thirty-five lines more.

The layman must remember that he is reading a play, and should be imaginatively translating it into performance as he reads. Into what sort of performance do the editors help him to translate this, and the whole stretch of action from the eve of the first battle with Cæsar to the carrying of Antony dying to the Monument? They parcel it into twenty-two scenes, two of four lines each, one of six, one of nine, one of ten, three of sixteen lines and two of twenty-two; the rest are of more normal length. Scenes, as the editors of the Folio understood the word, they may be; as localized scenes they make dramatic nonsense.

Do the modern editors mean us to envisage the play in performance with painted scenery shifting every minute or so, transporting us round Actium, from one camp to another, to Alexandria and back again? Apparently. They know that Shakespeare's theater provided for nothing of the sort; do they never stop to think what the effect of this cinematographic patchwork of their devising must be?[12] But strike out their place-headings, and still think in terms of "scenes," and even then where are we? For Sir Edmund Chambers, who carries the Elizabethan stage pretty vividly in his eye, can tell us that in these passages "Shakespeare is in some danger of outrunning the apprehensions of his auditory."

Is it so? Sir Edmund will be using the word "auditory" with

---

[12] Modern producers, never looking back past them, have, of course, solved the problem with a liberal blue-pencil.

intention; but is he thinking of its members, not as listening merely, and looking at the actors, but imaginatively staring beyond them, making efforts to conjure up backgrounds that are never described, barely indicated, and being kept on the jump, asking themselves—while Cæsar and his men leave the stage empty for Antony and his men to fill it, only to leave it in a moment to Cæsar again—"Where on earth are we now?"

If the play's first audiences sat trying to do anything of the sort, Shakespeare certainly did outrun their apprehensions; and if Sir Edmund supposes that Shakespeare meant them to, no wonder he is dubious about its stagecraft; and no wonder that critics with not a tithe of his knowledge, vaguely agreeing, will cry it down. But (with respect) Shakespeare's intentions were utterly different, and his audiences were not puzzled at all.

Convention in art is hard to discount, and we accept the accustomed conventions of the theater more unquestioningly than most. The visual side of our modern "realistic" drama is itself conventional; but it has come, by slow degrees, so fully to its own that we are apt to apply the laws of it, quite unconsciously, to every sort of theater and play, as if they were natural laws.[13] The "visual law" of drama was, to the Elizabethans, a very different, and an arbitrary and inconstant thing besides. It had existed, crudely, in the miracle plays, and it became elaborately, decoratively dominant in the Masques. But on the public stages it was, for various reasons, unprofitably hard to develop, and only in the candle-lit "private" theaters were its claims finally made good. By "visual law" must be understood, of course, not the sight of the actors and their acting, unescapable in any play, but their environment, the background, against which they show, and which can be as histrionic in its kind as they. We are now so used to seeing this pictured, be it as *A drawing room in Mayfair*, or as *Piccadilly Circus*, or *The Forest of Arden*, or *A street in Venice*, or *Verona*, or *Rome*, that if it is not set before us we set ourselves to imagine it there; and we assume that the Elizabethans did the same—for, after all, the characters in a play must be somewhere. Yes, they must be, if we push the enquiry. But the Elizabethan dramatist seldom encour-

---

[13] This is less true certainly than it would have been twenty years ago, before so many experiments in newfangled (which is really oldfangled) staging had been made. But the normal stage of today is still the realistic stage.

ages us to push it; and his first audiences assuredly, as a rule, did not do so in despite of him. For them the actors were very plainly on the stage, but the characters might, half the time, be nowhere in particular. It was, for the dramatist of that day, a privilege akin to the novelist's, who may, if he chooses, detach characters, through page after page, from fixed surroundings. It was a freedom which the promise of the scenic stage gradually sapped; but Shakespeare, at least, never surrendered it, and we here find him in the maturity of his craftsmanship, enjoying and exploiting it to the full.

He will always have, of course, as the novelist has, the whereabouts of his characters in mind, and casual allusion to it will crop out. There may also be the demands of the action for a house door, a balcony, a tree or a cavern to be satisfied; but these things will have rather the utility of furniture than the value of scenery. And—this is the point—he need never give more attention to his play's background than he feels will be dramatically profitable. Moreover, he can give it—yet again as does the novelist—the *sort* of attention he chooses. Look at *Richard II*. Poetry is lavished on the characters and the theme in general. But it is never put to use for the verbal painting of a background.

> Believe me, noble lord,
> I am a stranger here in Gloucestershire:
> These high wild hills and rough uneven ways
> Draw out our miles and make them wearisome.

is the extremest instance of it. We are left, as a rule, to judge by the tenor of the action where the actors are; and in many cases it would be impossible for the listener to say. If we need to know with any precision, the simple label of such a line as

> Barkloughly Castle call they this at hand?

will suffice to tell us.

Take two of the Comedies.

> Well, this is the Forest of Arden.

sets us (in *As You Like It*) accurately enough where Shakespeare wishes us to be.[14] Scene after scene, so called, once this impression

---

[14] This, however (to be accurate oneself), is not our first introduction there. But we only know *where* the Banished Duke should be when we first meet him by a reference to him in the scene before.

is given us, may be taking place anywhere thereabouts; and, as it is a comedy of character, not much time is spent upon picturing the forest itself. Such description of it as we do get is fantastic and reflects the artifice of the story. But *A Midsummer Night's Dream* is one long lyrical painting of the wood near Athens, with its English banks of primroses and thyme, the oxlip and the nodding violet; for this is what the play's theme demands.

From such direct simplicity as this turn to *Macbeth*, to such passages as

> This castle hath a pleasant seat; the air
> Nimbly and sweetly recommends itself
> Unto our gentle senses. . . .

as

> The west yet glimmers with some streaks of day;
> Now spurs the lated traveller apace
> To gain the timely inn. . . .

to the recurring chorus of the witches—the play's writing is full of pictorial suggestion. It is suggestion rather than description, an elaborate creating of atmosphere:

> Light thickens; and the crow
> Makes wing to the rooky wood. . . .

Description in this play is, indeed, as nothing compared with suggestion. Whereabouts in the castle at Inverness we are throughout the comings and goings of Duncan's tragic sojourn we should never know if the editors did not tell us, nor what the rooms or courtyards look like. But what scene-painter will create such darkness for us as that in which a magic of words wraps the night of the murder?

But all through, and in every phase of Shakespeare's development, it is a question of dramatic profit and the particular need of the play. In *Antony and Cleopatra* we find, except for the one episode of the sentries on guard listening to the mysterious music, no verbal scene-painting of any sort, direct or implicit, nor, as we have noted, more than the very minimum of reference to the locality of the scenes. The reason is plain. It is a play of action and of multiplied incident. The story is simple, but the tributary threads of it are manifold, and the interweaving conflicts of purpose complex enough. Its theme (once again) is not merely Antony's love for Cleopatra, but his ruin as general and statesman, the final ascension of Octavius, and the true end of

that work the ides of March begun.

Therefore the dead Fulvia's doings, Pompey's grievances, Cæsar's policy, Lepidus and his timeserving, Ventidius balked of a bigger victory—these things and their like are of first importance, and we must be kept alive to them. But an audience has only a certain amount of attention to bestow, and it must be economized. It does not matter much where Cæsar and Lepidus, Pompey and Mene-crates and Menas have their talks, nor whether the bargaining with Antony takes place indoors or out; so Shakespeare spends hardly a thought or a line upon it. Nor upon the beauties of the prospect —nor the weather! Antony and Cæsar, we feel, would certainly take a prosaic view of such things; and, for our part, we shall know them no better for viewing them against a picturesque background. But that each turn in the battle of their quick, ruth-less Roman minds should be made clear to us—this matters a great deal, and to this all else, if need be, is sacrificed. Emotion, and at full pitch, is in store; but it will not be freed till the issues of the action are narrowing to the point of solution. Meanwhile, we have clarity, the clarity of a desert landscape, the theme in its stark integrity. *Antony and Cleopatra* is, among other things, the most businesslike of plays.

And if, for a beginning, this has been Shakespeare's aim, how much more, when we come to the confusions of the three days' battle, with its blunders and false hopes, its chances and changes, must not perfect clarity be achieved? Nor in the writing only, and by suppressing picturesque inessentials. Could he do what he sets out to do if he did not now exploit to the full the freedom from circumstance which the convention of his stage allows him? For this in itself gives clarity; it lets the dramatist concentrate upon the single subject. Complicate these twenty-two "scenes" as they flash past us by thinking of their whereabouts, and our limited power of attention will certainly not suffice.[15] But listen without further conjecture to the mere tale as the dialogue unfolds it, and watch just what we are asked to watch, the characters as they

[15] And if our eyes are distracted by changing scenery the strain will, of course, be worse still.

come and go and the symbolic marching of the armies, and there
is no confusion whatever—only such, at any rate, as Shakespeare
is at positive pains to be painting for us, in the hectic uncertainties
through which Antony moves to his end.

An audience need do no more than listen and look at what there
is to see and ask no questions. And audiences, as a fact, do no
more than they are asked to do. Would that they always did that!
Nothing will be heard of Actium, nor of a plain near it, nor
anything of the sort. There is talk of the obviously distant Toryne
and Peloponnesos. But from the beginning of this long stretch of
action to the end, till Antony is carried dying to the Monument,
there is hardly a hint to let us know where, at any moment, we
may imaginatively be. Shakespeare does not set out to inform us,
and he might sometimes be hard put to it to say himself.

> Cæsar sits down in Alexandria . . . .

we are told. The next day he is to be beaten to his camp, and
Antony will give the order:

> Through Alexandria make a jolly march.

But that same night, with Cæsar still in occupation, Antony's
sentries are on guard "about the streets." What streets? What does
it matter? Just nothing at all. We not only do not want to know;
it would be worse than useless to trouble us with the information.

If Shakespeare knows these things himself (perhaps he does)
and wants to tell us, there are half a dozen ways open. He never
seems to have rejected simplicities of the

> Barkloughly Castle call they this at hand?

sort merely because they were simple. He can range from this to
the subtle expounding of geography and history, too, by which
Ventidius lets us know where he is in the first few lines spoken
upon his entrance *as in triumph.* But, simply done or subtly, this
sort of thing would overlengthen the action here, check its flow
and distract our attention—as badly, almost, as our own perverse
efforts to imagine a whereabouts for each "scene" distract it.

To give anything of the spaciousness of a true scene to the four
or five terse lines, by which now Cæsar, now Antony, show us the
quality of their generalship, they would need to be multiplied by
four; and this would weaken the present effect even in magnify-

ing it. The larger episodes could easily be localized; but the others would then lose substance by comparison; what is more, the unity of the whole complex event would be destroyed. And it is in this unity that its dramatic strength lies. It is by the welding of the mixed mass of incident and character into a consistent whole, freed from all irrelevant circumstance, that its value is isolated and made clear. Obliterate scenic locality, we have still the stage itself left, with its formal furnishings, certainly. But make-believe makes short work of those familiar features; and, once we are enthralled and they vanish, there is nothing left to stand between us and the essential drama; we are at one with its realities. Here, surely, is a technical achievement of some account.

Why show us this long panorama of detail? Why not (as a Greek and probably a modern dramatist would) plan a few full-charged organic, significant scenes, and shape and compress the story to fit them? Again (if we could imagine Shakespeare putting himself the question) the answer is plain. Antony's is a great captain's downfall, the end of a man who has ruled half the Roman world, and we are to see both why he ends and how; and to see, as near as may be, the very process of it. The poor strategy, the weak will, the useless bargaining, set against Cæsar's steady mind; these are as significant every whit as the passion that wreaks vengeance on the wretched Thidias[16] and storms at Cleopatra. And the strung-out sequence of events, that are tense often and feverish while they matter little, slackened to triteness though they matter much, now catching up, now shedding their actors as they pass, time and place apt to seem the most fortuitous things about them—does not this both show us the true process of the matter, and give us, besides, just the impression that in life will belong to our share in such a crisis? Bouts of noisy fighting with heart-rent love-scenes in between would doubtless make a good show. But here, if Plutarch tells true, is a picture of the business of war as these Roman realists waged it, with luck and cunning, passion and judgment and interest all at odds in leaders and followers too. It is history directly dramatized.

---

[16] So the Folio calls him, with a variation to "Thidius." Theobald, apparently, first made him into Plutarch's "Thyreus" again, and other editors have followed. But the change is surely too marked for Shakespeare not to have made it purposely.

Shakespeare neither takes nor uses his material haphazardly. If, with one dramatic aim, he frees himself from ties of place, with another he creates for himself ties of time. He telescopes Plutarch's vague weeks into a strict three days. They mark the ebb and flow and ebb of Antony's fortunes. First, there is the night's carouse after defeat, while the sentries keep their strange watch; then the next night's after victory, while Cæsar's sentries mark Enobarbus creeping out to die; then the third day's ebb to disaster. This gives him rhythm and form, and increases tension; it makes the story clearer, and our interest easier to hold. It is deliberate stagecraft.

The Play's Construction, *Continued*

THE THREE DAYS' BATTLE

WE are plunged, for a beginning to the business, amid the squabbling distractions of Antony's counsels. Enobarbus, level-headed, caustic of tongue, does what he can to stem the tide of folly. Antony stands, weakly obstinate, under Cleopatra's eye. Against all reason, he will meet the enemy at sea—

> For that he dares us to't.

The news accumulates of Cæsar's swift, unchecked advance. We have the veteran legionary breaking all bounds of discipline in a last desperate protest.

> O noble emperor, do not fight by sea;
> Trust not to rotten planks: do you misdoubt
> This sword, and these my wounds?

Then, as they disappear,

> *Enter Cæsar, with his army, marching.*

The first day's fighting is compressed into the symbolism (it is little more) of a dozen lines of dialogue and business. This is a sort of variation upon the old dumb show, to an Elizabethan audience a familiar and pregnant convention. But note the niceties of effect. Cæsar enters *with his army, marching*; a formal processional entrance, capping the news of his approach that has threaded the preceding scene. In two sentences he shows us his strategy and his quality in command. Next, Antony and Enobarbus appear alone on the emptied stage. Antony speaks four hurried and half-purposed lines, Enobarbus never a word, but his glum looks will be eloquent; and they vanish. Then comes the marching and countermarching of the armies that are not to fight (pure symbolism!), each with its subordinate general in command. The stage empties again, and its emptiness holds us expectant. Then, of a sudden, comes the climax, the significant event; *the noise of a sea-fight* is heard.[17] Then, actual drama reasserting itself, Enobarbus, with alarums to reinforce his fury, bursts upon us, tongue-tied no more, to interpret disaster with

> Naught, naught, all naught! I can behold no longer:
> Th' Antoniad, the Egyptian admiral,
> With all their sixty, fly and turn the rudder. . . .

He is reinforced by Scarus, younger and fiercer still[18]:

> Gods and goddesses,
> All the whole synod of them! . . .
> The greater cantle of the world is lost
> With very ignorance; we have kissed away
> Kingdoms and provinces.

This symbolism of war is not in itself dramatic, one sees. Shakespeare could hardly make it so, but he hardly needs it to be. He gives us, however, very little of it. His drama lies in the consequences of the fighting, as these are reflected in the conduct of his characters. We are shown, it is to be remarked, no actual fighting at all, come no nearer to it than the sight of young Scarus and his fresh wounds. He is marked out for us as the gallant warrior, and Antony gives him generous praise. Antony's own valor we may take for granted. But his challenge to Cæsar to fight him single-handed is stressed, and as a ridiculous thing. Says Enobarbus:

~~~~~~~~~~

[17] I cannot pretend to say how "the noise of a sea-fight" was made. Professor Stuart-Jones (who spoke with authority upon one aspect of the matter) suggested to me that what one heard was the breaking of the sweeps of the galleys. But is that—would it have been to Shakespeare's audience—a recognizable sound? I fancy that a hurly-burly flavored with "Avasts," "Belays" and other such seaphrases from the landman's vocabulary would be a likelier refuge in a difficulty for the prompter and his staff. But there may have been some recognized symbolism of a sea-fight.

[18] There is no authority (that I know of) for Scarus' age. But the dramatic value of the contrast between his keen youth and Antony's waning powers is indubitable.

Cæsar, thou hast subdued

His judgment too.

This is stressed because in it and all it implies lie his failure and his tragedy.

The sequel to the first battle is shown us at length. Scarus' boyish wrath spends itself; Enobarbus, shame rankling deeper in him, relapses to his gibing; Canidius coolly plans to make his peace with Cæsar, and departs, no man hindering him; Antony appears. The gradation from the convention of the battle to the actuality of the scene to come between the broken Antony and Cleopatra, all repentance, is nicely adjusted. First we have had the angry agony of defeat, which needs human expression; next, the few lines Canidius speaks give us an abstract of many happenings; then Antony, in the exhaustion of despair, sums up against himself and tells to the end the chapter of disaster. Here is Plutarch's ". . . and so Antonius . . . went and sat down alone in the prowe of his ship, and said never a word, clapping his head between both his hands . . . and so lived three days alone without speaking to any man. But when he arrived at the head of Tænarus there Cleopatra's women first brought Antonius and Cleopatra to speak together, and afterwards to sup and lie together. . . . Now for himself he determined to crosse over into Africk and toke one of his carects or hulks loden with gold and silver and other rich cariage, and gave it unto his friends, commanding them to depart, and to seeke to save themselves. They answered him weeping, that they would nether doe it nor yet forsake him. Then Antonius very curteously and lovingly did comfort them. . . ." And it is interesting to see how Shakespeare, contracting the circumstances, can yet keep the sense and temper of the events, can even, by the tune and rhythm of a dozen lines of verse, by a suggestive phrase or so, and by the indicated business of the scene, give us the slack sense of days of breathing-space following on the blow.

The encounter with Cleopatra brings us back to matter more his own, and of more immediacy, closer therefore in tension. It is to be the first of three in which Antony will face perforce the truth of what is between them, mounting the scale of suffering to madness at the last. This one, then, must be in a low key (Shakespeare even skirts the edge of the comic at its start, with the lead-

ing of Cleopatra, spectacularly pitiful, up to the weeping hero),
and it holds no contest; he is but too ready with his

> Fall not a tear, I say; one of them rates
> All that is won and lost . . . .

We pass to Cæsar's diplomatic exploiting of his victory, his
curt rejection of Antony's overtures, the sending of Thidias to
wean Cleopatra from him. Antony rises to nobility again, with his
"Let her know't" for sole comment upon the offer of peace to
Cleopatra if she will yield him up. But with his next breath he
falls to the fatuity of the challenge to Cæsar.

There follows Cleopatra's ignoble reception of Thidias. Enobarbus can have at least one taste of revenge upon her, and
Antony is fetched to see her smiling on Cæsar's messenger.

> 'Tis better playing with a lion's whelp
> Than with an old one dying.

The savage outburst, which sends the glib fellow back, dumb and
bleeding from his stripes, is, for all its passion, as futile—and is
meant to seem so—as were the heroics of the challenge; so is the
moral stripping and lashing of Cleopatra. For, his rage glutted
and appeased by the sight of the wretch half-slaughtered at his
feet, he can turn back to her, open-eyed to the truth about her,
and, listening to the easy lies, can end them with an easier—and a
hopeless—

> I am satisfied.

After this we may be sure that he is doomed. Enobarbus is sure
of it, and Cæsar's comment is contemptuous and brief. Shakespeare adds, for the ending of the day, the strange little hysterical
passage in which, by

> one of those odd tricks which sorrow shoots
> Out of the mind. . .

we find him melting his followers to tears as he pathetically paints
the prospects of his defeat and death—to show us yet again, one
supposes, how helplessly off the rails the man has run.[19]

Now comes, to mark the passing of the night, the episode of the
sentries on their watch. It is, as we have noted, the one piece of

---

[19] Shakespeare elaborates this from a couple of sentences in Plutarch; and the
suggestion (from Enobarbus) that Antony almost deliberately "makes a scene,"
is all his own.

scene-painting in the play; a developing of atmosphere, rather—
for the single line,

> Heard you of nothing strange about the streets?

is the only hint of locality—of the ominous atmosphere of a night
of reprieve between battles. The means to it are merely a few
whispering voices and the

> *Music of the hoboyes ... under the stage.*

It is after the couples have met, gossiped a moment and parted
with "good-night," that they hear this.

4TH SOLDIER.	Peace! what noise?
1ST SOLDIER.	List, list!
2ND SOLDIER.	Hark!
1ST SOLDIER.	Music i' the air!
3RD SOLDIER.	Under the earth.
4TH SOLDIER.	It signs well, does it not?
3RD SOLDIER.	No.
1ST SOLDIER.	Peace, I say.
	What should this mean?
2ND SOLDIER.	'Tis the god Hercules, whom Antony loved,
	Now leaves him.

They feel their way towards each other and whisper confusedly
in the darkness, their nerves a little ragged.

2ND SOLDIER.	How now, masters!
ALL TOGETHER.	How now?
	How now? do you hear this?
1ST SOLDIER.	Ay: is't not strange?
3RD SOLDIER.	Do you hear, masters? do you hear?
1ST SOLDIER.	Follow the noise so far as we have quarter.
	Let's see how it will give off.
ALL.	Content! 'Tis strange.

And, holding all together as the music dies into distance, they
vanish. The entire effect, simple in itself, is made with masterly
economy. The scene has two uses: it preserves the continuity of
the action, and is gloom before the bright beginning of the second day.

Antony has not slept. He comes jovial and confident from
night-long revelry, calling for his squire. Cleopatra, seeming a
lissom girl again, beneath the spell of this still magnificent spend-

thrift of fortune, plays at buckling on his armor; and with shouts and the flourish of trumpets and the clangor of the gathering of armed men Shakespeare rings up the dawn. Trumpets sound again; it is as if they set out to sure victory. Two notes of doubt are struck: by a shrewder Cleopatra with her

> That he and Cæsar might
> Determine this great war in single fight!
> Then, Antony—! But now—?

—before she retires to her chamber to recover what she may of her lost night's rest; and by the news, greeting Antony as he marches forth, that Enobarbus—Enobarbus!—has deserted. He puts the treason behind him with a gentle magnanimity which comes strangely—does it?—from a man who could have his enemy's ambassador half flayed alive. But this is Antony.

Next we see Cæsar. But this—upon a mere half-victory won—is an overconfident Cæsar, not the cautious general of the earlier battle. Between the brilliant opening and the brilliant end of Antony's day we have, for contrast, Enobarbus repentant. There is, of course, no strict measuring out of time; and we return to some degree of symbolism when, after alarum, drums and trumpets, Agrippa enters with

> Retire, we have engaged ourselves too far:
> Cæsar himself has work, and our oppression
> Exceeds what we expected.[20]

He and his staff pass, unflurried, across the stage. They have been quickly cured of their confidence. Antony and Scarus pursue them, the youthful elation of Scarus a foil to Antony's self-possession. He is the potent general still, one might believe—set him free from Cleopatra! Drums and alarums subsiding in the distance give us the battle's ending. The emptied stage here is the equivalent of a line of asterisks on a printed page. Then with

> *Enter Antony again in a march.*

comes the brilliant consummation of this last day of good fortune that he is to see. It ends as it began, with trumpets sounding; and

---

[20] The Folio's stage direction brings Agrippa on alone, but this, his speech pretty clearly shows, must be an error. He may have Dolabella or Mæcenas with him. It will hardly, however, be a symbolic army in full retreat. All the disorder of battle Shakespeare is giving us by sound, its thrills through individuals; and his massed entries are processional. The stage directions hereabouts are all rather cursory.

it has shown us Antony at his best, generous, gallant, a born leader of men.

Cæsar's sentries on their watch mark the second night's passing; and our sight of Enobarbus, sick of his ague, broken in spirit, crawling out into the misty moonlight to die, gives it a dreary coloring. The dawn breaks dully.

> *Drums afar off.*
> Hark, the drums
> Demurely wake the sleepers. . . .

The armies parade again. First Antony leads his across. He is smiling grimly, yet there is a desperate edge to his

> I would they'd fight i' the fire, or i' the air;
> We'd fight there too . . . .

Then we see Cæsar, sober caution itself this time. He passes, heading his men, and the stage stays empty a moment.

Antony and Scarus appear alone. No tokens of fighting so far, and Antony is in suspense. With

> Yet they are not joined: where yond pine does stand
> I shall discover all: I'll bring thee word
> Straight, how 'tis like to go.

he vanishes, leaving Scarus to turn suspense to misgiving with

> Swallows have built
> In Cleopatra's sails their nests: the augurers
> Say they know not, they cannot tell; look grimly,
> And dare not speak their knowledge. Antony
> Is valiant and dejected, and, by starts,
> His fretted fortunes give him hope and fear
> Of what he has and has not.

Through this comes sounding an

> *Alarum afar off, as at a sea-fight.*

—to our remembrance, a most ominous sound. And hard upon it, transformed, wrought to a grand climacteric of fury, Antony reappears.

> All is lost!
> This foul Egyptian hath betrayed me:
> My fleet hath yielded to the foe; and yonder
> They cast their caps up and carouse together

Like friends long lost. Triple-turned whore! 'tis thou
Hast sold me to this novice; and my heart
Makes only wars on thee. Bid them all fly!
For when I am revenged upon my charm,
I have done all. Bid them all fly: begone.[21]

From now till he is carried exhausted and dying to the Monument Antony's passion dominates the action. Eros, Mardian, the
Guard, Dercetas, Diomedes are caught distractedly in the wind of
it; we see nothing of Cæsar; panic quickly obliterates Cleopatra. It
is a long passage and highly charged; but Shakespeare can find
all the change and variety he needs in its own turbulent ebb and
flow. Nor, when the medium is rhetoric raised to such a pitch and
given such coloring, could any competition be admitted; the
audience must be caught and rapt by the mood. The shock of the
first outburst should capture us. Then, the brilliant Scarus, Enobarbus' successor, Antony's new right hand, having been sent
packing like a lackey (and as ready to go: or do we wrong him?)
we are held by the simple magnificence of

Oh, sun, thy uprise shall I see no more:
Fortune and Antony part here; even here
Do we shake hands. All come to this? The hearts
That spanieled me at heels, to whom I gave
Their wishes, do discandy, melt their sweets
On blossoming Cæsar; and this pine is barked
That over-topped them all.

---

[21] The Folio gives the stage direction

Alarum farre off, as at a sea fight.

in the interval between Cæsar's exit with his army and Antony's entrance with
Scarus. This is almost certainly wrong. Antony would not enter upon an alarum
with a "Yet they are not joined." But it does not as certainly follow that the editors
(from 1778 onwards, according to Furness) are right in transferring it to the
instant before his re-entrance with "All is lost." They may be. But it is an
"alarum afar off," and might come more effectively before, or even during, Scarus'
speech. The point is not a very important one. It is hard to tell what sheer
dramatic value there was for the Elizabethans in these symbolic alarums and the
like, and what variety of effect could be given them. Some without doubt; they
speak a language, if a simple one. The effect of that first *noise of a sea-fight*
which precipitated Enobarbus' outburst of "Naught, naught, all naught" is evidently not precisely the same—nor meant to be—as this *alarum afar off* which
brings Antony on to the greater crisis of "All is lost." We may note that, besides
the "symbolism," Shakespeare gives about a dozen illustrative lines of dialogue
to each of the first two battles, to the third about twenty.

His fury soon begins to work again; it is like yeast in him; and when he turns, expectant of Eros coming to his call, to find Cleopatra herself, he chokes for a moment, long enough for her smooth incongruity,

> Why is my lord enraged against his love?

to give a fresh twist to his torture. In this babyish line, and in her flabbergasted, tongue-tied, sudden, very unqueenlike bolting, in his frenzied pursuit of her, Shakespeare again skirts the ridiculous; and closely enough this time to provoke in us a sort of half-hysteria which will attune us to his next shift of key—into the delirium which brings Antony, exhausted, to a pause. We must picture the actor, transfigured to the terms of

> The shirt of Nessus is upon me: teach me,
> Alcides, thou mine ancestor, thy rage:
> Let me lodge Lichas on the horns o' the moon. . . .

and storming from the stage. While we still hear him we see Cleopatra with her scared women and her sapless eunuch scurrying across like rabbits. And as they vanish he follows, vertiginous, insensate! It is a wild, roundabout chase, hazardously raised to poetic power.

If we were not first thrown off our emotional balance we might find the fantasy that follows—for all its beauty—too much an intellectual conceit, and too long-drawn-out.

> Ant. Eros, thou yet behold'st me?
> Eros.   Ay, noble lord.
> Ant. Sometime we see a cloud that's dragonish,
>   A vapour sometime like a bear or lion,
>   A tower'd citadel, a pendent rock,
>   A forked mountain, or blue promontory
>   With trees upon't, that nod unto the world
>   And mock our eyes with air: thou hast seen these signs;
>   They are black vesper's pageants.
> Eros.   Ay, my lord.
> Ant. That which is now a horse, even with a thought
>   The rack dislimns and makes it indistinct,
>   As water is in water,
> Eros.   It does, my lord.
> Ant. My good knave Eros, now thy captain is
>   Even such a body. . . .

We should feel with Antony the relief this strange sense of dissolution brings from the antics of passion, and how, as he does, one would prolong the respite, playing with these fancies that the half-freed spirit conceives!

From this he sinks to quiet grief. The sight of the "saucy eunuch," on tiptoe with his glib tale, sets fury glowing for a moment again. Then comes the news, worded as piteously as ever Cleopatra, safe now in her Monument, could desire—the news that she is dead. He greets them as Antony must.[22] The fact that they are false is of a piece with the other futilities of these three days that have gone to his undoing. Yet another is to follow when he stands waiting for the merciful sword-stroke which Eros turns on himself; yet another when he bungles his own, and has to lie there, begging the guard to dispatch him—and, instead, off they go and let him lie![23]

With his carrying to the Monument the long phase of more particularly "unlocalized" action, germane to the three days of fighting, ends. We have been "ideal" spectators, we know what happened, and why; and just such an impression has been made on us as the reality itself would leave behind. It is a great technical achievement, and one of great artistry too.

Cleopatra Against Caesar

ANTONY dead, the domination of the play passes at once to Cleopatra. She asserts it in the lament over him; a contrast to his stoic greeting of the news of her death. And from now to the end, the action (but for one short scene) is definitely localized in the Monument. As suited, this, to the intensity and cunning of Cleopatra's battle with Cæsar as was diversity of place to the chances and changes of the other; and by contrast made more telling.

---

[22] If we remember his
> On:
> Things that are past are done with me.

[23] Eros is dispatched from the stage for a moment or so by an apparently motiveless "From me awhile." The practical need is probably to dispose of Antony's armor; for soon there will be both Antony and the body of Eros himself to be carried off by *four or five of the guard*, Diomed and (more doubtfully) Dercetas. But Shakespeare, by merely leaving it unexplained, lets it seem part of the general slack confusion.

But Antony's death leaves Shakespeare to face one obvious problem: how to prevent Cleopatra's coming as an anticlimax. Plutarch is still lavish of material, but it will need some choosing and molding.

Cæsar is surprised by the news—here is one risk of slackening tension avoided—and shocked into more feeling than we expect of him. Then at once the last round of the play's contest is opened, and we see what the struggle is to be. A humble anonymous messenger comes from Cleopatra, his message as humble. Cæsar sends him back with fair words; and promptly thereafter:

> Come hither, Proculeius; go and say
> We purpose her no shame: give her what comforts
> The quality of her passion shall require,
> Lest in her greatness by some mortal stroke
> She do defeat us; for her life in Rome
> Would be eternal in our triumph. . . .

It is to be Cæsar's wits against Cleopatra's pride and despair. He fought Antony to the death; it may take more generalship to secure Cleopatra alive. Proculeius, we notice, is sent; the one man about Cæsar, said Antony, that Cleopatra was to trust. Is it in some distrust of him (for his own part) that Cæsar sends Gallus too; and, on yet further thought, Dolabella to watch them both, lest Cleopatra wheedle her way round them? It turns out to be Dolabella that needs watching. But here, unfortunately, the text, as we have it, plays us false. There has been cutting and botching, and the niceties of the business we can now only guess at.[24] The main trend of it is clear, though. In their Roman fashion, Gallus and Proculeius add force to diplomacy and manage to capture Cleopatra in her Monument. Proculeius finds a few moments with this tiger in a trap quite enough for him, and gladly gives place to Dolabella.

The passage that follows is a notable one. He fancies himself, does Dolabella; he is a ladies' man, and quite the jailer, surely, for this most wonderful of wantons.

> Most noble Empress, you have heard of me?

is his ingratiating beginning. From a Roman there is flattery in the very title; it owns her Antony's widow and ignores Octavia.

---

[24] This is discussed in more detail on p. 39.

She is far from responsive. She sulks and snarls, gives him half a glance, and forthwith breaks into invidious praise of her dead hero. But she knows she can twist the conceited fellow round her finger. She has only to turn to him with a smile, with an "I thank you, sir," and a "Nay, pray you, sir," and he promptly betrays his master to her, blurts out that, for all these comforting messages, Cæsar does mean to lead her chained in his Triumph. At which point Cæsar himself appears.

He comes in full state and circumstance, his staff surrounding him, guards clearing the way. And if Cleopatra thinks to impress him in turn, his opening sally might well damp her somewhat. For he faces this marvel among women as she stands there with her mere maids beside her, and coolly asks which of them is the Queen of Egypt. Which? And once it was

> Remember
> If e'er thou look'st on majesty.

The duel of lies that follows—a pretty piece of fighting!—epitomizes this second and subtler struggle. We have Egyptian against Roman now, neither with much simplicity left to shed; but Cleopatra, passionate and unstable, shows a very child beside Cæsar. She kneels, and he raises her. He repeats his smooth promises, and she smiles her gratitude, alive to the worth of them—had she ever doubted it!—thanks to coxcomb Dolabella. But, surely, for a man so very indifferent to her, he is a little anxious to be gone. Has she any hope of winning him, and does he suspect this? It is second nature in her to be wily with men—and to lie. Seleucus and the false inventory of "money, plate and jewels" make illuminating matter of dispute. Are not these barbarians to be bribed, and tricked too? Cæsar is neither to be tricked—nor shocked by the attempt made on him. And as for her raging and her nobly pathetic attitudes, he counters them, her lies and her flatteries, too, with the same cold smile. She is beaten. Even Seleucus can withstand her scoldings now; it is Cæsar, contemptuously considerate, who orders the man off. She is helpless in his clutches, but for the one sure escape. And he thinks, does he, to lure her from that with his lies? She fawns on him as he leaves her; let him think he has!

> He words me, girls, he words me, that I should not
> Be noble to myself! . . .

If any doubt were left, any chance of yet another of her accustomed conquests, Dolabella—the paltry proof that she still can conquer—comes back to disperse it.

DOLABELLA.   Madam, as thereto sworn by your command,
Which my love makes religion to obey,
I tell you this: Cæsar through Syria
Intends his journey, and within three days
You with your children will he send before:
Make your best use of this: I have performed
Your pleasure and my promise.

CLEOPATRA.   Dolabella,
I shall remain your debtor.[25]

She again makes his name sound beautiful in his ears (it is a name that can be lingered on), perhaps gives him her hand to kiss (he does not pay Thidias' price for the honor) and he goes. Her way is clear now to death.

But she has still to rise to that final, secure nobility, with which the sight of the dead Antony inspired her.

> and then, what's brave, what's noble,
> Let's do it after the high Roman fashion,
> And make death proud to take us . . . .

She climbs there by no straight path. The longing to die never leaves her. But we all long to die at times; and there is much protesting, a stealthy look or so for chances of escape, some backsliding into the old twisted passions; and she must at last lash herself—with, for company, poor frail Iras—through agony and beyond it before she can repose upon

> My resolution's placed, and I have nothing
> Of woman in me: now from head to foot
> I am marble-constant. . . .

Then, for one more mitigation before the play's last tragic height is reached, Shakespeare gives us the countryman and his figs. By

---

[25] He made no promise. At most he is so enthralled by her that he would have— feels, perhaps, he must have done. Here is an interesting instance of the way in which Shakespeare makes an *ex post facto* effect, which he knows will pass muster.

now (here is the art of it) Cleopatra is past bitterness or fear, and can smile and take the simple pleasure in his simplicity that we do. She jokes with him. This must have been, if one comes to think of it, not the least of her charms. When she would royally

> Hop forty paces through the public street . . .

how the people—the common people, so despised by Cæsar and the politicians—how evidently they would adore her! It is very right that one of them should bring her the comfort of death in a basket slung on his arm, and that she should trust him, and joke with him, a great lady at her ease.

From this she turns to a queenliness unapproached before.

> Give me my robe, put on my crown; I have
> Immortal longings in me . . . .

Long ago, we learn, a dead king's servants would be slaughtered around him. This is a still more royal death; for Iras' heart breaks silently at the sight of it, and Charmian only lags behind to set a crooked crown straight once again, and to send triumphant mockery echoing to Cæsar's ears.

He accepts his defeat like a gentleman, let us own. The ceremony of his coming matches the ceremony of her dying; and the end of the play, we should note, is sensibly delayed while they stand gazing—tough soldiers that they are—at a queen so strangely throned:

> she looks like sleep,
> As she would catch another Antony
> In her strong toil of grace.

The Staging

THE action makes no extraordinary calls upon an Elizabethan stage as we now think we know it to have been. Two things are noticeable, however. There are, for five-sixths of the play, few definite indications of the use of the inner stage. This keys with the scant localization of the scenes; the inner and upper stages are always likelier to be "places" than the main stage will be. But the full stage, i.e. the main stage with the inner stage curtains open and the inner stage itself accessible, would probably be used from the general entrance of Charmian, Iras, Mardian, Alexas, the

Soothsayer and the rest to Antony's departure for Rome; for all Cleopatra's scenes while she sits waiting news of him—and receiving it; for the long scene of reconciliation between Antony and Cæsar; and for the scene in Pompey's galley.[26] The intermediate scenes will be played on the main stage, with the inner stage curtains closed. When the battles begin it looks as if Cleopatra's scenes again employed the inner stage (as hinterland at least to the outer); she and Antony retiring to it or through it at such points as

> Some wine within there, and our viands! . . .

> Let's to supper, come,
> And drown consideration.

—the curtains then closing on them. She may come from the inner stage when she welcomes him from his victory; and

> Through Alexandria make a jolly march . . .

may imply that they all pass back, as if into the city in triumph. Cæsar's scenes, the marching and countermarching and the swifter coming and going, take place on the main stage, that is clear.[27] Now comes disputable matter.

> *Enter Cleopatra and her Maides aloft, with Charmian and Iras.*

They are in the Monument, to which, in a moment, the dying Antony has to be hoisted. There are two slight difficulties. The hoisting of a full-grown man ten or twelve feet in the air asks some strength. However, this could be provided ostensibly by the "and her Maides," actually by stagehands helping from behind the curtains; and Shakespeare makes dramatic capital out of the apparent difficulty. But the upper stage of the public theater must have had a balustrade at least three feet high. Swinging a dying man over it and lowering him again asks some care. Granted this

---

[26] This, it may be said, was the normal way of employing the inner stage; the action would seldom be wholly confined there. But furniture, and the localization this implies, would tend to focus the action within its bounds. See also the Preface to *Cymbeline*, Vol. II, p. 87 *et seq.*

[27] But the stage direction

> *Canidius marcheth with his land army one way over the stage, and Taurus, the lieutenant of Cæsar, the other way: After their going in . . .*

could be more slickly obeyed if there were an inner as well as an outer stage to march over. With two doors only available, it will be a long-drawn-out affair.

done with skill and grace, what of the effect of the rest of the
scene, of Antony's death and Cleopatra's lament over him, played
behind the balustrade as behind bars? Clearly it would be a poor
one. The balustrade must, one presumes, have been removed for
the occasion or made to swing open, if the ordinary upper stage
was used.[28]

When we next see Cleopatra she is obviously still in the Monument; as obviously she is not still upon such an upper stage as we
believe the Globe's to have been. Nor is there any sign that—as
with Romeo's farewell to Juliet and her encounter with her mother
—the acting of the scene began above and finished below. The
stage directions, however, are incomplete, and the text may have
been altered. In the previous scene Proculeius and Gallus have
been sent to parley with Cleopatra and keep her, if they can, from
doing herself a mischief. By the Folio's stage direction only Proculeius arrives. A simple supposition is that he finds her on the
inner stage behind a barred gate and speaks to her through it.[29]
This at any rate reproduces Plutarch's "For Proculeius came to the
gates that were very thick and strong, and surely barred; but yet
there were some craneries through the which her voyce might be
heard. . . ." When she has protested her submission he evidently
makes as if to go, with

> This I'll report, dear lady.
> Have comfort, for I know your plight is pitied
> Of him that caused it.

But now, with no other speech nor stage direction intervening, the
Folio has

> Pro. You see how easily she may be surpriz'd;
> Guard her till Cæsar come.

Modern editors (following Theobald in the main) give the speech
to Gallus, whom they have brought on with Proculeius, and add:

> *Here Proculeius and two of the Guard ascend the
> monument by a ladder placed against a window,*

---

[28] There seems commonly to have been a trap in the floor of the upper stage. But
the use of this and the need to place Antony directly under it would rob the
dialogue—would rob the all-important "I am dying, Egypt, dying"—of much of
its effect.

[29] Just such a barred gate as shuts in Juliet's tomb.

> *and, having descended, come behind Cleopatra.*
> *Some of the Guard unbar and open the gates.*[30]

A minor objection to this is that Gallus in the Folio is *persona muta*; the full speaking strength of the company is, we may well suppose, already employed, and here is a super. A more serious one must be that so much climbing up and climbing down again would take time. There is no concurrent dialogue, and a long pause at such a moment is dramatically unthinkable.[31]

No great difficulty arises if we see Gallus and the guard left at the door while Proculeius advances to the gate that bars the inner stage. Cleopatra would not see them. Let him give them the order quietly as he returns to the door, and, with no climbing involved, they can be upon the inner stage by the back way in a couple of seconds, seize Cleopatra and unbar the gates; and Gallus may well go off to report to Cæsar; his exit as his entrance, if he stays *persona muta*, being a likely omission from stage directions, which would need to be unwontedly elaborate if all this were to be made clear.[32]

The discussion is fairly barren from a modern producer's point of view; he can provide for all these exigencies without violating the text or distorting the action.

But if for this and all the rest of the action the recognized Elizabethan stage does not content him, then he must devise one which will not violate its fundamental liberties and laws—its liberties, above all. He will probably find in the end that he has devised something not so very different. If he is for painted scenes of *Cleopatra's palace, Cæsar's house, Antony's camp, The plain near Actium* and a variety of "other parts of the same"—well, the

---

[30] Thus, at least, the (English) Arden edition. But it also presumes (in a footnote) and the Oxford edition definitely states that Cleopatra has so far been upon the upper stage. How and when she gets down is left a mystery.

[31] Johnson proposed to insert part of the speech earlier so that the guards could come quietly behind and seize Cleopatra at the cue. But the three previous speeches allow of no such interruption. If Cleopatra had to be *brought* down to the lower stage, it would be ten times worse.

[32] There remains the unnatural hiatus between Proculeius' two speeches, if they are both his. Suppose that the upper stage to which Antony is hoisted were not the usual balcony, but something a little more accessible, to which the guards might climb without delay, and from which Cleopatra might be as easily brought down. The hiatus *may* point to some change in staging, or in the stage itself, or to the shifting of the play from one theater to another of different resources.

reading of this Preface will only have wasted his time. He must somehow provide a staging free from actuality of place; that is his main problem. He may decorate it; but if the decoration distracts us from the hearing of Shakespeare's lines—and they ask, as we have noted, pretty close attention—it will be a positive nuisance. It is a hard problem to solve; for one thing, because self-effacement is the rarest of artistic virtues. And let the decorator set out, however discreetly, to interpret the play in his own terms, if he find himself—and it is an ever-present danger—competing with the actors, the sole interpreters Shakespeare has licensed, then it is he that is the intruder, and he must retire. Even if his picturesque effects are but an anodyne to our vigilance—and much modern stage decoration is of this sort—they will do the play negative harm. We need to have our minds kept clear and alert. Still, if we cannot take the Elizabethan stage for granted as the Elizabethans did, producer and decorator must certainly face the problem of providing something that we can.

Costume

ONCE we are freed from pictures of Rome and Alexandria, brought (so to speak) archaeologically up to date, the difficulty of costume is not acute.

> Cut my lace, Charmian.

summarizes it, and, upon a narrow view, may be said almost to exhaust it. Shakespeare's Cleopatra wore a stomacher of some sort, that is evident. But it is an error to suppose that Shakespeare dressed all his plays in the ordinary costume of his time. It is also an error, for that matter, to suppose that nowadays we all carry accurate pictures of the past in our minds. Dress Cleopatra as a Queen of the Tenth Dynasty instead of as an Alexandrian Greek, and how many of us would be the wiser? Careful research might find us an Alexandrian fashion plate of the right period with laces to cut (Sir Arthur Evans has brought us corsets from Knossos), but our conscientiously Egyptian Cleopatras have so far been left laceless and waistless, and the line without meaning.

In all this, as in everything else of the sort, the Elizabethans thought first and last—whether by choice or necessity—of dramatic profit. It is not likely that Shakespeare troubled to give a specifically French touch to *Love's Labour's Lost* and an Italian to *Much Ado About Nothing*; nor, had his knowledge run to it, would he probably have seen much gain in dressing Romeo and Juliet by "the paintings of Giotto and his pupils."[33] But when some dramatic end was to be served it is clear that he did not lack means of a kind, and he used them. In *Macbeth* the Scots and the English can be told apart, British and Romans in *Cymbeline*; and in this play, quite evidently, Roman and Egyptian stood in picturesque contrast. There would be little archaeology about the business and less consistency. We can guess at the sort of figures they made by turning to extant designs for the Court Masques. The theaters could not run, perhaps, to such splendor as that; but they were prosperous, finery was popular, and they probably did pretty well. Rome meant the romantic past, Egypt the exotic East; and Shakespeare would do what he could to capitalize both. The dialogue of the play is colored with every sort of allusion to the wonders of that far world, from the description of Cleopatra at Cydnus, to the talk of Syria and the Parthians, from the story of Antony in the Alps, from his call to Alcides his ancestor, to tales of "pyramises" and crocodiles.

We know better about all these things than did Shakespeare; but it is too late now to put him right. We have to interpret, not to correct him; we are committed even to his errors. Our concern is with the Egypt and Rome of his imagination, not of our own. The difference is manifest less in this detail or the other than in the whole texture of the play. Cut the knot of the "Cut my lace, Charmian" difficulty, and there is still the larger problem. In the National Gallery hangs Paolo Veronese's "Alexander and the Wife and Daughter of Darius." This will be very much how Shakespeare saw his Roman figures habited. Antony would wear Alexander's mixture of doublet, breastplate, sandals and hose. Here too is something very like Octavia's costume; and though Cleopatra might be given some Egyptian stigmata, there would

---

[33] This is how Charles Knight tells us they should be dressed (I quote from the quotation in Furness). "But," he adds, "for the younger and lighter characters ... some very different habit would be expected by the million, and indeed, desired by the artist." He is writing in the mid-nineteenth century. The quest for accuracy in these matters is a new thing.

still be laces to cut. It is all grievously incorrect; but we do not like the picture less for that, nor are students set to copy it and told to redraw the costume in the light of the latest information available. Its good painting apart, we even gain by its being a Renaissance view of a Classic subject, for the spirit of the picture is in that. Now, no one will contend that by clothing Antony and Cleopatra and Cæsar and ordering their Court and their armies according to our modern imagination we shall crush the dramatic life out of them, for this is rooted far deeper. But we shall at every moment, both on the main issue and in countless little ways, be falsifying Shakespeare, and doing him far more damage than the simple logic of the case implies. We do him, of all dramatists, great damage. For he has an extraordinary faculty of making the great things vivid to us by means of the little things, by just such strokes, in fact, as that

> Cut my lace, Charmian.

This play is exceptionally full of them, very homely things; and it is bare chance that one of the finest, Charmian's

> Your crown's awry:
> I'll mend it, and then play.

does not get us into more sartorial trouble. He has absorbed Rome and Egypt into his own consciousness; but it is a consciousness opening upon his own world, not the historical Antony's, and naturally not upon our vision of that.

Shakespeare in modern dress is as inappropriate as archaeological Shakespeare, and for the same good reason. And the very argument that great drama is not dependent upon its trimmings should surely help us to accept the trimmings that we find. Cleopatra in a farthingale! The orthodox playgoer may turn pale at the thought. But surrender to the idea that this is Shakespeare's Cleopatra we are looking at, not the product of our schoolbooks (is that more difficult than to look up from our program and admit that the well-known Miss Blank, lately seen as Nora in *A Doll's House*, is the real thing?), and by the end of the first scene the oddity will be forgotten; and thenceforward we shall be anachronism-proof. There will be one further gain. An historical play of any sort has a double victory to win; the play's own and a victory over our preconceptions of its history. The less familiar its figures the better the chance of the play with us—as a play.

The Music

TRUMPETS and cornets and drums are needed; and the flourishes, the sounding of a sennet, the beating of the drums have each their import. Enobarbus is borne away dying to the sound of *Drummes afarre offe*. A consort of woodwind is also used. The "hoboyes" play under the stage, and their pungent vibrations should make excellent assault on the nerves.

The music for the revels on Pompey's galley is given to woodwind (the accompaniment of the song included), trumpets and drums reinforcing it occasionally. The clamor is insisted on.

> Make battery to our ears with the loud music. . . .
> These drums! these trumpets, flutes, what!
> Let Neptune hear we bid a loud farewell
> To these great fellows: sound and be hanged, sound out!

It is a soldiers' revel. But it never slips from the distinction of poetry; and the song itself—the boy's voice singing it—is like light beside the darkness of Menas' whisper to Pompey:

> These three world-sharers, these competitors,
> Are in thy vessel: let me cut the cable;
> And, when we are put off, fall to their throats. . . .

The scene falls midway through the play. It is a rest point in the action. Shakespeare has taken care to give it solidity, variety and color.

Cleopatra calls once for music, but countermands it with her next breath. She would have needed a consort of viols; and it is possible that strings and woodwind both were more than could be always reasonably demanded at one performance.

The Verse and Its Speaking

ROME and its Empire are ever a clarion call to Shakespeare's imagination; and the strength of his answer to it lies in his power to make the alien characters his own. For he leaves them in no classic immunity, casting his care upon their impressive reputations. They must be sifted through his dramatist's conscience; he brings them to terms on the ground of common humanity. What is Cleopatra's passport to tragic heights?

> No more but e'en a woman, and commanded
> By such poor passion as the maid that milks
> And does the meanest chares. . . .

With this, of course, they risk the loss of their conventionally heroic stature. But it is preserved for them by the magic of poetry.

This is literally a sort of magic, by which the vibrations of emotion that the sound of the poetry sets up seem to enlarge its sense, and break the bounds of the theater to carry us into the lost world of romantic history. Conceive such a story and such characters so familiarly, and then tie their expression to plain prose—Dido will be in danger of becoming a dowdy indeed, and Cleopatra a gypsy. But Shakespeare has traveled far since Mercutio could thus mock Romeo's poetic prowess, and is now himself by no means "for the numbers that Petrarch flowed in." He has come to the writing of a verse which combines actuality and power, and is malleable to every diversity of character and mood. Here and there we may begin to feel a strain. Sometimes emotion will not quite vivify thought, which stays constricted or confused; or a too constant repetition of effect or an oversimplifying of simplicity may show fatigue. But Shakespeare has always had the tact to seize on the subject that will best fit his artist's mood, or to adapt mood and method to subject—which, it is not our business to inquire. And in its qualities and defects alike his present method and ability, resourceful, audacious, spontaneous, ripe if to over-ripeness, fit this subject most consummately well.

Big though the task will be, he feels no need to economize his strength. He begins at what a pitch!

> Nay, but this dotage of our general's
> O'erflows the measure; those his goodly eyes,
> That o'er the files and musters of the war
> Have glow'd like plated Mars, now bend, now turn,
> The office and devotion of their view
> Upon a tawny front: his captain's heart,
> Which in the scuffles of great fights hath burst
> The buckles on his breast, reneges all temper,

> And is become the bellows and the fan
> To cool a gipsy's lust.

Ample and virile in substance, consonant in its music! One tremendous sentence, the ends of the lines not answering to pauses either; these, such as they are, fall midway (a bare four of them in nine lines and more, though), so that fresh impulse may overleap the formal division, and the force be the force of the whole. Note, too, the placing of the dominant "o'erflows the measure" and its complement "reneges all temper" with the doubled parenthesis between them, and how the "now bend, now turn" saves this from slackness; how "files and musters" and "office and devotion" strengthen the beat of the verse, with "plated Mars" coming like the sudden blare of a trumpet, and "burst the buckles on his breast" to sound the exploding indignation which culminates in the deadly

> And is become the bellows and the fan
> To cool a gipsy's lust.

A fairly opulent dramatic allowance for this Philo, of whom we know nothing, are never to see again. But throughout the play we shall find the least considered characters, and on no special occasion, with as meaty stuff—is there a better term for it?—in their mouths. Mæcenas greets Octavia, upon her disillusioned return, with

> Welcome, dear Madam.
> Each heart in Rome does love and pity you:
> Only the adulterous Antony, most large
> In his abominations, turns you off;
> And gives his potent regiment to a trull,
> That noises it against us.

The anonymous legionary, even, has no less vivid and stirring a moment to his share than

> O noble emperor, do not fight by sea;
> Trust not to rotten planks: do you misdoubt
> This sword and these my wounds? Let the Egyptians
> And the Phœnicians go a-ducking: we
> Have used to conquer, standing on the earth,
> And fighting foot to foot.

And from Pompey in his first scene (Shakespeare himself well into his stride by this!) comes the full enrichment of

> But all the charms of love,
> Salt Cleopatra, soften thy waned lip!
> Let witchcraft join with beauty, lust with both!
> Tie up the libertine in a field of feasts,
> Keep his brain fuming; Epicurean cooks
> Sharpen with cloyless sauce his appetite;
> That sleep and feeding may prorogue his honour
> Even till a Lethe'd dullness.

Too much rich writing of this sort would be like Cleopatra's feasts, and clog the march of the action. But when mere argument is in hand we fall back to nothing less pedestrian than Antony's

> Sir,
> He fell upon me ere admitted: then
> Three kings I had newly feasted, and did want
> Of what I was i' the morning: but, next day,
> I told him of myself; which was as much
> As to have asked him pardon. Let this fellow
> Be nothing of our strife: if we contend
> Out of our question wipe him.

This, and such a passage as Cæsar's somewhat smug

> Let's grant it is not
> Amiss to tumble in the bed of Ptolemy;
> To give a kingdom for a mirth; to sit
> And keep the turn of tippling with a slave;
> To reel the streets at noon, and stand the buffet
> With knaves that smell of sweat; say this becomes him—
> As his composure must be rare indeed
> Whom these things cannot blemish—yet must Antony
> No way excuse his foils, when we do bear
> So great weight in his lightness.

or as Pompey's

> To you all three,
> The senators alone of this great world,
> Chief factors for the gods,—I do not know
> Wherefore my father should revengers want,
> Having a son and friends, since Julius Cæsar,
> Who at Philippi the good Brutus ghosted,
> There saw you labouring for him.

may be taken as the norm of the play's poetic method, upon

which its potencies are built up. And it is upon this norm, of course, that the actors must model their own style.

The elemental oratory of this verse needs for its speaking a sense of rhythm that asks no help of strict rule. Shakespeare is so secure by now in the spirit of its laws that the letter may go. He does not commonly stray far. A cæsura may fall oddly or there may be none distinguishable, a syllable or so may splash over at the end. Dramatic emphasis is the thing, first and last; to get that right he will sacrifice strict meter—yet never music—grammar now and then, and at a pinch, if need be, exact sense too.

These freedoms gain in effect as the play's temper heightens. Cæsar's calculated indignation is sounded in the two swelling catalogues:

> I'the common show place where they exercise.
> His sons he there proclaimed the kings of kings:
> Great Media, Parthia and Armenia
> He gave to Alexander; to Ptolemy he assign'd
> Syria, Cilicia and Phœnicia. . . .
>   He hath assembled
> Bocchus, the king of Libya; Archelaus
> Of Cappadocia. . . .

The latter passage has been quoted already; the scansion is highly individual.

But no Cleopatra, with an ear, can miss the shrill arrogance of

> Sink Rome, and their tongues rot
> That speak against us! A charge we bear i' the war,
> And, as the president of my kingdom, will
> Appear there for a man. Speak not against it;
> I will not stay behind.

The upward run of semiquavers in "A charge we bear i' the war" is as plain as any musical stave could make it; and the pauses seem to mark so many snaps of the jaw. The lines are not, of course, here or elsewhere to be reckoned by syllables, but by beat.

Listen, on the other hand, to the weary descent to depression's depths in Antony's

> Fall not a tear, I say; one of them rates
> All that is won and lost: give me a kiss;
> Even this repays me. We sent our schoolmaster;
> Is 'a come back? Love, I am full of lead.

—given us by a regular caesura, followed by an irregular one, followed by a mid-line full stop; the line then finished with an effort by the banal "We sent our schoolmaster" (who could get anything but exhaustion out of that "schoolmaster"?); the next line with its dead monosyllables dragging after, the pause in the middle made the longer because of them. Then comes a sudden rally in the rhymed couplet:

> Some wine, within there, and our viands! Fortune knows
> We scorn her most when most she offers blows.

—its irregular first line just saving it from sounding mechanical.

The violence of Antony's anger when he finds Thidias kissing Cleopatra's hand has its own notation and tune.

> Approach there! Ah, you kite! Now, gods and devils!
> Authority melts from me. Of late, when I cried 'Ho!',
> Like boys unto a muss, kings would start forth
> And cry 'Your will?' Have you no ears?
> I am Antony yet. Take hence this jack and whip him.

Long lines, giving a sense of great strength. Exclamatory phrases, prefacing and setting off the powerful center-phrase, with its ringing "kings" for a top note. The caesura-pause of two beats that the short line allows is followed by the repeated crack of two more short phrases, the first with its upward lift, the second with its nasal snarl and the sharp click of its ending; the last line lengthens out, and the business finishes with the bitten *staccato* of

> Take hence this jack and whip him.

Note the deadly flick of the last two words!

The sense apart, what an almost willful pathos we feel in the smoothly sustained, one- and two-syllable worded, predominantly thin-vowelled speech of Antony's to the weeping servants!

> Tend me to-night;
> May be it is the period of your duty:
> Haply you shall not see me more; or if,
> A mangled shadow: perchance to-morrow
> You'll serve another master. I look on you
> As one that takes his leave. Mine honest friends,
> I turn you not away; but, like a master
> Married to your good service, stay till death.
> Tend me to-night two hours. I ask no more;
> And the gods yield you for 't.

Note in particular the importance given to "A mangled shadow"
by the sustaining tripled consonant, and the two-beat pause that
follows ("to-morrow," with its weak ending, ranking for a dis-
syllable), and how the repeated, "Tend me to-night" rounds in
the speech a trifle artificially.

Throughout these scenes, throughout the play indeed, one can
so analyze the verse, find its rhythm and music, often transcending
rule, but always close fitted to mood and meaning. The best
moments need no analysis, and seem to defy it. One must not
appear to be praising.

> I am dying, Egypt, dying; only
> I here importune death awhile, until
> Of many thousand kisses the poor last
> I lay upon thy lips.
>   I dare not, dear—,
> Dear, my lord, pardon,—I dare not,
> Lest I be taken:

merely for the way in which a short first line allows for the two
silent breaths that will show Antony's flagging strength, nor for
the infallible accenting of Cleopatra's fear, first upon the "dare,"
and then, with repetition, upon the "not." But actors have to
concern themselves with such impertinences.

The passionate hysteria of her

>   Where art thou, death?
> Come hither, come! come, come, and take a queen
> Worth many babes and beggars!

PROCULEIUS.   O, temperance, lady!
CLEOPATRA.   Sir, I will eat no meat, I'll not drink, sir—
                If idle talk will once be necessary—
                I'll not sleep neither: this mortal house I'll
                ruin . . . .

asks neither comment nor analysis. Why waste time trying to
scan the last line? It is right, and not the extremest perversity
could speak it wrongly, one would suppose. Nor will much more
be gained by trying to extract meaning from the last line but
one. If it has any in particular (which seems doubtful) no audience could be made to grasp it. But as a setting of hysterical gib-
bering to verbal music, it is perfect.

But one technical excellence among many it is hard to pass by. As Shakespeare nears the last great moment, that of Cleopatra's death, he wants to give his verse solid strength and dignity; and the pulse of it now throbs with a steady intensity, goes processionally forward, as it were.

> Give me my robe, put on my crown; I have
> Immortal longings in me: now no more
> The juice of Egypt's grape shall moist this lip.
> Yare, yare, good Iras: quick! Methinks I hear
> Antony call; I see him rouse himself
> To praise my noble act; I hear him mock
> The luck of Cæsar, which the gods give men
> To excuse their after wrath. . . .

Regular meter, saved from formality by the subtle variety of the mid-line stopping; the whole welded into unity by the constant carrying-on of the sentences from line to line. But, lest the effect grow all too set, Charmian is let interpose, a little later, not a single line but one and a half. Then, lest life die out of it, we have—after the added emphasis of an irregular line, in which Cleopatra lays hands on the asp with a heavily accentuated "Come . . ."—the words clipped, the pace quickened. Twice more Charmian interrupts, but now with phrases that sustain rather than break the rhythm.

CLEOPATRA.	Come, thou mortal wretch,
	With thy sharp teeth this knot intrinsicate
	Of life at once untie; poor venomous fool,
	Be angry, and despatch. O, could'st thou speak,
	That I might hear thee call great Cæsar ass
	Unpolicied!
CHARMIAN.	O eastern star!
CLEOPATRA.	Peace, peace!
	Dost thou not see my baby at my breast,
	That sucks the nurse asleep?
CHARMIAN.	O break! O break!
CLEOPATRA.	As sweet as balm, as soft as air, as gentle!
	O, Antony!—Nay, I will take thee too:
	What should I stay—?

Not one beat has been missed till her dying breaks the last line; yet we have been no more conscious of the form than when the verse was at its loosest, only of the added power.

Shakespeare no longer divides his characters into speakers of verse and speakers of prose, nor makes this distinction regularly between scenes. The freedom and variety of his verse writing allow him to pass almost imperceptibly from poetry to prose and back again. Thus he ranges an unbroken scale, from a pedestrian exactitude in stating plain fact at one end of it to the conventional flourish of the rhymed couplet at the other. But he can still make the sharp contrast of a change effective between scene and scene; or in the midst of a scene he can bring passion or pretentiousness down to earth—and prose, or as suddenly restore force and dignity with rhythm and tone. And he can go to work more subtly than that. As in stagecraft, so in his play's actual writing, exploiting freedom to the full, he has forged a weapon of extraordinary suppleness and resource.

For instance, in the ostensibly prose scene that follows the play's more formal opening, we have the Soothsayer countering Charmian's impudent chatter with single lines of verse. Their recurrence lends him peculiarity and a slight portentousness; but the surrounding prose is so subtly adjusted that the device itself passes unnoticed.[34] Later, upon Cleopatra's entrance, the scene is suddenly braced to forcefulness by half a dozen consecutive lines of (not too regular, lest the effect be too noticeable) verse. Later still, with a strong dose of prose, Enobarbus turns Antony's philosophic realism very much the seamy side out.

Enobarbus (he in particular) speaks now verse, now prose, either as the scene requires it of him for harmony or contrast, or as his humors dictate; his character being just such a compound of contrasts. Antony only occasionally relapses to prose, and his verse is regular on the whole. Cleopatra hardly touches prose at all; her verse is apt to be a little freer. Cæsar speaks only verse; it is fairly formal, and expressive of his calculated dignity.

But the supreme virtue of the writing lies in its peculiar combination of delicacy and strength, of richness with simplicity. For simple strength take the quick passage in which Menas tempts Pompey to put to sea and then cut the throats of his guests.

MENAS.   Wilt thou be lord of all the world?
POMPEY.   What say'st thou?

---

[34] We also find Enobarbus entering with a blank verse line. The scene, it is true (see p. 6), shows some signs of rewriting.

MENAS.   Wilt thou be lord of the whole world? That's twice.
POMPEY.   How should that be?
MENAS.   But entertain it,
    And though thou think me poor, I am the man
    Will give thee all the world.

For simplicity, Cleopatra's

> O well-divided disposition! Note him,
> Note him, good Charmian, 'tis the man; but note him.
> He was not sad, for he would shine on those
> That make their looks by his; he was not merry;
> Which seemed to tell them his remembrance lay
> In Egypt with his joy; but between both:
> O heavenly mingle!

For delicacy, her

> But bid farewell and go: when you sued staying,
> Then was the time for words: no going then;
> Eternity was in our lips and eyes,
> Bliss in our brows' bent; none our parts so poor,
> But was a race of heaven. . . .

or Antony's

> Come, let's all take hands;
> Till that the conquering wine hath steeped our sense
> In soft and delicate Lethe.

or his picture of Octavia:

> Her tongue will not obey her heart, nor can
> Her heart inform her tongue—the swan's down-feather,
> That stands upon the swell at the full of tide,
> And neither way inclines.

For strength, his malediction of Cleopatra:

> You were half-blasted ere I knew you; ha!
> Have I my pillow left unpressed in Rome,
> Forborne the getting of a lawful race,
> And by a gem of women, to be abused
> By one that looks on feeders?

or his dismissal of the half-flayed Thidias.

> Get thee back to Cæsar;
> Tell him thy entertainment: look thou say
> He makes me angry with him; for he seems

> Proud and disdainful, harping on what I am,
> Not what he knew I was. He makes me angry;
> And at this time most easy 'tis to do't,
> When my good stars, that were my former guides,
> Have empty left their orbs, and shot their fires
> Into the abysm of hell.

We constantly have that favorite device, the enrichment of a simple effect by an echoing phrase; as when Cleopatra turns to Antony in pathetic dignity with

> Sir, you and I must part, but that's not it:
> Sir, you and I have loved, but there's not it. . . .

—as in the Soothsayer's response to Antony's command to him to speak no more:

> To none but thee; no more, but when to thee.

The thought also is echoed in Cleopatra's

> That time—O, times!—
> I laughed him out of patience; and that night
> I laughed him into patience: and next morn
> Ere the ninth hour, I drunk him to his bed. . . .

and in Enobarbus' remorseful

> This blows my heart:
> If swift thought break it not, a swifter mean
> Shall outstrike thought: but thought will do't, I feel.

Such devices easily degenerate into trick; as this comes near to doing with Cleopatra's

> These hands do lack nobility, that they strike
> A meaner than myself; since I myself
> Have given myself the cause.

—even as the power of concentration which can pack three clear thoughts into those seven words of hers:

> Therefore be deaf to my unpitied folly . . . .

has overreached itself a moment earlier in

> O, my oblivion is a very Antony,
> And I am all forgotten.

The most delicate and precise accenting of the "oblivion" and the "all" may fail to make the meaning of this last clear upon the instant.

But we have concentration, clarity, strength, simplicity all combined in the swift exchange between Alexas and Cleopatra when he brings her the first news of the absent Antony with

> His speech sticks in my heart.
> Mine ear must pluck it thence.

she answers; and in her dark misgiving as the unlucky second messenger faces her:

> But, sirrah, mark, we use
> To say the dead are well: bring it to that,
> The gold I give thee I will melt and pour
> Down thy ill-uttering throat.

and in the primitive

> Call the slave again:
> Though I am mad, I will not bite him: call!

Such things seem easy only when they are done—and well done.

Again, there is artistry of the subtlest in the freedom and apparent ease of this (the same wretched messenger is now atoning for his fault by disparaging Octavia, Charmian abetting him):

MESSENGER.   She creeps:
Her motion and her station are as one;
She shows a body rather than a life,
A statue than a breather.
CLEOPATRA.   Is this certain?
MESSENGER. Or I have no observance.
CHARMIAN.   Three in Egypt
Cannot make better note.
CLEOPATRA.   He's very knowing;
I do perceive 't: there's nothing in her yet;
The fellow has good judgment.
CHARMIAN.   Excellent.
CLEOPATRA. Guess at her years, I prithee.
MESSENGER.   Madam,
She was a widow.—
CLEOPATRA.   Widow! Charmian, hark!

—in the way the continuing swing of the verse keeps the dialogue swift while the dividing of the lines gives spontaneity.

Note how actual incoherence—kept within bounds by the strict rhythm of the verse—leads up to, and trebles the nobility of a culminating phrase. (She and her women surround the dead Antony.)

> How do you, women?
> What, what, good cheer? Why, how now, Charmian!
> My noble girls! Ah women, women, look!
> Our lamp is spent, it's out. Good sirs, take heart:
> We'll bury him; and then, what's brave, what's noble,
> Let's do it after the high Roman fashion,
> And make death proud to take us. . . .

The compelled swiftness of the beginning, the change without check when she turns to the soldiers, the accordant discipline of the line which follows, so that the last two lines can come out clarion-clear; here, again, is dramatic music exactly scored. In like fashion Antony's mixed metaphors (when he has been told she is dead), which include something very like a pun, lead up to and enhance a luminous close.

> I will o'ertake thee, Cleopatra, and
> Weep for my pardon. So it must be, for now
> All length is torture: since the torch is out,
> Lie down and stray no farther: now all labour
> Mars what it does: yea, very force entangles
> Itself with strength: seal then, and all is done.
> Eros!—I come, my queen: Eros!—Stay for me:
> Where souls do couch on flowers, we'll hand in hand,
> And with our sprightly port make the ghosts gaze:
> Dido and her Æneas shall want troops,
> And all the haunt be ours.

While, for a glorious and famous passage that is music itself—but what more?—take:

> O see, my women,
> The crown o' the earth doth melt. My lord!
> O, withered is the garland of the war,
> The soldier's pole is fall'n: young boys and girls
> Are level now with men; the odds is gone,
> And there is nothing left remarkable
> Beneath the visiting moon.

This, in analysis, is little better than ecstatic nonsense; and it is meant to sound so. It has just enough meaning in it for us to feel as we hear it that it may have a little more. Art must by so much at least improve on nature; in nature it would have less or none.

But it gives us to perfection the reeling agony of Cleopatra's mind; therefore, in its dramatic setting, it ranks as supreme poetry.

Utterly sure of himself, Shakespeare has, in fine, reached in the writing as in the shaping of this play limits of freedom and daring that he will not, but for the worse, overpass.

The Characters

ANTONY

In the two early episodes of his breaking from Egypt and of his welcome to Rome Antony is painted for us in breadth and detail; they give us the man complete, and thereafter the drama of his actions needs no alloy of analysis or explanation.

Shakespeare's first strokes seldom fail to be significant. The four words to the messenger, who crosses Antony's uncharted path as he and Cleopatra saunter by, with

> News, my good lord, from Rome.
> Grates me! The sum?

(the harsh, impatient, yet slightly conscience-stricken sound of it!); the next three to Cleopatra:

> How, my love?

(the softened vowels!), then the full diapason of the heroic, yet fustian-flavored

> Let Rome in Tiber melt, and the wide arch
> Of the ranged empire fall! . . .

—here, in a few phrases, we have the gallant grown old and the confident conqueror in decline. He passes on; the keynote has been struck. But Philo's sad, scrupulous

> Sir, sometimes when he is not Antony,
> He comes too short of that great property
> Which still should go with Antony.

promises, and Cleopatra's descent upon her giggling maids preludes another tune in him with

CLEOPATRA. Saw you my lord?
ENOBARBUS.   No, lady.
CLEOPATRA.   Was he not here?

CHARMIAN.   No, madam.
CLEOPATRA.   He was disposed to mirth; but on the sudden
             A Roman thought hath struck him. . . .

She sees him coming and will have him see her go, her offended
nose in the air. But if he does he ignores her.[35]

The so-lately snubbed messenger is with him, talking, and
encouraged to, as man to man. (These messengers, by the bye,
are not errand boys, but men of responsibility.) This is the Antony—or little less than he—that could coolly outface and out-
scheme the mob of Cæsar's murderers, outgeneral the ideologue
Brutus and Cassius the fanatic; it is Antony the realist, and never
a starker one than when he needs to see himself coldly and clearly
as he is. And he is enough a master of men to dare to let them see
him so!

        Who tells me true, though in his tale lie death,
        I hear him as he flattered.

This encounter with the messengers sets him very relentlessly
before us. Shakespeare has never had more illusions about Antony
than he about himself. In *Julius Cæsar* how swiftly the heroics of
the Capitol and the flattering eloquence of the Forum were followed by the calm proposal to Lepidus and Octavius to cheat the
citizens, whose hearts he had just won, of part of their legacies;
and, Lepidus being sent on this errand, to jockey *him* next out of
his share of the spoils. But, whatever he was at, there was a sportsmanlike gaiety about him then. He has grown colder with the
years, cynically philosophical. It is a quality of greatness in a man,
no doubt, that seeks the truth and sees it even in himself, boldly
lets others see it. But such truth, seen and shown with such indifference! Colder; and callous, one adds.

The second messenger's appearance is heralded by ominous
hesitations. (The play abounds in these delicacies of craftsmanship.) And, when he does appear, Antony, by that unusual

---

[35] The Folio gives us Antony's entrance before Cleopatra's line

        We will not look upon him; go with us.

Modern editions are too apt to place it after, and after her departure, quite
obliterating the intended effect. There is even the shadow of a further one. If
Enobarbus has already gone to look for Antony, it is with a little train of Egyptians
that Cleopatra sails off, leaving the barbarian Romans to their business.

> What are you?

reads trouble in the sight of him. The answer comes straight:

> Fulvia thy wife is dead.

The response, the curt question,

> Where died she?

makes no sentimental pretenses; and, the messenger dismissed, he is as honest with himself.

> There's a great spirit gone! Thus did I desire it.
> What our contempts doth often hurl from us,
> We wish it ours again: the present pleasure
> By revolution lowering, does become
> The opposite of itself.—She's good, being gone . . . .

And Enobarbus, summoned to make ready for departure, is in talk with him a minute or more before, casually abrupt, he says

> Fulvia is dead.
> Sir?
> Fulvia is dead.
> Fulvia!
> Dead.

We recall Brutus and Cassius and Portia's death.[36] This also, then, would seem to be in "the high Roman fashion." But how truly English, too, the avoidance of the subject, the curt exchange to hide emotion—which, it may be, is not there to hide!

Enobarbus' frank brutalities lend by contrast dignity to his chief, as, lost now in "Roman thoughts," he passes on to take his leave of Cleopatra. He knows her

> cunning past man's thought. . .

He is free of her forever if he would be; and it is hardly, one would say, a very fatal passion that shows in his farewell. He looks for tantrums.

> I am sorry to give breathing to my purpose . . . .

An uncomfortably polite opening; it is an awkward business.

---

[36] *Brutus.*   No man bears sorrow better. Portia is dead.
   Cassius.   Ha! Portia!
   Brutus.   Dead.

She plays her every pretty trick on him; but she can tell that the Roman thought has, for the moment, conquered.[37] His protests come easily; she makes short work of them. She stirs him to candor by twitting him with "Liar"; but she unmasks more reality than she bargained for.

> Hear me, queen.
> The strong necessity of time commands
> Our services awhile. . . .

—and when Antony bites thus on his words, it is as well to be silent and listen. We are at the pivot of the scene, its revealing moment. He unfolds for her, with all the force of his mind, his tangled task ahead. She listens indifferently: what are politics and Sextus Pompeius to her? Then he adds—as if it were an item forgotten in the sum—

> My more particular,
> And that which most with you should safe my going,
> Is Fulvia's death.

Spoiled wanton of a woman she may be, but she has a sensitiveness he lacks and a humanity he has lost. On the instant there possesses her such a sense of the pitiful transient littleness of life:

> Though age from folly could not give me freedom
> It does from childishness. Can Fulvia 'die'?

—of her own life too, and of their love:

> Now I see, I see,
> In Fulvia's death, how mine received shall be.

Yet the next instant she is trifling it away and at her tricks again.

The duel goes on, he obstinately asserting that it is all to her queenly advantage he should go, she pricking and stinging him with her woman's grievances. She cannot change his purpose, but she knows how to conquer in retreat.

> But, sir, forgive me,
> Since my becomings kill me when they do not
> Eye well to you! Your honour calls you hence:
> Therefore be deaf to my unpitied folly,
> And all the gods go with you. Upon your sword

---

[37] Note a technicality. Cleopatra has not to be told that he is going; she guesses or has already heard; she saw him, indeed, confabulating with that fatal messenger. This starts the scene at the needed pitch; no time is wasted working up to it.

> Sit laurel victory! and smooth success
> Be strewed before your feet!

That, she sees to it, shall be his remembrance of her.

He is found next in Rome, confronting Cæsar and outtopping him; and by how much more the lesser men around, Lepidus, Agrippa, Mæcenas and the rest. In this scene and those deriving from it we have Antony at his ablest, the seasoned statesman. That prefatory hint at his soldiership, peaceably though he now comes,

>   'Tis spoken well,
> Were we before our armies and to fight,
> I should do thus.

the quick opening of the argument, when courtesies with Cæsar have been exchanged,

> I learn, you take things ill that are not so,
> Or, being, concern you not.

give him vantage of position. He has, it would appear, a poor enough case to plead. He makes neither useless defense nor impulsive apology, but with clever dialectic shapes the issue, as far as may be, to his liking. Cæsar is pettish, but Antony—diplomatist that he is—remains proof against pin-pricks. He even jokes about the dead Fulvia and her "garboils."

>   As for my wife,
> I would you had her spirit in such another.
> The third o' the world is yours, which with a snaffle
> You may pace easy, but not such a wife.

He makes shrugging confession of his own failings; and in all so takes the wind out of Cæsar's sails that that self-conscious respectability is stung at last into taxing this elderly scapegrace point blank with perjury—very much to Lepidus' alarm. Antony still stays unruffled. But, with his adversary trapped into such rashness, we can feel his wrist harden and see the steely eye above the easy smile.

>   No,
> Lepidus, let him speak:
> The honour is sacred which he talks on now,
> Supposing that I lacked it. But, on, Cæsar;
> The article of my oath.

Cæsar does not shirk; but he speaks now by the card. Antony (in his own phrase) paces them all with a snaffle. Let them take no liberties, though. He may jest about Egypt; they had better not.

Then Mæcenas and Agrippa take up their allotted part in the peacemaking. The marriage with Octavia is broached.

> great Mark Antony
> Is now a widower.

The outmatched Cæsar cannot resist a malicious gibe.

> Say not so, Agrippa:
> If Cleopatra heard you, your reproof
> Were well deserved of rashness.

He earns the snub direct.

> I am not married, Cæsar: let me hear
> Agrippa further speak.

But business is business, and a peace is patched up between the two, "according to plan."

From now to the consummating of the treaty with Pompey, and thereafter to the brotherly parting with Cæsar, Antony stands in the sun. These men know his worth to them and he knows it. Secure in reputation, he can be generous to Pompey, who girds at him too; he is even civil to Lepidus. And he brings to Octavia such a boyish penitence—

> My Octavia,
> Read not my blemishes in the world's report:
> I have not kept my square; but that to come
> Shall all be done by the rule.

—that how should we not, with the good Mæcenas, trust to her beauty, wisdom and modesty to settle his chastened heart? But Enobarbus has warned us betimes; and we see him, on the instant, turn from her to the Soothsayer, that sinister shadow of his bewitchment; and the very next we hear is

> I will to Egypt:
> And though I make this marriage for my peace,
> I' the East my pleasure lies.

He is lost. And the significant thing is that he sinks without an effort from sanity to folly. He has won back his lost ground. We have seen him, with easy authority, outmatching Cæsar, and

Cæsar, for all his jealousy, shrewdly content to be outmatched. Yet here he is flinging everything away. This is not the Antony of Philippi, of the Capitol and the Forum. His spirit all afraid to govern him near Cæsar! Is it, indeed!? Cæsar has all the luck at dicing and cockfighting. No doubt! But the naked truth is that the sensual man in him must find excuse for the

> I will to Egypt. . . .
> I' the East my pleasure lies.

and any is better than none.

This is the nemesis of the sensual man. Till now Antony's appetites have not fatally played him false. Such gifts and vitality as his can for long enough make the best of both worlds, the sensual and the world of judgment too; for life is bred in passion, and has continuing need of it. But the time comes when Nature finds no more profit in a man, and her saving graces fail him. Antony has never learned to bargain with life; his abundant strength could take politics and love-affairs, interest and inclination in its stride. And now that judgment does pull one way and appetite another there is neither struggle nor dispute, no overt choice made, even. Appetite wins, while judgment winks and ignores defeat. He knows what going back to Cleopatra means.

> These strong Egyptian fetters I must break,
> Or lose myself in dotage.

Yet in the very knitting-up of the new ties that are to save him from her he can say, "I'll go," nor seem to count the cost. He speaks his own doom in a careless phrase—and forgets it. He will have his chance to make a brave show still and a nobler end; but shameful, secret moments such as this are the true counterpart to that earlier conscienceless success. No agony, nor darkening of the spirit before defeat, nor a Promethean defiance of the partial gods. This hero's fate is sealed quite casually, in a talk with a soothsayer about dice and fighting cocks.

Shakespeare adds yet one more touch to his disintegrating. Antony, we shall remember, came with Ventidius to the conference, saying

> If we compose well here, to Parthia.

—to avenge his Egypt-bred defeats there. But now it is

> O, come, Ventidius,
> *You* must to Parthia.

while he will wait the chance to step back to his sty.

This phase of the study of him, in sober businesslike relation to Cæsar and his fellow-Romans, gives great ballast to the play. Cleopatra's hectic scenes stand in current contrast to it, and it is steadying preparation for the violence of the end. It is prose in its temper, but the pitch and swing of the actual verse lend it a more heroic life. There come no exciting clashes; but these close-woven contrasts of character that are its substance are the very stuff of drama.

Shakespeare is never the vindictive moralist, scourging a man with his sins, blind to all else about him. Antony's ending, when we reach it, is of a piece with his life. It is the garment of his good fortune turned inside out; and if some virtues have more luster, some vices are more tolerable in failure than success. Once again, here is no spiritual tragedy of ideals betrayed. The man has had what he wanted from the world; with luck, daring and judgment to bring it him. A debauched judgment, no luck left to draw upon, mere daring become folly, and he loses it; that is the whole story. But he loses like a man, and there is some spiritual tragedy in it too; for if no ideals betray him, yet at every turn he is conscious that he betrays himself. He knows—who better?—that he should not fight Cæsar by sea. He has no reasons to give but

> For that he dares us to't.

All his answer to argument, as he stands supine under Cleopatra's eye, is a weakly obstinate

> By sea, by sea!

though he adds, for excuse, a futile

> But if we fail,
> We then can do't at land.

His mind seems a blank. He has no plan of battle; and with one defeat his nerve and self-respect are gone.

This is his lowest fall, and there in helpless ignominy we might have to leave him

> unqualitied with very shame . . .

to humble himself before his conqueror, to

> dodge
> And palter in the shifts of lowness . . .

—but for Cæsar! Thanks to his enemy, the old courage and a new nobility are made to stir in him. There is a cold unloveliness about Cæsar. With Antony at his mercy—well, he might accord it or refuse it; but surely he need not so promptly send an envoy to win Cleopatra from him who has lost everything for her sake, to tempt her at any price to drive from Egypt

> her all-disgraced friend,
> Or take his life there . . .

Conquerors, it would seem, cannot even learn the common sense of magnanimity. The clever trick comes near, though, to costing Cæsar all he has won and more.

Antony has been no great precisian in such matters himself; but he is thinking now, we may suppose, less of his own shortcomings than of old days of comradeship with Cæsar when the diffident schoolmaster-ambassador returns.

> Is *that* his answer?
> Ay, my lord.
> The queen shall then have courtesy, so she
> Will yield us up.
> > He says so.
> > > Let her know't.

He recovers some at least of his stature as hero with that.

But if this is not spiritual tragedy, still less is it a moral tale, with the scales of vice and virtue neatly tipped for our edifying; Shakespeare has left all that behind with artifice of plot and characters cut to suit it. The light is shining for us here upon things as they were and men as they are. So the heroic gesture can be followed by the folly of the challenge to Cæsar and the savagery of the whipping of Thidias; by the bitter purging of the illusion that was Cleopatra, and at her beck, the prompt re-embracing of it with a narcotic

> I am satisfied.

Yet if Cleopatra is all that in his fury he says she is, and even readier, it may be, to betray him than he thinks, she is not cold-hearted toward him, strange though that may seem.[38] And while

---

[38] Enobarbus believes the very worst of her. But, of course, *he* would!

(by every rule of ready-made morality) his open-eyed return to bondage and debauch should bring him swiftly to defeat,—and fact-facing Enobarbus makes sure it will—on the contrary, it preludes temporary victory, and it is the overconfident Cæsar that must learn a lesson.

But Cæsar is quick to learn, and Enobarbus will prove right in the end (though remorse and malaria end him before he finds it out), and Shakespeare forthwith shows us very plainly the flaws in the prospect. There is the omen of the strange music that the soldiers hear, the sign that

> the god Hercules, whom Antony loved,
> Now leaves him.[39]

and the strange mood in Antony himself that sets him, on the eve of battle, to making his followers weep his likely death.

> The gods make this a happy day to Antony!

is the old legionary's greeting to him as he marches out in the morning; and the response is generous:

> Would thou and those thy scars had once prevailed
> To make me fight at land!

The gods do grant him one more happy day, and we see him at his best in it. Shakespeare shows it as the briefest of the three; a ray shooting through sunset clouds.

He begins it with what may be called the single touch of romantic sentiment in the play. Antony and Cleopatra come out in the early dawn—come from a night of revel, moreover!—like a young bride and bridegroom, laughing together at her pretty fumblings as she helps him put his armor on. A spoiled child's useless fingers; Octavia would have made a neater job of it, one fears! He flatters and pets her:

> Well, well:
> We shall thrive now!

Her glee when she has slipped a strap into place!

> Is not this buckled well?
>   Rarely, rarely! . . .

---

[39] Shakespeare finds this in Plutarch, of course; but there it occurs before the last defeat. He adds an ironic value to it by setting it before the intermediate day of victory.

> Thou fumblest, Eros, and my queen's a squire
> More tight at this than thou.

Seen among his soldiers he is still the Antony of her worship:

> The demi-Atlas of this earth, the arm
> And burgonet of men.

But there are qualities in him that a little pass her understanding, perhaps. For, even as he sets forth, he learns that Enobarbus has deserted; and, very quietly, with no touch of anger, and but one most human shade of bitterness, comes

> What say'st thou?

SOLDIER.   Sir,
> He is with Cæsar.

EROS.   Sir, his chests and treasure
> He has not with him.

ANTONY.   Is he gone?

SOLDIER.   Most certain.

ANTONY.   Go, Eros, send his treasure after; do it;
> Detain no jot, I charge thee: write to him—
> I will subscribe—gentle adieus and greetings;
> Say that I wish he never find more cause
> To change a master. O, my fortunes have
> Corrupted honest men! Despatch. Enobarbus!

He goes to fight, not confident of the issue (not stained with such overconfidence as Cæsar's, certainly), nor braggart of his cause. And when he beats his enemy and returns in triumph, his first thought is to thank his soldiers and to praise before them all the young and wounded Scarus, the hero of the day, who, for his reward, shall kiss Cleopatra's hand. Does she remember Thidias at this juncture, and *his* wounds?

Not much is made of the third day's fighting; nor does Shakespeare trouble with the question which Plutarch leaves unanswered, whether Cleopatra did "pack cards" with Cæsar or no. It is enough that fortune crashes upon Antony in final ruin. There is little noble about him now, in his beastlike rage and thirst for her blood; much though that is pitiful in the wreck of such a man.

> The soul and body rive not more in parting
> Than greatness going off.

For, if but in his folly, he has been great. He has held nothing back, has flung away for her sake honor and power, never weighing their worth against her worthlessness; there is a sort of selfless greatness in that. The lust to kill her before he kills himself is the due backwash of such spendthrift love. He sees her and cannot; folly is folly and weakness is weakness still, he can only damn her to a shamefuller end. Fury racks him again; and then the merciful riving of spirit from body begins. Shakespeare turns, as we have seen, to pure poetry to express it:

> ANTONY.   Eros, thou yet beholdest me?
> EROS.   Ay, noble lord.
> ANTONY.   Sometimes we see a cloud that's dragonish . . . .

He is coming to the end of his strength—even his!—and the body's passions begin to seem unreal, and he to be slipping free of them. Yet another wrench or so of anger, suffering and shame; and the news comes that, in despite of him, she it is that has slipped free.

It is a lie; and he will be a laughingstock in death. What more fitly tragic end for the brilliant general and statesman, the great realist and paragon of worldly wisdom, than to be tricked into emulating the heroism of a Cleopatra, who is, we know, even now safe in her Monument; than to be outdone in quiet courage by his servant; than to bungle his own death-stroke and have to lie begging, in vain, to be put out of his misery? And, as he lies there, he learns the ridiculous truth.

Shakespeare spares him no ignominy; yet out of it rises, not, to be sure, an Antony turned angel, but a man set free of debt to fate, still abiding in his faith, justified of it, then, at the last. When the news of Cleopatra's death comes, he reproaches her no more, says not a word of any loss but this, has no thought but to follow her. What purpose is left him?

> Unarm, Eros; the long day's task is done,
> And we must sleep.

He is nothing without her; the world is empty and time has no meaning.

> Since Cleopatra died,
> I have lived in such dishonour, that the gods
> Detest my baseness . . . .

Since she died, the single minute's passing has been to him as years. And when, dying, he learns that she lives he makes no comment upon that; what do Fate's pettinesses matter now? He asks only to be carried to her that he may die in her arms. Even of this he comes near to being cheated. She will not risk her safety for his sake. But she has them draw him up to her; and his thoughts are for her safety and peace of mind.

> The miserable change now at my end
> Lament nor sorrow at; but please your thoughts
> In feeding them with those my former fortunes,
> Wherein I lived the greatest prince o' the world,
> The noblest; and do now not basely die,
> Not cowardly put off my helmet to
> My countryman—a Roman by a Roman
> Valiantly vanquished. Now my spirit is going;
> I can no more.

He has loved her, the worst and the best of her; and given her the best and the worst of him. He won much from the world, so he had much to lose. Losers ought not to whine. Antony stays a soldier and a sportsman—and a gentleman, by his lights—to the end.

CLEOPATRA

Shakespeare's Cleopatra had to be acted by a boy, and this did everything to determine, not his view of the character, but his presenting of it. Think how a modern dramatist, a practical man of the theater, with an actress for his Cleopatra, would set about the business. He might give us the tragedy of the play's end much as Shakespeare does, no doubt—if he could; but can we conceive him leaving Cleopatra without one single scene in which to show the sensual charm which drew Antony to her, and back to her, which is the tragedy's very fount? Yet this is what Shakespeare does, and with excellent reason: a boy could not show it, except objectionably or ridiculously. He does not shirk her sensuality, he stresses it time and again; but he has to find other ways than the one impracticable way of bringing it home to us. What is the best evidence we have (so to speak) of Cleopatra's physical charms? A description of them by Enobarbus—by the misogynist Enobarbus—given us, moreover, when she has been out of our sight for a quarter of an hour or so. Near her or away from her, Antony himself never speaks of them. He may make such a casual joke as

> The beds i' the East are soft.

or reflect in a fateful phrase,

> I will to Egypt . . . .
> I' the East my pleasure lies.

but Shakespeare will not run even so much risk of having a lover's ecstasies discounted. Enobarbus may grumble out gross remarks about her; but Antony's response, as he plans his escape, is

> She is cunning past man's thought.

The lovers are never once alone together; and the only approach to a "love-scene" comes with our first sight of them, walking in formal procession and reciting antiphonally:

CLEOPATRA.   If it be love indeed, tell me how much.
ANTONY.   There's beggary in the love that can be reckoned.
CLEOPATRA.   I'll set a bourn how far to be beloved.
ANTONY.   Then must thou needs find out new heaven, new
             earth.

This is convention itself. Antony's

> Here is my space.
> Kingdoms are clay: our dungy earth alike
> Feeds beast as man: the nobleness of life
> Is to do thus; when such a mutual pair
> And such a twain can do't. . . .

is pure rhetoric.[40] And the poetry of

> Now, for the love of Love and her soft hours,
> Let's not confound the time with conference
>   harsh.
> There's not a minute of our lives should stretch
> Without some pleasure now. What sport to-
>   night?

CLEOPATRA.   Hear the ambassadors.
ANTONY.   Fie, wrangling queen!
> Whom everything becomes, to chide, to laugh,
> To weep; whose every passion fully strives
> To make itself in thee, fair and admired! . . .

is sensuality sublimated indeed.

---

[40] The "embracing" which Pope and editors after him tagged on to "thus," is not Shakespeare's direction. Whether he means the two to embrace here may be a moot point; but this sort of thing was not what he meant by suiting the action to the word and the word to the action.

Not till their passion deepens as tragedy nears does Shakespeare give it physical expression. Antony leaves her for battle with "a soldier's kiss" (it is the first the action definitely shows) and, returning triumphant, hails her with

> O thou day o' the world,
> Chain mine armed neck: leap thou, attire and all,
> Through proof of harness to my heart, and there
> Ride on the pants triumphing.

A very open and aboveboard embrace. And not till death is parting them do we reach

> I am dying, Egypt, dying; only
> I here importune death awhile, until
> Of many thousand kisses the poor last
> I lay upon thy lips.

with, for its matching and outdoing, her

> welcome, welcome! die where thou hast lived:
> Quicken with kissing: had my lips that power,
> Thus would I wear them out.

By which time, if dramatist and actors between them have not freed the imaginations of their audience from the theater's bonds, all three will have been wasting it. Throughout the play Cleopatra herself gives us glimpses enough of her sensual side.

> Thou, eunuch Mardian!
>   What's your highness' pleasure?
> Not now to hear thee sing. I take no pleasure
> In aught an eunuch has: 'tis well for thee
> That, being unseminared, thy freer thoughts
> May not fly forth of Egypt.

But Shakespeare never has her turn it towards a flesh-and-blood Antony, inviting response.

His only choice, then, is to endow her with other charms for conquest: wit, coquetry, perception, subtlety, imagination, inconsequence—and this he does to the full. And had he a veritable Cleopatra to play the part, what other and what better could he do? How does a Cleopatra differ from the common run of wantons but in just such gifts as these? It would take a commonplace dramatist to insist upon the obvious, upon all that age does wither, while custom even sooner stales its infinite monotony!

It is, of course, with his magic of words that Shakespeare weaves Cleopatra's charm. To begin with, we may find ourselves somewhat conscious of the process. Though that first duet between the lovers is with good reason conventional, they seem slightly self-conscious besides; less themselves, at the moment, than advocates for themselves. Not till Cleopatra reappears has this cloud about her vanished; but nothing of the sort ever masks her again.

CLEOPATRA.	Saw you my lord?
ENOBARBUS.	No, lady.
CLEOPATRA.	Was he not here?
CHARMIAN.	No, madam.
CLEOPATRA.	He was disposed to mirth; but on the sudden
	A Roman thought hath struck him. Enobarbus!
ENOBARBUS.	Madam.
CLEOPATRA.	Seek him and bring him hither. Where's Alexas?
ALEXAS.	Here, at your service. My lord approaches.
CLEOPATRA.	We will not look upon him; go with us.

And when she returns:

> See where he is, who's with him, what he does:
> I did not send you: if you find him sad,
> Say I am dancing: if in mirth, report
> That I am sudden sick: quick, and return.

Here is actuality; and forged in words of one syllable, mainly. This is the woman herself, quick, jealous, imperious, mischievous, malicious, flagrant, subtle; but a delicate creature, too, and the light, glib verse seems to set her on tiptoe.

For the scene with Antony, Shakespeare rallies his resources. We have the pouting

> I am sick and sullen.

the plaintive

> Help me away, dear Charmian; I shall fall:
> It cannot be thus long, the sides of nature
> Will not sustain it.

the darting ironic malice of

> I know, by that same eye, there's some good news.
> What says the married woman? You may go. . . .

and pretty pettishness suddenly throbbing into

> Why should I think you can be mine and true,
> Though you in swearing shake the throned gods,
> Who have been false to Fulvia? . . .

Then the vivid simplicities melt into a sheer magic of the music of words.

> But bid farewell and go: when you sued staying,
> Then was the time for words: no going then;
> Eternity was in our lips and eyes,
> Bliss in our brows' bent; none our parts so poor
> But was a race of heaven. . . .

And so, up the scale and down, she enchants the scene to its end.

For a moment in the middle of it we see another Cleopatra, and hear a note struck from nearer the heart of her. She is shocked by his callously calculated gloss upon Fulvia's death. Vagaries of passion she can understand, and tricks and lies to favor them. But this hard-set indifference! She takes it to herself, of course, and is not too shocked to make capital of it for her quarrel. But here, amid the lively wrangling, which is stimulus to their passion, shows a dead spot of incomprehension, the true division between them. They stare for an instant; then cover it, as lovers will. Fulvia's wrongs make the best of capital; there are poisoned pin-pricks in them, and the second round of the fight leaves him helpless—but to turn and throttle her. The rules of the ring are not for Cleopatra. She takes woman's leave to play the child, and the great lady's to outdo any wench in skittishness; she matches vulgar gibing with dignity and pathos, now loses herself in inarticulate imaginings, now is simple and humble and nobly forgiving. He must leave her; she lets him go. But to the unguessed riddle that she still is he will return.

Let the actress of today note carefully how the brilliant effect of this first parade of Cleopatra is gained. There is no more action in it than the dignity of a procession provides, and the swifter coming and going and returning which ends in this duel of words danced at arm's length with her lover. There is no plot to be worked out; Antony is departing, and he departs, that is all. What we have is the transposing of a temperament into words; and it is in the changing rhythm and dissolving color of them, quite as much as in the sense, that the woman is to be found. Neither place nor time is left for the embroidery of "business," nor for the overpainting of the picture by such emotional suggestion as the author of today legitimately asks of an actress. Anything of that sort will cloud the scene quite fatally. If the shortcomings of a boy Cleopatra were plain, we can imagine his peculiar virtuosity. To the adopted graces of the great lady he would bring a delicate aloofness, which would hover, sometimes very happily, upon the edge of the absurd. With the art of acting still dominantly the art of speech—to be able to listen undistracted an audience's chief need—he would not make his mere presence disturbingly felt; above all, he could afford to lose himself unreservedly—since his native personality must be lost—in the music of the verse, and to let that speak. So in this scene must the Cleopatra of today, if *we* are not to lose far more than we gain by her. There will be the larger demands on her later, those that Shakespeare's indwelling demon made on him; he had to risk their fulfillment then, as now.

But her presenting continues for awhile to be very much of a parade. She is never, we notice, now or later, left to a soliloquy.[41] Parade fits her character (or if Shakespeare fits her character to parade the effect is the same). She is childishly extravagant, ingenuously shameless; nothing exists for her but her desires. She makes slaves of her servants, but she jokes and sports with them, too, and opens her heart to them in anger or in joy; so they adore her. It is not perhaps an exemplary Court, in which the Queen encourages chaff about her paramours, and turns on her lady-in-waiting with

> By Isis, I will give thee bloody teeth,
> If thou with Cæsar paragon again
> My man of men.

but it is at least a lively one, and its expansiveness would be a boon to any dramatist.

She is indeed no sluggardly sensualist; double doses of mandragora would not keep her quiet. What she cannot herself she

---

[41] Nor is anyone else in the play for more than a few lines; another token of it as drama of action rather than of spiritual conflict. We see in this too how far Shakespeare's stagecraft had outgrown the older, conventional, plot-forwarding use of soliloquies. In his earlier plays of action they abound.

must do by proxy; she cannot follow Antony, but her messengers gallop after him every post. Her senses stir her to potent imagery:

> O happy horse, to bear the weight of Antony!
> Do bravely, horse! for wot'st thou whom thou movest. . . .

—if perverted a little:

> now I feed myself
> With most delicious poison.

And in that

> **Think on me,**
> That am with Phœbus' amorous pinches black,
> And wrinkled deep in time.

there is elemental power. And if her praise of Antony for his "well-divided disposition" seems incongruous; why, a nature so sure of itself can admire the qualities it lacks.

Shakespeare shirks nothing about her. What will be left for us of her womanly charm when we have seen her haling the bringer of the news of Antony's treachery up and down by the hair of his head, and running after him, knife in hand, screaming like a fishfag? But this also is Cleopatra. He allows her here no moment of dignity, nor of fortitude in grief; only the pathos of

> CLEOPATRA. In praising Antony, I have dispraised Cæsar?
> CHARMIAN. Many times, madam.
> CLEOPATRA. I am paid for't now.

—which is the pathos of the whipped child, rancorous against its gods, resigned to evil. There is the moment's thought, as she calls the scared messenger back again:

> These hands do lack nobility, that they strike
> A meaner than myself; since I myself
> Have given myself the cause.

And this is a notable touch. It forecasts the Cleopatra of the play's end, who will seek her death after the "high Roman fashion"; it reveals, not inconsistency, but that antithesis in disposition which must be the making of every human equation. It is the second touch of its sort that Shakespeare gives to his picturing of her; and both, in the acting, must be stamped on our memories.[42]

---

[42] The first, her stinging reproach to him for his callousness at Fulvia's death.

The end of the scene sees her, with her maids fluttering round her, lapsed into pitifulness, into childish ineptitude. But again, something of spiritual continence sounds in its last note of all, in the

> Pity me, Charmian;
> But do not speak to me.

The complementary scene, in which the unlucky messenger is re-examined, would be more telling if it followed a little closer; but, as we have seen, Shakespeare has hereabouts an overplus of Roman material to deal with. It is pure comedy, and of the best. She is calm again, very collected, making light of her fury; but an echo of it can be heard in that sudden nasty little snarl which ends in a sigh. Charmian and Iras and Alexas have evidently had a trying time with her. They conspire to flatter her back to confidence—and she lets them. The messenger has been well coached too. But the best of the comedy is in Cleopatra's cryptic simplicity. She likes flattery for its own sake. There is a sensuality of the mind that flattery feeds. What does it matter if they lie to her; of what use is the truth? Anger is crippling; but in the glow of their adulation she uncurls and feels her lithe strength return, and this is her only need.

> All may be well enough.

Yet the words savor faintly of weariness too.

Now comes the war and her undoing. Her disillusion first; for Antony, won back, is no longer the all-conquering captain, from whom she may command Herod of Jewry's head—or Cæsar's!— nor does her own reckless generalship prove much help. We do not, as we have noted, see the reuniting of the lovers; we find her at a nagging match with Enobarbus, and turned, with her Antony, to something very like a shrew. And if to the very end she stays for him an unguessed riddle, "cunning past man's thought," there is much in which Shakespeare is content to leave her so for us— thereby to manifest her the more consummately. By what twists of impulse or of calculation is she moved through the three fateful days of swaying fortune? How ready was she to "pack cards" with Cæsar? What the final betrayal amounted to, that sent Antony raging after her, Shakespeare, it may be said, could not tell us, because he did not know; and her inarticulate terror at this point may therefore show us his stagecraft at its canniest. But in retrospect all this matters dramatically very little; what does matter is that as we watch her she should defy calculation.

It is futile, we know, to apply the usual moral tests to her, of loyalty, candor, courage. Yet because she shamelessly overacts her repentance for her share in that first defeat it by no means follows that she feels none. She lends an ear to Thidias, and the message to Cæsar sounds flat treason; this is the blackest count against her. But soft speech costs nothing, and perhaps it was Cæsar who was to be tricked. Can we detect, though, a new contempt for Antony as she watches him, his fury glutted by the torment of the wretched envoy? She might respect him more had he flogged her instead! Is there in the sadly smiling

> Not know me yet?

with which she counters his spent reproach, and in her wealth of protest, something of the glib falsity of sated ardors? Next morning she buckles on his armor and bids him good-bye like a happy child; but, his back turned:

> He goes forth gallantly. That he and Cæsar might
> Determine this great war in single fight!
> Then, Antony—! But now—?

It is a chilling postscript.

She is like Antony in this at least—and it erects them both to figures of heroic size—that she has never learned to compromise with life, nor had to reconcile her own nature's extremes. To call her false to this or to that is to set up a standard that could have no value for her. She is true enough to the self of the moment; and, in the end, tragically true to a self left sublimated by great loss. The passionate woman has a child's desires and a child's fears, an animal's wary distrust; balance of judgment none, one would say. But often, as at this moment, she shows the shrewd scepticism of a child.

From now till we see her in the Monument and Antony is brought to die in her arms, Shakespeare sinks the figure into the main fabric of the play. He makes a moment's clear picture of the welcome to Antony returned from victory. The

> *Enter Cleopatra, attended.*

might be radiance enough; but, for surplus, we have her ecstatic

> Lord of lords!
> O infinite virtue, comest thou smiling from
> The world's great snare uncaught!

When defeat follows quickly, her collapse to terror is left, as we saw, the anatomy of a collapse and no more. Then, from being but a part of the general swift distraction, she emerges in fresh strength to positive significance again; and—this is important—as a tragic figure for the first time.

From wantonness, trickery and folly, Shakespeare means to lift her to a noble end. But, even in doing it, he shirks no jot of the truth about her. She loses none of her pristine quality. If she victimizes the complacent Dolabella with a glance or two, who shall blame her? But how far she would go in wheedling Cæsar— were there a joint to be found in that armor of cold false courtesy —who shall say? She cheats and lies to him as a matter of course, and Seleucus would fare worse with her than did that once unlucky messenger. Misfortune hardly lends her dignity, the correct Cæsar may well think as he leaves her there. He will think otherwise when he sees her again. But it is not till the supreme moment approaches that she can pretend to any calm of courage. She must sting herself to ever fresh desperation by conjured visions of the shame from which only death will set her free; we hear that "Be noble to myself," "my noble act," repeated like a charm. Yet she is herself to the end. It is the old willful childishness, tuned to a tragic key, that sounds for us in

> O Charmian, I will never go from hence.
> CHARMIAN. Be comforted, dear madam.
> CLEOPATRA.   No, I will not:
> All strange and terrible events are welcome,
> But comforts we despise. . . .

and in the extravagant magnificence of her grief she is the Eastern queen, who could stir even an Enobarbus to rhapsody, and beggar all description. She has no tears for Antony.[43] The shock of his death strikes her senseless, but her spirit is unquelled. Defiant over his body:

---

[43] Throughout the play Cleopatra never weeps. Antony does.

> It were for me
> To throw my sceptre at the injurious gods;
> To tell them that this world did equal theirs
> Till they had stolen our jewel. . . .

The rest may find relief in grieving; not she!

Shakespeare allows her one touch of his favorite philosophy. She reappears, confirmed in her loss.

> My desolation does begin to make
> A better life. 'Tis paltry to be Cæsar;
> Not being Fortune, he's but Fortune's knave,
> A minister of her will. . . .

This is the note, once struck by Brutus, sustained by Hamlet, of failure's contempt for success. We hear it in life, more commonly, from quite successful men, who also seem to find some needed comfort in the thought. It is a recurring note in all Shakespearean tragedy, this exalting of the solitary dignity of the soul; and he will not end even this most unspiritual of plays without sounding it. He passes soon to a somewhat truer Cleopatra—here is the same thought pursued, though—when she counters Dolabella's bland assurance with

> You laugh when boys or women tell their dreams.
> Is't not your trick? . . .
> I dreamt there was an Emperor Antony.
> O, such another sleep, that I might see
> But such another man!

and utterly bewilders him with the hyperbole that follows, strange contrast to Cæsar's recent decorous regret. But it is on such ridiculous heights that genius—even for wantonness—will lodge its happiness. And the next instant he appears, the manikin Cæsar, who has triumphed over her "man of men"! She stares, as if incredulous, till Dolabella has to say

> It is the emperor, madam.

Then she mocks their conqueror with her humilities. But the scene is, besides, a ghastly mockery of the Cleopatra that was. Compare it with the one in which she laughed and pouted and turned Antony round her finger. She is a trapped animal now, cringing and whining and cajoling lest the one chink of escape be stopped. There is no cajoling Cæsar. He betters her at that with his

> Feed and sleep:
> Our care and pity is so much upon you,
> That we remain your friend.

Even so might a cannibal ensure the tenderness of his coming meal. She knows; and when he is gone:

> He words me, girls, he words me, that I should not
> Be noble to myself!

One last lashing of her courage; then a flash of glorious, of transcendent vanity—

> Show me, my women, like a queen: go fetch
> My best attires: I am again for Cydnus,
> To meet Mark Antony.

—a last touch of the old frolicsomeness as she jokes with the clown, peeping the while between the fig-leaves in which the aspics lie; and she is ready.

> Give me my robe, put on my crown; I have
> Immortal longings in me: now no more
> The juice of Egypt's grape shall moist this lip.
> Yare, yare, good Iras: quick! Methinks I hear
> Antony call; I see him rouse himself
> To praise my noble act; I hear him mock
> The luck of Cæsar, which the gods give men
> To excuse their after wrath. Husband, I come:
> Now to that name my courage prove my title! . . .

The dull Octavia, with her "still conclusions," defeated and divorced!

> I am fire and air; my other elements
> I give to baser life. So; have you done?
> Come then, and take the last warmth of my lips.
> Farewell, kind Charmian, Iras, long farewell. . . .

Iras so worships her that she dies of the very grief of the leave-taking.

> Have I the aspic in my lips? Dost fall?
> If thou and nature can so gently part,
> The stroke of death is as a lover's pinch,
> Which hurts and is desired. Dost thou lie still?

> If thus thou vanishest, thou tell'st the world
> It is not worth leave-taking.

Sensuous still, still jealous; her mischievous, magnificent mockery surpassing death itself.

> This proves me base.
> If she first meet the curled Antony,
> He'll make demand of her, and spend that kiss
> Which is my heaven to have. Come, thou mortal wretch,
> With thy sharp teeth this knot intrinsicate
> Of life at once untie; poor venomous fool,
> Be angry and despatch. O, couldst thou speak,
> That I might hear thee call great Cæsar ass
> Unpolicied!

Charmian sees her uplifted, shining:

> O eastern star!

Then follows the consummate

> Peace, peace!
> Dost thou not see my baby at my breast,
> That sucks the nurse asleep?

and in another moment she is dead.

Very well, then, it is not high spiritual tragedy; but is there not something still more fundamental in the pity and terror of it? Round up a beast of prey, and see him die with a natural majesty which shames our civilized contriving. So Cleopatra dies; defiant, noble in her kind, shaming convenient righteousness, a miracle of nature that—here is the tragedy—will not be reconciled to any gospel but its own. She is herself to the very end. Her last breath fails upon the impatient

> What should I stay—?

Her last sensation is the luxury of

> As sweet as balm, as soft as air, as gentle!

And what more luminous summary could there be of such sensual womanhood than the dignity and perverse humor blended in this picture of her yielded to her death—suckling an asp? It defies praise. So, for that matter, does Charmian's

> Now boast thee, death, in thy possession lies
> A lass unparalleled.

—the one word "lass" restoring to her, even as death restores, some share of innocence and youth.

This scene shows us Shakespeare's artistry in perfection, and all gloss upon it will doubtless seem tiresome. But though the reader be teased a little, it cannot hurt him to realize that this close analysis of every turn in the showing of a character and composing of a scene—and much besides—must go to giving a play the simple due of its acting. As reader he cannot lose by knowing what demands the play's art makes on the actor's. The greater the play, the more manifold the demands! When he sees them fulfilled in the theater his enjoyment will be doubled. If they are not, he will a little know why, and so much the worse for the actor; but, at long last, so much the better.

OCTAVIA

Octavia speaks a bare thirty lines, and they are distributed, at that, through four scenes. She is meant to be a negative character, set in contrast to Cleopatra; but if only as an instance of what Shakespeare can do by significant "placing," by help of a descriptive phrase or so, and above all by individualizing her in the music of her verse, she ranks among the play's achievements. She first appears hard upon the famous picturing of Cleopatra in her barge on Cydnus, with this for preface:

> If beauty, wisdom, modesty can settle
> The heart of Antony, Octavia is
> A blessed lottery to him.

—turned, though, to irony by the comment of Enobarbus' grimmest smile and shrug. We then have but a passing sight of her, and only hear her innocently answer Antony's most ambiguous

> The world and my great office will sometimes
> Divide me from your bosom.

with

>   All which time
> Before the gods my knee shall bow my prayers
> To them for you.

She departs with her brother; but before the scene ends the ambiguity is resolved. Antony, we learn, will take his first chance to go back to Cleopatra, and Octavia is already befooled. An unpromising beginning for her.

Next we see her parting from her brother, setting out with an already faithless husband, pledge of an amity between the two as hollow to the sound as mocking comment and bland protest can show it; she helpless to make the false thing true. She weeps at the parting. Antony is kindly in deceit—

> The April's in her eyes: it is love's spring.
> And these the showers to bring it on. Be cheerful.

—and, as she turns back to whisper some woman's misgivings to Cæsar, he sums up their usage of her, and paints her quite inimitably in the sense and very music of

> Her tongue will not obey her heart, nor can
> Her heart inform her tongue—the swan's down-feather,
> That stands upon the swell at the full of tide,
> And neither way inclines.

A gentler victim of great policies one could not find. Another scene shows her shaken off by Antony with the same kindly deceit, grown colder now; another, her return to Cæsar, to a welcome humiliating in its sympathy; and so, impotent in goodness, she vanishes from the play. But we should remember her, if only by such melodies as

> A more unhappy lady
> If this division chance, ne'er stood between,
> Praying for both parts.

as

> The Jove of power make me most weak, most weak,
> Your reconciler! . . .

The gentle and sustained purity of the cadence is all her own. To Cleopatra, of course, she is "dull Octavia," and Antony, in the fury of defeat, can credit her with revengefully "prepared nails"; their obvious tribute to a woman they have wronged.

OCTAVIUS CÆSAR

Cæsar is the predestinate successful man. Beside his passionate rival, he is passionless; no puritan though. If, as he says, Antony merely

> filled
> His vacancy with his voluptuousness. . .

it would be his own affair. But how not lose patience with a part-
ner, and such a man as Antony, when he behaves even as boys will,

> who being mature in knowledge,
> Pawn their experience to their present pleasure,
> And so rebel to judgment.

Still, it is his business as politician, to see things as they are, and he
knows well enough that his prosaic virtues will never fire the
enthusiasms of the Roman mob. He must have the gallant Antony
to counter the danger that the gallant Pompey has now become.
Not that he undervalues himself—far from it! Much as he needs
Antony, he makes no concessions to him; insists rather on his own
correct conduct:

> You have broken
> The article of your oath; which you sháll never
> Have tongue to charge me with.

He must not only be in the right, but keep proving that he is.
This alone labels him second-rate.

But is not this the sort of man that Rome now needs to bring
the pendulum of conflict to a stand? Such genius as Julius
Cæsar's was not to be endured. There was small profit in the
zealotries of a Cassius and a Brutus; and to what Antony will
bring the Empire we see. Octavius Cæsar may seem no great
general. Doubtless at Philippi he "dealt in lieutenantry"; but at
least he does not now send a Ventidius to Parthia to do his work
for him, while he is yet so jealous that the work stays half done.
And is not the best general the one who does deal in lieutenantry
—when he has chosen his lieutenants well? Here is, at any rate,
the industrious, unflagging, cautious man, who wins through in
the end, and can say and mean, most luckily for Rome, that

> The time of universal peace is near.
> Prove this a prosperous day, the three-nook'd world
> Shall bear the olive freely.

though, as we saw, the moment's overconfidence in which he
says it is followed by a day's defeat. Not even the best-regulated
characters can wholly discipline fortune!

Personally he is in many ways, no doubt, an estimable man. If
he sells his sister to Antony— and we should not, of course, take
a sentimental view of such a marriage—he still holds her dear,

and is jealous of her honor. His grief for Antony's death, for his one-time

> mate in empire,
> Friend and companion in the front of war. . .

is not hypocrisy, even though he has, in his own interest, just passed from trying to bribe Cleopatra to have "the old ruffian's" throat cut to orders that he be "took alive," to be brought to Rome to walk (as Antony well knows) chained in his conqueror's Triumph. And if he lies to Cleopatra he does but pay her in her own coin. Nor when she outwits him is he angry; he respects her rather.

> Bravest at the last;
> She levelled at our purposes, and, being royal,
> Took her own way. . . .

Not a lovable man, but a very able one; and we see him growing in ability—such ungenerous natures do—as opportunity matures. If he were not rather humorless, we might suspect him of irony in giving as his excuse for getting rid of Lepidus—having had his use of him—that this meekest of incompetent parasites "was grown too cruel." And there is a savor of cant, perhaps, in the assurance to poor wronged Octavia that

> the high gods
> To do you justice, make their ministers
> Of us and those that love you.

But one may poke fun at a Lepidus with safety; and righteousness —even self-righteousness—is an asset in public life. In sum, he knows the purblind world for what it is, and that it will be safer in his hands than in a greater man's. And while this is so, does it become us, who compose that world, to criticize him very harshly?

ENOBARBUS[44]

When at last this good friend turns traitor Antony says remorsefully:

> O, my fortunes have
> Corrupted honest men! . . .

---

[44] Enobarbus, it is worth remarking, is wholly Shakespeare's own, with nothing owed to Plutarch but the incident of the restored treasure and the (altered) name.

And Enobarbus himself very early shows a sense of some small part of the corruption:

> Mine and most of our fortunes to-night shall be—drunk to bed.

His is the tragedy of cynic mind coupled with soft heart, a tragedy of loyalty to something other than the best one knows.

He is a misogynist confessed, and his talk about women is brutal. Misogyny is recognized armor for a soft-hearted man. But he is as plain-spoken about men, and to their faces besides; nor sparing of himself. Nor is this mere bombast. He sees these chaffering traders in the event as they truly are, and sees further into consequences than do any of them. Antony is his master, and when things go ill he does his best to save him; but good sense and plain speaking will not serve. So far he is a simple variant of the outspoken, honest, disillusioned fellow, a type very useful to the dramatist lacking a chorus; Shakespeare has found it so often enough.

But Enobarbus is not all prose and fault-finding. The rhapsody upon Cleopatra stands out significantly; and when, later, the disintegrating rays of his mind turn inward, they discover him to himself a part and a victim of this timeserving world that he so scorns. It is in the process of his lapse from loyalty, in his sudden collapse from cynicism to pitifulness, that we find Shakespeare's maturer mind and art.[45] We see the moral self-destruction of the man upon whom no man's weakness has imposed, and the completing of a figure of far subtler purport than the conventional, plain blunt image which, at a too careless glance, he may seem to be.

The competent soldier rages against Antony's blundering. But when, with the rest, he could save himself from its consequences, he will not. He chooses the losing side, though his reason "sits in the wind" against him.

-----

[45] This minor tragedy is worked out in a few asides. It is done, as it seems, very casually, but it shows what can be done with thrifty skill in the freedom of the Elizabethan stage; divorced from this, it will be ineffective, probably. It is worth remarking that the asides might well, most of them, be joined up into a long soliloquy; and by Shakespeare's earlier method they probably would be. But by parceling the matter out he preserves the unity and prominence of the main action, and keeps it flowing on. And the whole episode, in its detached quietness, helps to throw Antony's vociferation into high relief.

The loyalty well held to fools does make
Our faith mere folly. Yet he that can endure
To follow with allegiance a fall'n lord,
Does conquer him that did his master conquer,
And earns a place i' the story.

This is strange doctrine for an admitted cynic. Then he argues back and forth as things go from bad to worse; at last cold reason conquers, and he rats. It is too late now; and he is but half-hearted in treason. We next see him standing silent, aloof, ignored by the sufficient Cæsar—and not sorry to be. Then Antony, by one simple, generous gesture of forgiveness, breaks his heart.

There is excellent irony in his end. That the rough-tongued, thick-skinned Enobarbus, of all men, should expire sentimentally, by moonlight, of a broken heart! But the superficial effect is not all. Thus ends another unbalanced man; and whether the inequity lies between passion and judgment as with Antony, or, more covertly, as with Enobarbus, between the armored and the secret self, here was tragedy prepared. And we have seen the waste of a man. For this it is to bring sound sense and loyalty into the service of the Antonys of the world. With blind folly to serve, loyalty and good sense must come to odds; then one will oust the other, and master and man and cause go down in disruption.

POMPEY, LEPIDUS AND THE REST

If in a scheme of things so warped by passion, jealousy and self-seeking, the robust Enobarbus is broken, how shall such weaklings as Pompey and Lepidus survive? "Fool Lepidus" is doomed from the start. He must be everybody's friend; and, while the patching-up of quarrels is in train, who more useful than this mild-mannered little man, with his never-failing, deprecating tact, his perfect politeness?[46] Cæsar condescends to him with scarcely veiled contempt.

'tis time we twain
Did show ourselves i' the field. . . .

But the "twain" are Antony and Cæsar; Lepidus, the "poor third" (as Eros calls him later), counts for nothing. The colleagues "Sir" each other in this scene, we notice, with suspicious

---

[46] One sees him, for the play's purposes, physically also, as a little man.

courtesy. There is a touch of mockery in Cæsar's. Later, the generous Antony pays him compensation for one quite undeserved snub. The little man has started off the critical debate with Cæsar by a reconciling speech, his only eloquent effort:

> then, noble partners,
> The rather for I earnestly beseech,
> Touch you the sourest points with sweetest terms,
> Nor curstness grow to the matter.

and thereafter is so ready—yet never too ready—with cooing interjections, all ignored. Difficulties resolved, he does mildly assert himself; but Cæsar still ignores him, and is departing. Whereupon Antony:

> Let us, Lepidus,
> Not lack your company.
>   Noble Antony,
> Not sickness should detain me.

The little man is grateful.

He cannot carry his liquor, and they laugh at him for that. And all but the last we hear of him is in the mocking duet between Agrippa and Enobarbus.[47]

AGRIPPA.   'Tis a noble Lepidus.
ENOBARBUS.   A very fine one: O, how he loves Cæsar!
AGRIPPA.   Nay, but how dearly he adores Mark Antony!
ENOBARBUS.   Cæsar? Why he's the Jupiter of men!
AGRIPPA.   What's Antony? The god of Jupiter.
ENOBARBUS.   Spake you of Cæsar? How! the nonpareil!
AGRIPPA.   O Antony! O thou Arabian bird!
ENOBARBUS.   Would you praise Cæsar, say 'Cæsar'; go no
             further.
AGRIPPA.   Indeed, he plied them both with excellent
             praises.
ENOBARBUS.   But he loves Cæsar best: yet he loves Antony:
             Hoo! hearts, tongues, figures, scribes, bards,
                poets, cannot
             Think, speak, cast, write, sing, number—hoo!—
             His love to Antony. But as for Cæsar;
             Kneel down, kneel down and wonder.

---

[47] Shakespeare also throws him into contact with Enobarbus for a brief exchange before the reconciling of Cæsar and Antony begins, and the smoothness and roughness make an illuminating contrast.

He comes to no heroic end. Cæsar stows him away somewhere, as one puts a pair of old boots in a cupboard.

> the poor third is up, till death enlarge his confine.

It is a sketch of a mere sketch of a man; but done with what skill and economy, and how effectively placed as relief among the positive forces of the action! Shakespeare (as dramatist) had some slight affection for the creature too. For a last speech, when Octavia is tearfully taking leave as she sets forth with her Antony, he gives him the charming

> Let all the number of the stars give light
> To thy fair way.

Should one call Pompey a weakling? He makes a gallant show; but we suspect from the first that facile optimism:

> I shall do well:
> The people love me, and the sea is mine;
> My powers are crescent, and my auguring hope
> Says it will come to the full . . . .

And in a moment we are finding him out. Bad news must be denied; and when it persists, and there is no doubt that the Triumvirs, all three, are to be in the field against him, why,

> let us rear
> The higher our opinion, that our stirring
> Can from the lap of Egypt's widow pluck
> The ne'er lust-wearied Antony.

The scene ends with an empty flourish:

> Be't as our gods will have't! It only stands
> Our lives upon to use our strongest hands.

Pompey is full of flourishes; for he seems to be conscious of a certain intellectual hollowness within him, he whistles to keep his followers' courage up, and his own.

He is a great man's son. He must not forget it, for no one else will, and there is a certain debility in this. He makes peace discreetly, is magniloquent, scores a verbal point or so; no one may say he is overawed. Then comes Menas' offer to cut the throats of his new allies and make him lord of the world; and he answers

> Ah, this thou shouldst have done
> And not have spoke on't. In me 'tis villainy;

> In thee't had been good service. Thou must know
> 'Tis not my profit that does lead mine honour;
> Mine honour, it.

These gallant gentlemen who look to their honor to profit them, and will profit by other men's dishonor! When the Cæsars of the world override them, the world loses little, one must confess. Pompey fades out of the play. To fit him with an appropriate metaphor, he carries too much sail for his keel.

Relays of minor characters, each with a life of its own, help keep the play alive. Shakespeare's fertility in this kind is here at its full; but so forthright is the work that the action is never checked, each character answers its purpose and no more. Nothing very startling about any of them, nothing very memorable as we look back; but this is as it should be, they are accompaniment to the theme, and, at their liveliest, should never distract us from it. Demetrius and Philo, soldiers ingrain, move for a moment in contrast, make their indignant protest against epicene Egypt and Antony in its toils; they have served their purpose, and we see them no more. The Soothsayer does his mumbo-jumbo, a peculiar figure; and Egypt and what it stands for will flash back to us when we see him, in Roman surroundings, again. The messengers are conventional figures merely; but Shakespeare gives to the person of each one the weight that belongs to his errand, and so augments the strength of the scene. Menecrates and Menas come out of Plutarch as famous pirates. Menas sustains the character most colorfully (and his admittance to distinguished company may throw a little light upon the Elizabethan conscience in this matter), but Menecrates is needed to offer a sententious check to Pompey's soaring confidence.

> We, ignorant of ourselves,
> Beg often our own harms, which the wise powers
> Deny us for our good; so find we profit
> By losing of our prayers.

A philosophic pirate, indeed; and we may see, if we will, the more pragmatic Menas, chafing, but scornfully silent in the background.

Agrippa and Mæcenas hover after Cæsar to the end, putting in the tactful word—which ripens to flattery, we notice, the minute he is secure in power. Such men, of such a measure, are always forthcoming. Shakespeare once spices their utility with the humor of their hanging back to hear the latest Egyptian scandal from Enobarbus; they are gleefully shocked by the eight wild boars at a breakfast and the goings-on of that royal wench Cleopatra. Their names apart, there is no history in them, of course. Ventidius, with good dramatic reason, dominates a single scene; and Eros, Thidias, Scarus, Dolabella and the others give vigor and variety to incident upon incident. They and the rest of the incidental characters provide, one might say, a fluid medium of action with which the stronger colors of the play may be mixed.

Of Charmian and Iras there is rather more to be said. They attend upon Cleopatra and she puts them in the shade; but Shakespeare has touched them in with distinct and delicate care. To give them betimes a little importance of their own we have the scene with the Soothsayer with the irony of its prophecy.

> find me to marry with Octavius Cæsar, and companion me with my mistress.

laughs Charmian. And he answers her:

> You shall outlive the lady whom you serve.

So she does, by one minute!

Thereafter the two of them decorate the Egyptian scenes; deft and apt, poised for their mistress' call. Iras is the more fragile, the more placid; Charmian, the "wild bedfellow," will be the quicker of her tongue, when a word may be slipped in. It is an impudent tongue too; she has no awe of her betters. Worthless little trulls, no doubt! But when disaster comes, and Antony's men, all save one, make their peace with the conqueror, for these two there is no question. They also see what lies behind Cæsar's courtesy; and the timid, silent Iras suddenly breaks silence with

> Finish, good lady; the bright day is done,
> And we are for the dark.

—revealing herself in a dignity of spirit of her own. Another moment and she is trembling again; one would think she could hardly carry her share of the heavy robe and crown. Her service consummated by her mistress' kiss, she dies, as the people of the

East can, so they say, by pure denial of life. Charmian, we know, is of fiercer breed. Quick, desperate, agonized, sticking to her task to the end—when all is over she is at it still, fighting her Queen's battles still, mocking the enemy. She laughs in triumph as she too dies.

Coriolanus

CORIOLANUS cannot be ranked with the greatest of the tragedies. It lacks their transcendent vitality and metaphysical power. But while neither story nor characters evoke such qualities, those they do evoke are here in full measure. The play is notable for its craftsmanship. It is the work of a man who knows what the effect of each stroke will be, and wastes not one of them. And while ease and simplicity may sometimes be lacking, an uncertain or superfluous speech it would be hard to find. Was Shakespeare perhaps aware of some ebbing of his imaginative vitality—well there may have been after the creation in about as many years of *Othello, King Lear, Antony and Cleopatra* and *Macbeth*! and did he purposefully choose a subject and characters which could make the most of by judgment and skill?

The play follows close, it would seem, upon *Antony and Cleopatra.* Between the two there is the general likeness of a setting in Roman history. For the rest, the contrasts are so many and so marked as hardly to be fortuitous. To that large picture of an imperial Rome and a decadent Egypt and of

> The triple pillar of the world transformed
> Into a strumpet's fool.

succeeds this story of earlier and austerer days, of a Rome still challengeable by her neighbors, and of a very different hero. Antony and Caius Marcius are men of action both. But Antony is the astute politician too, and by that talent could save himself from disaster if he would—does save himself and has the game in his hands, only to throw it away because

> The beds i' the East are soft.

Antony—and Othello and Macbeth too—are soldiers, famous generals; but that is not the side of them we come to know. Coriolanus is the man of action seen in action, and among the heroes of the maturer canon unique in this.[1] He is the younger man, a fighter and a brilliant one, but effectively no more. He is at heart—and despite his trials remains to the end—the incorrigible boy, with "Boy!" for the final insult flung at him by Aufidius that he will at no price swallow. And save in physical valor (of which in the elder, by the plan of the action, we hear but see nothing) in every trait he and Antony radically differ. To the one his men are "my good fellows." He jokes with them, praises them impulsively and generously for their pluck. The other is curt, even to friends and equals, self-conscious, and incapable of the least appeal to the populace he despises. In his contempt for spoils and rewards, in his stubbornness, his aristocratic pride, in his chastity—Virgilia greeting him on his minatory return, it is

> Now, by the jealous queen of heaven, that kiss
> I carried from thee, dear; and my true lip
> Hath virgined it ever since.

—in every significant feature the two stand contrasted.

Then in Cleopatra's place we have Volumnia; for the exotic mistress the Roman mother. Yet each in her fashion brings ruin, to lover or son. And for the Egyptian Court, in which, says Enobarbus,

> Mine and most of our fortunes to-night shall be—drunk to bed.

we exchange that picture of the simple Roman home, its great ladies content to

> *set themselves down on two low stools and sew.*

The contrasts are pervasive too. In the one play the action is spacious and varied beyond comparison; Shakespeare's every resource is drawn upon, his invention finds full scope. In *Coriolanus* it is disciplined, kept to its single channel, and the story moves lucidly and directly to its retributive end. And in one

[1] And even Henry V, at war, is not seen fighting. He is the didactic hero, and this is far less mature dramatic work.

major difference most of the rest are rooted: in the part played in
each by the idea of Rome. In each, of course, it is a vital part.
Antony early forecasts his own ruin in that reckless

> Let Rome in Tiber melt, and the wide arch
> Of the ranged empire fall!

Cleopatra's first note of alarm lest she lose him sounds in the

> He was disposed to mirth; but on the sudden
> A Roman thought hath struck him.

and throughout she is a prey to her jealousy, hatred and dread
of Rome. Still, this is little more than a background for the
personal passion. But in *Coriolanus* everything centers upon
Rome. It is the play's one sounding board. The springs of the
action are there. Coriolanus himself sinks at last by comparison to
something like second place. He returns for his revenge, and all
thoughts and eyes are on him. He departs, self-defeated; and it is
Volumnia who re-enters the city in triumph, hailed by a

> Behold our patroness, the life of Rome!

And his death thereafter in Corioles even approaches anticlimax.

But this fidelity to the larger, less personal theme lends the play
a very Roman strength and solidity, which compensates to some
degree, and in its kind, for the lack of such plenary inspiration as
has given us Lear or Macbeth, colossal and then stripped to the
soul. The play gains strength too from the keying of its action
throughout to strife of one sort or another. Of no other of the plays
can it be said that, but for an incidental scene or so, and for the
stilled suspense in which we listen to Volumnia's ultimate
pleadings, the quarreling and fighting scarcely cease from beginning to end. It is dramatically the more important, then,
that the opposing stresses should be kept fairly balanced, in
sympathy as well as in force. Amid mere ebb and flow of
violence the interest of the action could not be sustained. But the
balance is adjusted and continually readjusted, the tension never
quite relaxed. And the skill of the play's workmanship shows
largely in this.

The story allows for scene after scene of actual fighting, and
Shakespeare contrives for these every sort of variety: ranging in
the war with the Volscians from the amazing sight of Marcius

pitted against a whole city-full to the duel with Aufidius; in the struggle with the citizens from the victory where, sword in hand, he leads a handful of his friends against the rabble, a victory he is persuaded not to pursue, to the defeat in which this same rabble, better disciplined by the Tribunes, combine to banish him. And in the play's closing passages, the happy shouts of the Romans, freed from their fears, are contrasted with the spurious triumph of the Volscians.

The balance of sympathy also is fairly adjusted, neither side capturing—and keeping—overmuch. Shakespeare has been freely charged, in an age apt to be prejudiced in its favor, with bias against the populace. Allow for a little harmless ridicule and it is really not so. They are no match for Menenius in a contest of wit— although one of them, to his surprise, gamely stands up to him— but they see through Marcius' mockery, for all that they are too polite to tell him so. In that scene of the "garment of humility," indeed, his manners contrast most unfavorably with theirs. Individually, they seem simple, kindly creatures; collectively, they are doubtless unwise and unstable. They are human. Marcius has been their enemy, and they do not forget it. He declares that he remains so, and when he attacks them, they retaliate. They follow their leaders blindly, are misled and turn on them savagely at last. It is not a very sentimental survey, certainly. But why should it be?

The Tribunes are left the unqualified "villains of the piece"; a surface of comic coloring—which by making them amusingly contemptible may make them a little less detestable—is the only mitigation allowed them. But not one of the characters with a capital share in the melee of the action is very sympathetically drawn. Not, certainly,

> Worthy Menenius Agrippa; one that hath always loved the people.

—so acclaimed by them at our first sight of him, but in fact, as we soon find, cajoling them and sneering at them by turns. Not Aufidius, unstable in good and ill. The untender Volumnia remains so to the last, heedless in her triumph of the price her son must pay for it; a point made implicitly only, but clearly enough to leave us feeling cold towards her. And Shakespeare treats Caius Marcius himself detachedly, as a judge might, without creative warmth. Both sides of his case are to be heard; and we see him first at his worst (an unusual introduction for a titular hero), bullying the hungry citizens. The balance is soon adjusted by evidence—the fighter seen actually fighting—that his valor exceeds all tales of it; in battle and after it he stands out as hero supreme. And his trial of character, when this begins, is lifted, at its crisis, to high ground. It is not his ill-conditioned egoism but his fervent championship of an unpopular faith that gets him driven from Rome. The balance shifts violently when he seeks recreant revenge for this, to be shifted again when at the last moment he abandons it and pays the penalty. Finally, something like justice is done.

The play's range of characters is not a wide one, for it is kept closely relevant to the demands of the action, and these do not by much overspread the direct channel of the story. But within this range Shakespeare works with complete surety. We have that most leisurely of openings, the tale of the Belly and the Members, and Marcius' first attack on the citizens—much of a distractingly different sort having to happen before that full quarrel is joined— is given good scope. The geography of the battle-scenes by Corioles is schemed for us as concisely as clearly. But we have their action at length; for this serves to fill out the characters of Marcius, of Cominius and Titus Lartius too, each the more himself by contrast with the others; the prudent Consul and the old warrior, so young at heart, who will

> lean upon one crutch and fight with t'other,
> Ere stay behind this business.

generously happy, both of them, in their arrogant young hero's glory. The dispute that leads to the banishment is thrashed out at fullest length, argued back and forth, and yet again, nothing significant left uncanvassed. Later, in the scene at Antium, which brings us the renegade Coriolanus, we note that Shakespeare gives as much space to the sly, flunkey commentings of Aufidius' servants upon the amazing business and their master's romantic aberration as he has to the encounter itself. This, besides lowering the tension, helps resolve the new combination into the unheroic key in which it will be worked out.

Shakespeare has now come to ask for more sheer acting from his actors than he did, for more meaning and feeling to be compressed occasionally into half a dozen words than would once have flowed from a rhetorical hundred, for expressive listening as well as expressive speech, for silence itself sometimes to be made eloquent.

Holds her by the hand, silent.

—the play's most tragic moment, in which Marcius accepts defeat and in the sequel death at his mother's hand, confided to a simple stage direction.[2] Throughout the play action and words are expressively keyed together, the action of as great an import as the words. Marcius' share in the scene of the wearing of the gown of humility is as much picturing as speaking; and the mere sight of him later in his Roman dress, surrounded by the Volsces in theirs, sitting in council with them, marching into Corioles at their head—the graphic discord vivifies the play's ending.[3] The sight of the silently approaching figures of Volumnia, Virgilia and Valeria makes double effect; directly upon us, and upon us again through the effect made upon Marcius. And little though Virgilia says (and Valeria not a word), Volumnia so insistently joins them to her plea that their simple presence has an all but articulate value; while the actual spectacle of Marcius fighting singlehanded "within Corioles gates" is better witness to his prowess than any of the "acclamations hyperbolical" which he somewhat self-consciously decries. The memory of it, moreover, will not fade, only lie dormant until at the last it is rekindled by the magnificently trenchant

---

[2] And it is pretty certainly Shakespeare's own. Such moments of eloquent silence are to be found indicated, more or less explicitly, in all the later plays. A very notable one comes with Macbeth's hearing of his wife's death. Another follows upon the blow that Othello publicly deals Desdemona.

[3] In *Cymbeline*, certainly, costume marks the difference between Roman and British, and in *Macbeth* between Scots and English; in *Antony and Cleopatra*, probably, between Roman and Egyptian. We may take for granted, I think, that Volscians and Romans were dressed distinctively. A "realistic" reading may suggest that Marcius would cast off his Roman garb with his allegiance. But I believe that, quitting the "mean apparel" in which he went to encounter Aufidius, he would reappear as a Roman general, the dramatic effect being worth more than any logic.

"Boy"! false hound!
If you have writ your annals true, 'tis there,
That, like an eagle in a dove-cote, I
Fluttered your Volscians in Corioles:
Alone I did it.

Here, then, we have a play of action dealing with men of action; and in none that Shakespeare wrote do action and character better supplement and balance each other.

The Characters

CAIUS MARCIUS

MARCIUS is by no means a sympathetic character, and Shakespeare's attitude towards him seems, as we say, to be less that of a creator than a judge. There is a sense in which—brought to it by the art of dramatist and actor—we can come to "sympathize" even with the murderer Macbeth, as we can pity the murderer Othello, having learned to put ourselves imaginatively in their place. But we are left detached observers of Coriolanus; now admiring his valor, now exasperated by his harsh folly, touched occasionally by the flashes of nobility, the moments of gentleness. Yet we are never wholly at one with him, never made free of the inward man. And the juncture which could best bring this into play, the spiritual crisis in which he decides for his renegade revenge on Rome, is boldly and neatly side-stepped. It is strange, says Marcius in that one short soliloquy, how quickly enemies may become friends and friends turn enemies.

So with me:
My birth-place hate I, and my love's upon
This enemy town.

We are (this is to tell us) past the play's turning point already. The crucial change in the man has already taken place; and of the process of it we learn nothing. But this is not necessarily a shortcoming on Shakespeare's part—as were Marcius a Hamlet it would be. *Was* there any such explicable process? He is not a man of reason, but of convictions and passionate impulses, which can land him in a sudden decision—and he will not know how he came by it. That may help make him a good fighter, less good, probably, as a general, certainly a poor politician. And it justifies Shakespeare's treatment of him here. By his mere looks, in the bitter humility—the old pride so quickly breaking through, as the unlucky Third Servingman discovers—with which he encourages Aufidius' servants to mock him, we are to discern the sufferings of his lonely exile, and surmise the pent-up wrath, vented at last in that blind resolve to be revenged on his own ungrateful people or let the Volsces take revenge on him. Shall we now, on such evidence, sufficiently surmise all this? That the thing, when it did happen, will have happened in a flash; we have seen amply enough of him by now to believe so. Critics have combed the text for some sign of the actual moment of its happening; since surely, they argue, Shakespeare could not have let such a significant one slip by unmarked; and one has been found hidden in an exclamatory "O, the gods!" wrung from him at the very time of his banishing when he is taking leave of his mother and his wife. But this will not do. Tell the actor concerned that he is expected to convey to his audience in those three detached and unacknowledged words a sudden resolve to be revenged on the ungrateful city, and he will reasonably reply that it cannot be done. And while the maturer Shakespeare may certainly present his actors now and then with all but insuperable difficulties— creative imagination beckoning the interpreter towards very steep places indeed—never does he ask of them the impossible. What he does in this instance by a mere stroke of omission may seem to the *reader* of the play only to leave a rent in the texture of story and character. But in effect, and to the *spectator*, it is not so. Marcius could not appropriately be made to argue himself into such treason, as a Hamlet might, or discover the seeds of it in his nature, as might Macbeth. But picture and action significantly "placed" are as legitimate and often as important a dramatic resource as the spoken word can be. And what, at this juncture, could be more fittingly eloquent than the simple sight—and the shock it must give us—of this haggard, hardly recognizable figure? It will flash into our imaginations, as words might not, a sense of the suffering that has brought him to such a pass.

Shakespeare does not shirk the less tolerable aspects of the character. Indeed he stresses them, since he first shows us the man at his worst—strange treatment for a hero!—and in the theater first impressions cut deep. After the long and exceptionally leisurely opening of the tale of the Belly and the Members comes Marcius, like a tornado, bullying and abusing the hungry citizens; and while what he says of them may be true, it is no satisfying answer to their empty stomachs. But if this is the worst side of him the best side of that is turned to us a minute later, and within a few more the various contending forces of this most contentious of plays have been deployed, their differences established, Marcius in the center of them.

Word comes that the Volsces are in arms, threatening Rome. He turns happily to welcome the news, and the war itself, which he has shrewdly foreseen. It will help "vent our musty superfluity"; here is something quite other than the complaint that has driven the despised citizens (who listen in glum silence) to mutiny. To "our best elders," the Consul Cominius and the Senators, who now appear, he is all disciplined deference, accepting, though, besides, their tributes paid to him as if these were his right, nor forgetting as he goes to fling a parting sneer at the "worshipful mutiners."

The new-made Tribunes, Brutus and Sicinius, have been listening in silence too; and now we have their comments on him, as unfriendly, truly, as his own conduct to the people they are to stand for has been unfair—unfair to the best in his nature, but an undeniable part of that truth about him which the play is so judicially to unfold. Proud, disdainful, insolent; the three notes are hit hard. The Tribunes attach to him by implication besides— as such men are apt to—some of their own politician's cunning. But in this, it will soon be made plain, they mistake him. Better for him had he had that sort of weapon with which to fight them.

The battle-scenes bring his most trenchant qualities into play. The amazing spectacle of his singlehanded fight "within Corioles gates" is to be matched by his duel with Aufidius in which he takes on "certain Volsces" too who come to their leader's aid, *till they be driven in breathless*, later by his stand against his fellow Romans, drawing his sword with a "No; I'll die here," and contrasted with the yet later sight of him, truly alone, *in mean apparel, disguised and muffled*. Throughout the battle he is in his glory, and at his happiest, outshining and outtopping all the rest; hero indeed. But the more portraying strokes are not neglected. When his troops fall back he abuses them as roundly as he did the citizens; still this is in the stress of the fighting. When he calls inspiringly for volunteers to follow him in a desperate venture—

> If any such be here,
> As it were sin to doubt, that love this painting
> Wherein you see me smeared; if any fear
> Lesser his person than an ill report;
> If any think brave death outweighs bad life,
> And that his country's dearer than himself . . .

—these surly cowards of such a short while since, now *all shout and wave their swords; take him up in their arms, and cast up their caps.*[4] Marcius could win men if he would, it is plain, had he but a tithe of the confidence in them that he has in himself. Nor is it that he is mere cold-hearted egoist. At the very instant of victory he can remember the "poor man," a prisoner, who once used him kindly, even as later, in the midst of his triumph he can think of the widows left in Corioles and the "mothers that lack sons." He shows contempt for the spoils of war, honest distaste for the praises his prowess wins him, and under their lavishing an all but boyish self-consciousness.

This last trait (of Shakespeare's own importing: it has no place in Plutarch) is turned to varying account throughout the play. In the boyishness, the reckless high spirits with which he flings himself into battle, there is saving grace; even the thrasonical bragging to Aufidius before they fight is purged of offense if it comes as their mere overflow.[5] The question is not one of years. Marcius' actual age is not determined, and in North is only implied by the fact that he first went to the wars "being but a stripling," and that when he stands for Consul he has seen seventeen years' service. He might then, by this, be about thirty-two, and as mature a man as the maturer Hamlet. But more than one thing in the story gives color to youthfulness of temper. His

---

[4] It was not, truly, this division of the army which fled and left him to his fate "within Corioles gates." But while we shall remark the contrast in spirit and conduct, we shall not, I think—and are not meant to—make the nicer distinction.

[5] Note, too, that there is something of the duelists' conventional salute in this, as it might be a clashing of sword against shield.

boyish prowess, repeatedly stressed, suggests it; so do his rash decisions; so does his continued deference to his mother. And Shakespeare takes and enlarges on this means of mitigating the harshness which makes him—as North has it—so "churlish, uncivill and altogether unfit for any man's conversation," to touch him with an unruly charm instead.

It is in the self-consciousness that the flaw lies. His repeated protests against the praises lavished on him become somewhat less then genuine. During the traffic of the battle, to generous old Titus Lartius:

> Sir, praise me not;
> My work hath yet not warmed me. . . .

And again:

> Pray now, no more: my mother,
> Who has a charter to extol her blood,
> When she does praise me, grieves me. . . .

And yet again, in protest to his general, not very graciously:

> You shout me forth
> In acclamations hyperbolical;
> As if I loved my little should be dieted
> In praises sauced with lies.

—this is not modesty (as Cominius kindly calls it), rather an inverted pride. Neglect to praise him; he will be the first to resent that!

We are shown one aspect after another of this obsessing self-consciousness. He will not even make himself sit still and listen respectfully to the Senate's official tribute to him, but must be up and away in the middle of it with a

> I had rather have one scratch my head i' the sun
> When the alarum were struck than idly sit
> To hear my nothings monstered.

His desperate discomfort standing in the market place in the gown of humility is positively comic.

> May I change these garments?

—his first request when the ordeal is over. He pictures himself with dramatic clarity returning there shamefaced to ask pardon of the despised citizens; he cannot resist, even at this critical moment, the false modesty of

> Scratches with briers;
> Scars to move laughter only.

when his friends once more be-laud his "war-like service" and cite his many wounds. Later, he is most conscious of the effect he is making in his picturesque disgrace upon Aufidius and the lackeys. Lastly, he provokes his own death by losing all control under the petty insult of Aufidius' "Boy!"

Yet such self-consciousness is not self-knowledge. Possessing but a spice of *this*, would he ever have taken his rash, revengeful vow to destroy Rome?—which, put to the ultimate test, proves no more stable than does Aufidius' febrile conversion to his cause. At the critical moment he stands firm against Cominius, certainly. But with Menenius—though he dismissed him harshly—he has afterwards to own that, under guise of firmness, he *has* yielded, even if it be only "a very little." And the mere news of the coming of his wife and mother seems to paralyze him:

> Shall I be tempted to infringe my vow
> In the same time 'tis made? I will not.

—the desperate "I will not" telling us plainly that in his heart he knows already that he will. He is no true renegade. Striving to be false to Rome, he is false to himself. And this his instinct—his unclouded, unself-conscious self-knowledge—has warned him more than once that he cannot afford to be. He was so—if harmlessly; for it was a trivial matter, and Shakespeare stresses the comic aspect of it—when after swearing he never would he *did* put on the gown of humility. He is about to be again, and in a matter of more consequence, when, under protest—

> Would you have me
> False to my nature? Rather say I play
> The man I am.

—he is letting Volumnia persuade him to recant before the people the faith he has just so ardently professed to them. But he finds when he tries to that he cannot. And it is in the violent recoil from this attempt to be other than he is that he strikes his most genuinely heroic note, with the ineffably proud retort to his sentence of banishment, the "I banish you."

Wrong-headed, intolerant and intolerable in his dealings with the citizens he may be, but upon the actual issues between them is he so wrong? He foresaw the first Volscian attack when the Senators—"our best elders"—did not, and the hungry populace could think of nothing but their hunger. Victory won and a "good" peace granted the enemy (a little to his impatience), himself made Consul, he foresees another attack—

> So then the Volsces stand but as at first,
> Ready, when time shall prompt them, to make road
> Upon's again.

—not imagining, however, who, in the amazing irony of events, will lead it! He has foreseen, besides, from the beginning, that the new-made Tribunate

> will in time
> Win upon power, and throw forth greater themes
> For insurrections arguing.

And who is to say that he is wrong in his protest against the "popular shall . . . the greater poll . . . the yea and no of general ignorance" being let outweigh experienced wisdom. What answer is there to his passionate

> my soul aches
> To know, when two authorities are up,
> Neither supreme, how soon confusion
> May enter, 'twixt the gap of both and take
> The one by the other.

Wrong or right, however, he must abide by his own convictions: honestly he can no other. He foresaw that too from the beginning, when Volumnia first held him out hopes of the consulate and he told her:

> Know, good mother,
> I had rather be their servant in my way
> Than sway with them in theirs.

For a man can do no better than be himself at his best. Sometimes it may even strangely seem that his quality lies rather in the worse than the better part of him; then we must take the rough with the smooth.

Play and character become truly tragic only when Marcius, to be traitor to Rome, must turn traitor to himself. The actual turning, as we said, we do not see, we are shown the thing already inwardly done. And the tragedy is uncovered in something like a reversal of the process, in the tragic failure to undo the thing once done, once begun even. It is ironic tragedy, too. Marcius has been used to meet fortune, good or bad, in the open. But from that dark moment in Antium, of the bitter

> My birth-place hate I, and my love's upon
> This enemy town.

everything with him and within him turns to mockery. Aufidius' extravagant homage to him will soon show itself a cheat. It is a false façade of him seeming to sit there

>   in gold, his eye
> Red as 'twould burn Rome . . .

And when he has finally yielded to his mother's prayers he looks up to find that

>   the heavens do ope,
> The gods look down, and this unnatural scene
> They laugh at.

He could go back to Rome—the "clusters who did hoot him out o' the city" now as ready to "roar him in again"—thanked for his weakness and kindness, and forgiven—he Coriolanus forgiven! But nor is that his nature. He is at least no weathercock. He has turned aginst the Romans, he will stay loyal now to the Volsces.[6]

Mockery piles on mockery in Corioles. The people there are something the same problem that they were in Rome. Aufidius, with his great repute, has still to observe their temper. And of Coriolanus, even of him, it can be said that he

> Intends to appear before the people, hoping
> To purge himself with words . . .

And—though first, truly, to the lords of the city—so, *the Com-*

---

[6] Tennyson finds a similar thought for

> His honour rooted in dishonour stood
> And faith, unfaithful, kept him falsely true.

moners being with him, he does, boasting of the spoils and the
full third part
The charges of the action . . .

he has brought back. When till now did he value such pinchbeck
glory? In Rome he was plunged from triumph into obloquy.
Now it is the fickle commoners of Corioles that turn on him,
cheering him back at one moment, tearing him to pieces the next.
When last these same Volsces swarmed round him he was one
against all of them, and victor. They make better business of it
now.

Coriolanus, then, is a character not inwardly evolved, as the
greater tragic characters are, but seen from without. Seen and
molded, however, in the round; and as consistent and solid a
figure as Shakespeare ever put in motion.

VOLUMNIA

The relations between mother and son and the likeness and
difference between them are at the core of the play. The likeness
is patent. It is she, he is wont to say, whose praise first made him
a soldier. She rejoices in his prowess, gleefully in his very wounds,
has the tale of them by heart, could dance for joy at his return for
the third time with the oaken garland, wounded yet again. If
martial spirit were all she would seem to be almost more soldier
than he. And when the fateful struggle between them comes it is
the grimmer for this.

As a woman she has no overt part in the political quarrel with
the Tribunes; and, in that phase of the action, it is not until, amid
the violence of its crisis, Marcius seeks a breathing-space in his
house and hers, that we see or hear from her at all. But then she
astonishes us—and him. For until now she has seemed as stiff, and
stiffer than he, in pride. As to the Tribunes and their kind, she
has ignored them, but had been wont, he says,

> To call them woollen vessels, things created
> To buy and sell with groats, to show bare heads
> In congregations, to yawn, be still and wonder
> When one but of my ordinance stood up
> To speak of peace or war . . .

Yet now, when trouble comes, from unashamed policy she

would have him humble himself to them, recant his word and cheat them even in recanting, "mountebank their loves." He is to be, he protests, false to his nature; and she is setting him an example by being false to hers. She persuades him to it: yet fruitlessly since, tested, his nature rebels. It will take more than this: defeat and banishment and, later, suffering and blind anger, to trap him into swearing that oath of unnatural vengeance which it will prove beyond his power to keep. She will set out again to persuade him to break it, and, spending her last ounce of strength and influence, she will succeed. And then it will bear fruit; salvation for Rome, but, for him, bitter fruit indeed.

In a central scene, then, and at one of the play's chief turning points, we have this truly unexpected exhibition of difference between the two. Willful and stubborn he may be, but, to his credit, he is not the mere overgrown spoiled child which the extravagance of her praise might so easily have made him. He turns from praise with the touch of affectation we have noted; from hers the more genuinely, remembering how much he once owed to it. But in his quarrel with the Tribunes he stands fearlessly for a cause. This is enshrined in egoism doubtless, but is not, he proudly feels, the poorer for that; since he stands, in what he has done and is, for what is best in Rome and he will never shrink from proclaiming it and his faith in it, no matter the moment's consequence. Volumnia, astonishingly the opposite, shows herself at once shrewdly critical, worldly-wise—

> O, sir, sir, sir,
> I would have had you put your power well on
> Before you had worn it out.

—and shrewder yet:

> You might have been enough the man you are
> With striving less to be so. . . .

with irony to follow for the deflating of his anger, and the cold realism of

> I have a heart as little apt as yours,
> But yet a brain that leads my use of anger
> To better vantage.

—a calculated use of it. And it will no more dishonor him (she

easily argues) to maneuver a crooked way back into his fellow
countrymen's favor than it would in wartime to

> take in a town with gentle words.

She herself, here and now, lavishes the gentlest on him; these
failing, tries her "use of anger," pretended or real, with a

> At thy choice, then:
> To beg of thee it is my more dishonour
> Than thou of them. Come all to ruin. . . .
> Do your will.

He is the cause she stands for—that is the truth; and that he
will not help her, and himself, by unscrupulously putting it
before all other, exasperates her. He pays in banishment the
penalty of his scruples. She is passionately for him in defeat as in
victory, and but the more enraged with his enemies for their
profiting by his high-minded unwisdom. After this, again, she is
absent from the action for many scenes; and again, re-entering it,
she sounds an unexpected note.

Mark now the dramatic strategy, as Shakespeare plans it, of
her share in the women's appeal to Marcius for mercy upon Rome.
Simply the sight of her and of his wife and son stirs him. She
does not speak at first; only

> My mother bows,
> As if Olympus to a molehill should
> In supplication nod. . . .

The constricted figure has an eloquence of its own. His wife,
softly reproachful, wins the first response from him. Not until he
kneels does Volumnia speak, outdoing him then by herself
kneeling, a shade of irony—no more!—in the ostentation of her
gesture. After which, as with a certain confidence in this their
meeting again, the plea is launched. She can be eloquent now, as
never before. It is an eloquence inspired by that clarity of vision
which imminent tragedy brings:

> for how can we,
> Alas! how can we for our country pray,
> Whereto we are bound, together with thy victory,
> Whereto we are bound? Alack! or we must lose
> The country, our dear nurse, or else thy person,
> Our comfort in the country. We must find

> An evident calamity, though we had
> Our wish, which side should win; for either thou
> Must, as a foreign recreant, be led
> With manacles through our streets, or else
> Triumphantly tread on thy country's ruin,
> And bear the palm for having bravely shed
> Thy wife and children's blood.

The new note follows; a new note indeed:

> If it were so that our request did tend
> To save the Romans, thereby to destroy
> The Volsces whom you serve, you might condemn us
> As poisonous of your honour: no; our suit
> Is that you reconcile them: while the Volsces
> May say "This mercy we have showed"; the Romans,
> "This we received"; and each in either side
> Give the all-hail to thee, and cry "Be blest
> For making up this peace!"

If he "mused" before at her indifference to his heroic stand against the mob for his proud conscience' sake, what will his retort be now to this talk of peace—of peace for its own sake; to such a warning from her as

> Thou knowest, great son,
> The end of war's uncertain. . . .

to her disparaging

> Thou hast affected the fine strains of honour. . . .

her

> Think'st thou it honourable for a noble man
> Still to remember wrongs?

It has taken truly a terrible revolution to bring her to this: no less than the sight of her son, his country's hero, turned his country's enemy, her own son, her enemy. And she begins to feel nevertheless that she is beaten, that her high arguments are breaking against his stubborn silence. Yet she is as tenacious a fighter in her way as ever we have found him to be, and she flings herself and the forces with her—mother, wife, child, the whole womanhood of Rome—desperately into the struggle:

> Daughter, speak you:
> He cares not for your weeping. Speak thou, boy:

> Perhaps thy childishness will move him more
> Than can our reasons.

Their silence had begun it, as they stood ranged accusingly before him; by some means they must break his silence now. Volumnia chides and clamors:

> There's no man in the world
> More bound to's mother; yet here he lets me prate
> Like one i' the stocks. Thou has never in thy life
> Shewed thy dear mother any courtesy. . . .

By whatever means let her win! But she can fight a losing battle as fiercely as he could a winning one:

> Down, ladies; let us shame him with our knees.

Then with a Parthian scorn:

> Come, let us go:
> This fellow had a Volscian to his mother:
> His wife is in Corioles, and his child
> Like him by chance.

Yet she has won. Throwing her strength in to the very last, even at the admitted moment of defeat—

> Yet give us our despatch:
> I am husht until our city be a-fire,
> And then I'll speak a little.

—she had already won.

The very moment during his tenacious silence when his will yielded has been covered by silence too. And now she does not answer his low, searching

> O, mother, mother!
> What have you done?

when it emerges from the silence, nor respond at all to the unequivocal

> O, my mother, mother! O!
> You have won a happy victory to Rome;
> But for your son, believe it, O, believe it,
> Most dangerously you have with him prevailed,
> If not most mortal to him.

So possessed by her victory, is she, as to be incapable of a second thought? Is she so spent with the strain of her pleading that she faces Rome again a little later, and its frenzied welcome, in a very daze? Marcius, in any case, as with a new-learned magnanimity, shepherds away more talk of his defeat, thoughts of his fate. And her part in the play is done.[7]

It ends, as does her son's—as may be said of the whole play—amid the ironic laughter of the gods; she is unaware, that is all, of the successive mockeries in the event, made at last so bitterly plain to him. She has bred him to be at once Rome's hero and Rome's enemy. She has begged Rome's life of him, and, in

~~~~~~~~~~

[7] What exactly is the effect that Shakespeare means to have made here? The mere suggestion of his danger in Marcius'

> O, mother, mother!
> What have you done? . . .

Volumnia, not yet certain of her victory, might easily overlook. But the repeated

> O, my mother, mother! O!
> You have won a happy victory to Rome;
> But for your son, believe it, O, believe it,
> Most dangerously you have with him prevailed,
> If not most mortal to him.

—to ignore this practically plain statement that he is most likely to be going to his death she must be prostrated indeed. And that I think on the whole is the intention. He then turns and goes to Aufidius, and Volumnia, left among the women, quickly recovers. She has not fainted, there must be no such weakness; it is simply a moment's reaction from the extreme strain of the victory. He turns back, and apostrophizes them from where he stands:

> O, mother! wife!

and stands still gazing while Aufidius speaks his aside. This is the heartfelt farewell he takes.

Editors hereabouts insert

> *The Ladies make signs to Coriolanus.*

presumably to account for the "Ay, by and by . . ." with which he breaks the silence of his gaze. They stand expectantly where he has left them; there is no need of more. Then he joins them, as if bidding them dismiss all forebodings, gallantly congratulating them on their victory; and our query, if there was risk of one: why does not Volumnia see that in saving Rome she has sent her son to his death? has been fended off. It may return on reflection when the play is over. It probably will not. And if it takes the shape of the memory of a Volumnia as peremptory and passionate as her son, as stubborn in her own cause and as oblivious to all besides, that is a not unjust one.

Shakespeare the practical playwright, having had his full use of a character, and the whole action being near its end, will add nothing needlessly. Volumnia has saved Rome, and the action asks no more of her. Care for her son's fate would prolong or complicate it, and, in doing so, upset the balance of interest. It must suffice, then, that we do not remark any such omission; and circumstance and character are shaped so that we shall not. It is in these instances of dramatic tact that Shakespeare the playwright shows at his most skillful.

winning it, is obviously sending him to his death. And we last see her welcomed triumphantly back to Rome even as he once was, flowers strewed before her, amid cries of

> Unshout the noise that banished Marcius;
> Repeal him with the welcome of his mother. . . .

But it is too late for that. And tragedy of character does not work out in such happy confusions of popular acclaim.

It is a chill parting, this with Volumnia; our last sight of her—nothing nearer—parading through Rome, her back turned upon Marcius himself and the essential tragedy's imminent consummation.

AUFIDIUS

It takes all Shakespeare's skill to make Aufidius fully effective within the space which the planning of the action allows him—and perhaps he does not wholly succeed. For a while it is not so difficult. He is admitted on all hands to be Marcius' rival and to come short of him by little. Marcius' first word of him is that

> I sin in envying his nobility,
> And were I anything but what I am,
> I would wish me only he.

He is secondary hero. And when within a moment or so we see the man himself he is telling the Senators of Corioles:

> If we and Caius Marcius chance to meet,
> 'Tis sworn between us we shall ever strike
> Till one can do no more.

Volumnia, imagining glorious things, can see her Marcius

> pluck Aufidius down by the hair . . .

In the battle the Corioles taunt the Romans with

> There is Aufidius: list, what work he makes
> Amongst your cloven army.

while to Marcius, whether far off—

> There is the man of my soul's hate, Aufidius. . . .

—or within reach—

> Set me against Aufidius and his Antiats. . . .

—he is an obsession. And when they do meet and fight, Aufidius, if bettered, is not beaten. To this point, then, however little we may see of him, he is brought to our minds in each succeeding scene, and is emphatically lodged there when he is so unconsentingly rescued in the duel with his famous enemy by "certain Volsces" (anonymous: common soldiers presumably, therefore):

> Officious, and not valiant, you have shamed me
> In your condemned seconds.

And, since we shall not see him thereafter for some time, this note of shame, and of the crooked passion it can rouse in the man, is enlarged and given what will be memorable place in a scene coming but a little later.

> Five times, Marcius,
> I have fought with thee; so often hast thou beat me,
> And wouldst do so, I think, should we encounter
> As often as we eat.[8]

Frank confession! But now

> mine emulation
> Hath not that honour in't it had; for where
> I thought to crush him in an equal force,
> True sword to sword, I'll potch at him some way
> Or wrath or craft may get him. . . .
> Where I find him, were it
> At home, upon my brother's guard, even there,
> Against the hospitable canon, would I
> Wash my fierce hands in's heart.

We shall certainly recall that—and be given good cause to—when, all amazingly, the event so falls out. The scheme of the action allows Aufidius very limited space; but we have thus far been kept conscious of him throughout. From now, even until he emerges into it again, he does not go quite without mention, and we shall have lodged in mind what he may mean to it when he does. It is able stagecraft.

In a cruder play Aufidius and the Volsces might be made to serve as "villains of the piece." But Shakespeare is not painting in such ultra-patriotic black and white. We are on the Roman

---

[8] Later on, in Antium, Aufidius makes it "Twelve several times" that he has been beaten. But nothing hangs on the precise number, and he is not on his oath.

side, and they are "foreigners"; so their worse, not their better,
aspect is naturally turned towards us. The victorious Romans
give them a "good" peace, Titus Lartius being commanded to
send back from their captured city

> to Rome
> The best, with whom we may articulate,
> For their own good and ours.

They, when their victorious turn comes, so we hear,

> looked
> For no less spoil than glory . . .

Shakespeare shades them somewhat. But the balance is not
unfairly held.

Aufidius, then, re-enters the action at its most critical juncture,
and to play for the moment a surprising part in it. Here, in this
wine-flushed host to the nobles of Antium, is quite another man;
and not only in the look of him but, yet more surprisingly—
suspense resolved—in the deep-sworn enemy turned ecstatic
comrade. From that

> Nor sleep, nor sanctuary,
> Being naked, sick, nor fane nor Capitol,
> The prayers of priests, nor times of sacrifice,
> Embarquements all of fury, shall lift up
> Their rotten privilege and custom 'gainst
> My hate to Marcius.

we are at a glowing

> Let me twine
> Mine arms about that body, where against
> My grained ash an hundred times hath broke
> And scarred the moon with splinters: here I clip
> The anvil of my sword, and do contest
> As hotly and as nobly with thy love
> As ever in ambitious strength I did
> Contend against thy valour.

It is a turning point indeed, and doubly so; the revolution in
Marcius is barely set forth before it is matched with this. The two
revolutions differ as the two men do; the one a plunging
through defeat and misery from confident pride to obdurate
bitterness; that in Aufidius a sudden emotional overthrow,

sprung by this startling proffer, this attack upon a weakness in him which he would never think to defend. Yet there is a likeness between them too. And they are in keeping, both, with the rest of the play, its extremes of passion and their instabilities; the weathercock-swaying of the citizens, Volumnia's violence and arbitrary shifts. Marcius himself we shall see will be unable to abide by his treason to the end; and Aufidius, we shall very quickly guess, will not long sustain this unnatural change. Recurring ironies fitting into the scheme of tragic irony which informs the whole action.

This "strange alteration"—reflected too in the freakish comment of the servants—gives us a fresh, and, for the moment, an alert interest in Aufidius. From now to the end the stagecraft actuating him remains as able; and if here and there the figure seems to lack vitality, to be a little word-locked, why, livelier development of this new aspect of the man might well make more demands on the play's space than could be spared, or such a turn of inspiration as Shakespeare (even he!) has not unquestionably at command. But he does not dodge nor skip a step in the completing of the character. And, within a scene or so, to begin this, we see Aufidius again—quite disillusioned.

Thinking better of things is a dry business; and this ancillary scene, shared with an anonymous Lieutenant, will appropriately be none of the liveliest. But the matter of it is a strengthening rivet in the character scheme of the play. Aufidius' sobered reaction from his rhapsodies to the coldest common sense—hints dropped moreover of revengeful traps already laid for Marcius; Aufidius to be revenged on him for his own access of too generous folly, the hardest thing forgivable—this will redress any balance of sympathy lost between the two for the action's last phase. We have no violent swing back to the fanatically sportsmanlike hatred with which they started. On the contrary, to Aufidius is given in the scene's last speech the most measured and balanced of summarizings of his rival's qualities and failings. And for Marcius it is in this quiet reasonable accounting that his worst danger can be foreseen. Mastery in soldiership—who has ever denied him that? He has not even to exercise it now:

> All places yield to him ere he sits down;
> And . . .

—despite his treason; because of it indeed—

> the nobility of Rome are his:
> The Senators and Patricians love him too. . . .
> I think he'll be to Rome
> As is the asprey to the fish, who takes it
> By sovereignty of nature. . . .

Aufidius, lacking just that sovereignty, could not look his own problem more fairly in the face. For, indeed, he had better know just where he has the worse of it, that being the second-rate man's due approach to getting the better of it after all. He may next encourage himself by listing—though with every scruple and reserve—Marcius' failings too: pride, temper, intolerance and the rest, and by recognizing that in this discordant world men have the defects of their qualities and the qualities of their defects; and that at best, what is more,

> our virtues
> Lie in the interpretation of the time. . . .

—which may prove for us or against us; and whichever way

> One fire drives out one fire; one nail, one nail;
> Rights by rights founder, strengths by strengths do fail.

Fortune, with a little patient aid, is ever ready to turn her wheel:

> When, Caius, Rome is thine
> Thou art poor'st of all; then shortly art thou mine.

Both speech and scene demand of their audience close attention, closer, perhaps, than such detached argument will currently command at this juncture in a play unless it be embodied in some central, radiating figure. It is the more notable that Shakespeare should here, so to speak, be forcing his meaning through the recalcitrant lines.[9] But his aim, it would seem, is to give a rational substance to the figure, of such a sort as will keep us an Aufidius expressively if cryptically observant through succeeding scenes while we await the due restoring of the natural open enmity between the two.

It comes with relief.

> How is it with our general?

---

[9] One or two lines in this last speech are doubtless corrupt. But rectify them as we may, we shall hardly make them lucid.

his fellow conspirators ask.

> Even so
> As with a man by his own alms empoisoned,
> And with his charity slain.

But he is free now of his false position and on his own ground
again, and the ills done him are glib upon his tongue. He must
be cautiously in the right at all points:

> And my pretext to strike at him admits
> A good construction. I raised him, and I pawned
> Mine honour for his truth. . . .

More than so, he

> took some pride
> To do myself this wrong . . .

—he is fueling up with virtuous indignation, until, at the touch
of a match, Coriolanus himself can be trusted to fire out in fury,
no moral excuses needed. "Traitor . . . unholy braggart . . . boy
of tears . . . boy!"—it is the last spark that sets all ablaze.

Aufidius' philosophic mind has not endured; nor does the
one-time gallantry. "My valour's poisoned . . ." —we are back at
that. He is no coward, we know; has ever been ready to fight.
It is only that, now or never, he must have the best of it, and he
has made all sure. So, duly provoked

> *The Conspirators draw, and kill Coriolanus, who falls. . . .*

Upon which, though, he cannot resist it:

> *Aufidius stands on him.*[10]

Shakespeare, in the maturity of his skill, knows how to give
as much meaning to a significantly placed gesture as to a speech
or more. There are two gestures here, the insolent treading of
the slain man under foot, with the quick attempt in face of the
shocked outcry to excuse it:

> My noble masters, hear me speak.

then the response to the reproach:

> O, Tullus!
> Thou hast done a deed whereat valour will weep.
> Tread not upon him. Masters . . .

---

[10] Shakespeare's own stage direction, we may once more be pretty sure.

which can but be its shamed and embarrassed lifting, the more
eloquent of Aufidius, this. The more fittingly unheroic, besides,
the ending. The lords of the city have been honourable enemies.

> Peace, ho! no outrage: peace!
> The man is noble and his fame folds in
> This orb o' the earth. His last offences to us
> Shall have judicious hearing.

The sight of the outrage done him horrifies them. But as Aufidius
promptly argues,

> My lords, when you shall know, as in this rage
> Provoked by him, you cannot, the great danger
> Which this man's life did owe you, you'll rejoice
> That he is thus cut off.

and, truly, as they'll in fairness soon admit:

> His own impatience
> Takes from Aufidius a great part of blame. . . .

Common sense supervenes:

> Let's make the best of it.

And Aufidius can say with truth, the man being safely dead:

> My rage is gone,
> And I am struck with sorrow.

MENENIUS

Menenius makes one in the ironically figured pattern of
character. He is set outwardly—and at the play's very start—in
sharp contrast to Coriolanus himself:

> Worthy Menenius Agrippa; one that hath always loved the
> people.

—so even the disgruntled citizens admit. Jovial, humorous,
reasonable; what could be less like the intolerant, rough-tongued
young soldier, whose pride it is that

> He would not flatter Neptune for his trident,
> Or Jove for's power to thunder.

But soon enough we notice that behind the cajoling

> Why, masters, my good friends, mine honest neighbours . . .

and the merry tale that sets them laughing—at each other it is, too!—his complete indifference to their troubles. Marcius, storming, would have had

> the nobility lay aside their ruth,
> And let me use my sword.

Menenius has taken the cannier way; and here already, at no cost but fair words,

> these are almost thoroughly persuaded;
> For though abundantly they lack discretion,
> Yet are they passing cowardly.

Nor does he scruple, it would seem, to say so in their hearing.

Menenius is to pervade the play, yet as an auxiliary character only. This full and vivid shaping of the figure so early has one incidental advantage then; the lightest future touch—and however slight be its connection with the main action—will be effective. And in all the plays there are few livelier or more individual characters.

An old gentleman of "character," an "original," to his friends the best of friends; his fighting spirit has not flagged either with the years, and he fights the more cleverly with his tongue for his sole weapon, if the more spitefully now and then. Would Marcius but profit by it his counsel might steer him to safety. He loves him as a man his own son, delights in his prowess and fame. He knows him too, better than does Volumnia, and is quick to persuade him that, willy-nilly, he must don that vext "gown of humility," sticks to him too till he has it on, shepherds him to the very verge of the actual ordeal, only quits him then with almost comic misgiving, to return at the first moment as proud as a nurse of a well-behaved child at a party.

The rioting in the market place tells on his age. While he stands loyally by Marcius he pleads breathlessly with each disputant in turn, flatters even the loathed Tribunes. But he never loses his head, nor his sense of humor either, gives a savingly comic twist to Marcius' militant

> On fair ground
> I could beat forty of them.

(as indeed we know and see) by his own merry

> I could myself

Take up a brace of the best of them; yea, the two Tribunes.

Nor does he ignore his own side's failings. Of Marcius, momentarily relieved of his incendiary presence:

> His nature is too noble for the world. . . .
> What the vengeance!
> Could he not speak 'em fair?

—into which combination of tempers do these heroes drive us. But here he is at his best, with that frank

> As I do know the Consul's worthiness,
> So can I name his faults.

and in his plea for Rome's honor, threats of death and banishment overhanging the man who has so fought for her:

> Now the good gods forbid
> That our renowned Rome, whose gratitude
> Towards her deserved children is enrolled
> In Jove's own book, like an unnatural dam
> Should now eat up her own! . . .
> What has he done to Rome that's worthy death?
> Killing our enemies, the blood he hath lost—
> Which, I dare vouch, is more than that he hath,
> By many an ounce—he dropped it for his country;
> And what is left, to lose it by his country,
> Were to us all, that do't and suffer it,
> A brand to the end o' the world.

—the artful old man with his crotchets turned to the grave patrician; the verse as fittingly strong and clear.

But to the last moment he is pliably for give-and-take, real or pretended, wailing to his self-wrecked hero a despairing

> Is this the promise that you made your mother?

and past the last moment staying faithfully by him, till he finds place in that sad journey to the gates.

> Thou old and true Menenius,
> Thy tears are salter than a younger man's,
> And venemous to thine eyes.

—yet more quickly dried to calm, it seems. (Here comes one of Shakespeare's incidental touches of veracity.) The fight finished

and lost, the women—Volumnia, even Virgilia—pass from tears
to anger, Menenius to all that is most pacific. There is no more
to be done, and he is very, very weary; though if he

> could shake off but one seven years
> From these old arms and legs . . .

he'd tramp it too by Marcius' side with the best. But Marcius
gone, not even the sight of the swaggering Tribunes rouses him.
Finally, for the distraught and shaken mother and wife he has
nothing but a kindly

> Peace, peace! be not so loud.

unless it be, as Brutus and Sicinius sheer off, the consolation of

> You have told them home,
> And, by my troth, you have cause. . . .

with the yet solider comfort of

> You'll sup with me?

It is unheroic, doubtless, thus to finish such a day. But he is
not heroic!

Tit for tat is hard to resist; nor, certainly, is Menenius a man
to miss a chance of it when it comes. While Marcius is banished
and the Tribunes are in power he keeps a stiff lip in opposition,
foxing enough to warrant their sarcastic

> O! he is grown most kind
> Of late. Hail, sir!

But when the sudden, startling turn of fortune comes, tidings of
Marcius' and Aufidius' dread approach, the old Menenius
reappears, lively and ready as ever:

> What news? what news? . . .
> What's the news? what's the news? . . .
> Pray, now your news? . . .
> Pray, your news?

News suiting his ironic temper in defeat, of the prospect of his
hero's sacking of his city; a pretty contradiction, however deserved.
But here even Menenius' sense of irony will be stretched a little.
He can turn, however, sarcastically on the Tribunes:

> You have made good work,
> You and your apron men. . . .
> You and your crafts! You have crafted fair!

If they shirk the blame, what can the answer to that be but

> How! was't we? . . .

But it was.

> We loved him; but, like beasts
> And cowardly nobles, gave way unto your clusters,
> Who did hoot him out o' the city.

And will mere words now win pardon for either lot of them?
Menenius takes delight in assuring the wretched citizens—a troop
of them arriving at this juncture—in assuring them under the
crestfallen Tribunes' very noses that

> not a hair upon a soldier's head
> Which will not prove a whip: as many coxcombs
> As you threw caps up will he tumble down,
> And pay you for your voices.

He once more finds himself, indeed, the old racily tongued
Menenius of our first acquaintance, haranguing the biddable
crowd. Brutus and Sicinius make a last effort to regain their
followers' confidence, but with little enough left in themselves,
it seems. The one-time winners throw in their hands, and the
losers are left to make the best of a bad job between them.

Menenius does not fancy suffering himself the great man's
treatment of Cominius. It was Cominius' business (who preceded
him as Consul) to be the first to go begging forgiveness. Once

> He called me father:
> But what o' that? . . .
> Nay, if he coyed
> To hear Cominius speak, I'll keep at home.

But what he wants is to be pressed into going; and for that he
flagrantly plays, until flattery in full measure sends the old man
off, breezily confident that with him to do it the task is as good
as done.

Menenius makes, dramatically speaking, a good end. He plays
the statesman with the soldiers guarding Coriolanus, they, enjoy-
ably, the soldier with him. He is "an officer of state," and he and
Rome, things at the worst, retain, one hopes, their dignity. But
he's not the first to come (here the close-packing of the action,
the tale of Cominius' attempt, adds to the effect of this); and

> our general
> Will no more hear from thence.

Then begins the tussle, familiar to any wartime, between soldier and civilian, the Somebody in peace and Nobody in war, whose condescending

> Good my friends,
> If you have heard your general talk of Rome,
> And of his friends there, it is lots to blanks,
> My name hath touched your ears: it's Menenius.

earns from a sentry under orders no more than a cool

> Be it so; go back: the virtue of your name
> Is not here passable.

Menenius adds to his credit one civilian virtue after another:

> I tell thee, fellow,
> Thy general is my lover: I have been
> The book of his good acts, whence men have read
> His fame unparalleled, haply amplified:
> For I have ever verified my friends,
> Of whom he's chief. . . .

—and it is true!—

> with all the size that verity
> Would without lapsing suffer . . .

each as unavailingly as the last. Indignation does not serve.

> Sirrah, if thy captain knew I were here, he would use me with estimation.
> Come, my captain knows you not.
> I mean thy general.
> My general cares not for you. Back, I say, go; lest I let forth your half-pint of blood. . . .

—the soldier's conclusive argument. Marcius' own appearance, with Aufidius in quiet partnership, puts the matter to the proof.

Nowhere in the play do we find the pattern of its character-planning more effectively turned and colored. The comic charged with emotion; what more human? Old Menenius fatuously insisting upon the sentries discomfiting him, yet heartbroken in his pleading; and it is—we see it—with a cracked heart that Marcius repulses him, that harsh "Away!" little better than a blow in the face. And he must accept Aufidius' praise for it, the dry

> You keep a constant temper.

The sentries allowed their mockery, if they fancy they can out-mock this gallant old patrician in defeat they are vastly mistaken. He can still give back better than he gets: .

> I neither care for the world, nor your general: for such things
> as you, I can scarce think there's any, y'are so slight. . . .

Civilian though he be, he has a weapon of which they cannot rob him:

> He that hath a will to die by himself, fears it not from another.
> Let your general do his worst. For you, be that you are, long; and
> your misery increase with your age! [His does!] I say to you, as
> I was said to, Away!

—and he is gone; bearing off the honors with him, thinks one of these Volscians, duly impressed:

> A noble fellow, I warrant him.

the other of tougher mind:

> The worthy fellow is our general: he's the rock, the oak not
> to be wind-shaken.

The closely contrived action allows for yet one small turn more in the pattern of character, and typical—fully so—it shall be. The trembling Sicinius awaits tidings; not to be mitigated. But if Menenius has been beaten, let there be no belittling the battle lost; and, if *he* cannot come home winner, who may? Did not Cominius tell them how

> The tartness of his face sours ripe grapes; when he walks he
> moves like an engine, and the ground shrinks before his
> treading. . . . He sits in his state, as a thing made for Alex-
> ander. . . .

Sicinius may bleat that

> He loved his mother dearly.

Forlornest of hopes, retorted on by

> So did he me; and he no more remembers his mother now
> than an eight-year-old horse. . . . Mark what mercy his mother
> shall bring from him: there is no more mercy in him than there
> is milk in a male tiger. . . .

Menenius, be it remembered, does not know what has passed since his plea was repulsed. For all that he does know it is the right sort of medicine he is administering—having first swallowed it himself with that cheerful courage, which it is lets him in turn so enjoy forcing it down the unhappy Tribune's own throat. Once more comes the solacing refrain:

> and all this is 'long of you.

with, for a closing chord, each striking his own note, Sicinius' pitiful

> The gods be good unto us!

the old politician, gamer:

> No, in such a case the gods will not be good unto us. When we banished him we respected not them, and, he returning to break our necks, they respect not us.

Take the rough with the smooth and look facts in the face; as wholesome a lesson in politics as lay in the tale of the Belly and the Members. Whereupon, the concluding good news brought and confirmed, Menenius can take this also as coolly—for all that he'll let the two scurvy cowards of Tribunes discover! And with this he is caught back into the ending central stream of the play's action, lively to his last word.

THE TRIBUNES

Brutus and Sicinius make a listening and a not promptly identifiable first appearance. The aristocrats, assembled by the rumors of war, depart elated, the humiliated citizens steal away, leaving these two—the new Tribunes, will they be?—to savor their comments:

> Was ever man so proud as is this Marcius?
> He has no equal.

They are not of the simple caliber of their followers, that is at once made plain; the craftiest of politicians, rather, with Brutus to belittle—and slander—Marcius, true politician-wise:

> Fame, at the which he aims,
> In whom already he's well-graced, can not
> Better be held nor more attained than by

> A place below the first; for what miscarries
> Shall be the general's fault, though he perform
> To the utmost of a man; and giddy censure
> Will then cry out of Marcius, "O, if he
> Had borne the business!"

Sicinius joining in. The twenty-five-line interchange of cynical judgment stamps them vividly enough on our memory: a binding-up of the story; for between now and our next encounter with them the whole Volscian war is to pass.

We find them again still in Rome (where they are is always Rome); of consequence now, evidently, among the people, but uneasily awaiting the hero's return, decrying him, fearing for their chances beside him. It is now that they take color as comic villains; this thanks to Menenius, who finds ridicule, in which he is bluffly expert, the best weapon with which to torment them. One effect of this will be that while we, with the more sympathetic Menenius, may detest and make fun of them, in other bearings they are still the two sharp politicians. Shakespeare disposes his sides for the coming combat with great address. Here are these two, playing the game by its rules, yielding smoothly to their mastery, condoning no smallest breach of them, pursuing that, indeed, as far and as bitterly as vengeance may. It will be at no point a pretty picture. Set against it we have the cool comment of the neutral Senate House officials upon Marcius as he opens his political career:

> That's a brave fellow; but he's vengeance proud, and loves not the common people.
>
> Faith, there have been many great men that have flattered the people, who ne'er loved them; and there be many that they have loved, they know not wherefore: so that, if they love they know not why, they hate upon no better a ground. Therefore, for Coriolanus neither to care whether they love or hate him manifests the true knowledge he has in their disposition; and out of his noble carelessness lets them plainly see't.

"Noble carelessness"—that phrase alone, with what we have seen of him besides, would weight the sympathy well upon Marcius' side. But the yet cooler, the ironic

> but he seeks their hate with greater devotion than they can render it him . . .

caps it. A political play; the hero, under this aspect of it, with no more skill at the game than makes him his own worst enemy—a fruitful theme. Nor will he take counsel; Menenius could save him more than once. It is between him and the Tribunes that the earlier maneuvering mostly proceeds; Marcius—if he would but let himself be so!—a glorious figurehead, the citizens poor puppets. And it is not so easy to pick holes in the Tribunes' conduct at first. They demand their people's rights: that is only their duty. Is it their fault if Marcius so grudgingly grants these? They slyly incite them to test him at his weakest point. Are they to blame if he not merely yields under the test, but unrepentingly proclaims that here he is, to their despite, at his strongest instead? It is something of a trap, but need he so recklessly walk into it?

But from now on they grow ever more contemptible. They promptly abuse the success they so easily win. Says Marcius scornfully,

> I do despise them;
> For they do prank them in authority
> Against all noble sufferance. . . .
> It is a purposed thing, and grows by plot. . . .

and—though they may safely deny it—we know this is true.

They overplay their hands when they demand Coriolanus' death, show their last sign of political good sense when they'd accept Menenius as mediator in the quarrel. Otherwise they had better have pressed for death, since exile is but to bring back revenge. And something of this they do actually, in the midst of the turmoil, perceive—

> To eject him hence
> Were but one danger, and to keep him here
> Our certain death. . . .

—it being only that their insensate vanity, bred in the flush of success, so blinds them. Marcius gains tragic dignity in defeat and departure; they, tarring the rabble on to hoot him "out at gates," swaggering ludicrously through the streets themselves—"our noble Tribunes"!—touch depth.

When the tide of fortune has turned, although we know what is coming, we see them still sunning themselves fatuously for a while

i' the present peace
And quietness o' the people . . .

Then, foolishly, futilely, denying the plain unpleasant fact,
feebly protesting, when they cannot, against Menenius' mockery.
Nor that the worst. While one still tries, and yet again, to argue
facts away:

Enter a Messenger.

Sir, if you'd save your life, fly to your house:
The plebeians have got your fellow-Tribune,
And hale him up and down: all swearing, if
The Roman ladies bring not comfort home,
They'll give him death by inches.

Such politics have their revenges.

The Action of the Play

Enter a company of mutinous Citizens, with stones,
clubs and other weapons.

But let not the unwary producer be led by that *mutinous*, and
by the *stones, clubs and other weapons*, into projecting a scene
of mere quick confusion, violence and high-pitched noise. Shakespeare has further reaching intentions. These citizens form a
collective character, so to call it, of capital importance to the first
half of the play; at its very start, therefore, we are to be given a
fully informing picture of them. A homespun lot, but with a man
or so among them that can both think and talk. They are
certainly in an ugly temper at the moment and ripe for mischief,
since plaints and a fortnight's threats have, it seems, proved
futile; and they are not of the breed (Roman or British) that sits
down to starve in patience. So if nothing is left them to do but to
rid themselves and the world of this man they take to be their
"chief enemy," Caïus Marcius—why, no more speech-making, nor
parliamentary acclamations of "Resolved, resolved!": let the
thing be done! But they can be halted and made to listen yet once
more. First it is to the chief rebel amongst them ruthfully justi-
fying their intent, protesting that

the gods know I speak this in hunger for bread, not in thirst
for revenge. . . .

then to a last-minute defender Marcius finds among them, bidding them remember the "services he has done for his country." For even though he be "a very dog to the commonalty," all that can be said for him must be heard.

The distant shouts of some kindred company of mutineers rouse them again; such temper is infectious. And they would be off to make common cause with these others; but Menenius Agrippa's arrival once again quiets them. They like old Menenius. He is "one that hath always loved the people." Even the First Citizen will grudgingly admit that

> He's one honest enough: would all the rest were so!

"Honest," perhaps; but little proof of his love for the people is in fact ever forthcoming, and the chief token of his honesty would seem to be that he speaks his mind bluntly to them. But he does so in a sort of rough good fellowship, giving himself no high and mighty airs. How far with them even a show of kindliness will go! He knows how to tackle them. They are his "countrymen," his "good friends," his "honest neighbours"; and within a few minutes he has this mutinous mob quietly gathered round him while he tells them a fairy tale. It is the parable of the Belly and the Members. Only that ruthful rebel the First Citizen is mildly recalcitrant:

> you must not think to fob off our disgrace with a tale. . . .

—which, of course, is just what Menenius means to do. And most readily he does it, going his own leisurely pace, giving the homely humor its full value; and while he holds them there absorbed the mutinous mood ebbs out of them. With the recalcitrant First Citizen he spars offhandedly. A dash of ironic flattery (but indeed the creature is intelligent!), a tolerant snub, flooring him finally amid the merriment of his fellows with a stroke of something less than good-humored ridicule:

> What do you think,
> You, the great toe of this assembly? . . .
> being one o' th' lowest, basest, poorest
> Of this most wise rebellion . . .

After which Caius Marcius himself—Coriolanus to be—strides in.
It is for Shakespeare an unusual opening—the plays offer indeed

none comparable to it—with its hundred and sixty lines of abortive revolt and elaborate parable; he will habitually have swung his main theme into action within half the time or less. But it accomplishes a variety of purposes. The mutinous entry having furnished initial impetus enough, its slackening, the debate, and their equivocally mild response to Menenius' bluff bullying, give us a fair view of the citizens not yet in leash to their Tribunes, a sample of their native quality, upon which the lash of Marcius' contempt is next so precipitately to fall. The telling of the parable holds back the action, even as Menenius means it to hold up the revolt, yet bears directly on it, is no mere digression (that, at the play's outset, would be a weakness), but enlarges it at, so to say, one remove. This factor of the citizens and their condition is thus given ample preparatory display. Marcius' castigation will cow them now to silence. While the war with the Volsces is waging they will be absent from the scene. When they return to it Brutus and Sicinius will be their spokesmen, maneuvering and coloring their cause for them.

Marcius, abruptly appearing, at once spurs the action to the swift pace his dominance of it befits. To Menenius' affectionately admiring tribute of a

Hail, noble Marcius!

he—though young man to old—returns no more than a curt "Thanks," so impatient is he to round on the mutineers. Plainly, Menenius' milder methods have already prevailed; but he must still vent his spleen. They are rogues and curs, hares in cowardice, geese in folly, ingrates, their own worst enemies, inconstant and perverse. They say, do they, that there is grain enough in the city, yet they are hungry, that though they be dogs, yet dogs must eat? But

> Would the nobility lay aside their ruth,
> And let me use my sword, I'd make a quarry
> With thousands of these quarter'd slaves, as high
> As I could pick my lance.

Doubtless! And all he says of them and more may be true; but such scorn for starving fellow-countrymen has no very chivalrous ring. Nor is Menenius' placatory

> Nay, these are almost thoroughly persuaded;
> For though abundantly they lack discretion,
> Yet are they passing cowardly.

the most generous comment possible upon their surrender to his
wiles. Marcius, it may be, is the angrier with them since the other
"troops," whose shouts we heard, whom he has just quitted, have
by their plaints prevailed with this same nobility to grant them

> a petition . . . a strange one . . .
> Five tribunes to defend their vulgar wisdoms . . .
> S'death!
> The rabble should have first unroofed the city
> Ere so prevailed with me. . . .

He foresees, shrewdly enough, that

>   it will in time
> Win upon power and throw forth greater themes
> For insurrection's arguing.

There lies, indeed, the obstacle against which he is to bruise and
break himself, and it is embryonic already in this group of
sullen, silenced, confuted men over which he now rides so
contemptuously roughshod. Marcius is about the least sympathetic
of Shakespeare's heroes, and he is first shown to us in his
unloveliest light.

He is happy to be freed from these cankerous domestic politics
by the sudden news of war:

>   we shall ha' means to vent
> Our musty superfluity. . . .

And "our best elders," whose coming follows the news—Cominius
the Consul, old Titus Lartius and other Senators—will have
worthier duties to perform than playing blackmail to the populace.
He himself is consequently in great credit:

> Marcius, 'tis true that you have lately told us;
> The Volsces are in arms.

He can smell the chance of a fight, from wherever the wind of it
blows. And at once, in sharp contrast, he is at his best: his sword
his country's, no questions asked; chivalrous tribute paid to its
chief enemy:

Tullus Aufidius . . .
>   he is a lion
> That I am proud to hunt.

It may all go to a somewhat too self-sufficient tune, yet pardonably stimulated, this—were stimulus needed—by the deference Rome's great men offer him. He cannot resist, moreover, a parting gibe at the "worshipful mutiners," become sullenly silent onlookers, bidding them follow him to play rats among the abundant Volscian corn, which such a little valor will win. But, says the stage direction,

> *Citizens steale away.*[11]

(the empty stomach not being one for fighting), while Marcius, and old Titus, who'd

> lean upon one crutch and fight with t'other,
> Ere stay behind this business.

and Cominius the Consul and the Senators, depart high-heartedly to the Capitol, their place of honor and authority; from it to proclaim the war.

There have been two other onlookers, silent so far, who now remain behind: Brutus and Sicinius, the newly appointed Tribunes. And in the twenty-five lines or so with which they finish the scene Shakespeare etches them in memorably for the caustic element in the play they are to prove; politicians sizing up their destined adversary and, dispassionately, cynically, the weakness and the strength of his position. Nothing to be done now. They must "wait and see."

THE VOLSCIANS

The succeeding scene shows us the Senators of Corioles in council of war, Aufidius bringing news to them of the Roman preparations, and receiving his commission as general in the field. The scene is but forty lines long; yet we learn besides that much "intelligence" passes between Rome and the Volsces—a point to be made more than once; Rome, civilly distracted, has her fifth column—and from Aufidius, clinchingly, that

---

[11] For the argument that those and other stage directions are Shakespeare's own, see p. 238ff.

> If we and Caius Marcius chance to meet,
> 'Tis sworn between us we shall ever strike
> Till one can do no more.

The Senators are airily confident:

> Let us alone to guard Corioles. . . .

The clash is nearing.

With the scene which follows all the main factors of the play will have been assembled, and its opening stage direction is illuminating:

VOLUMNIA AND VIRGILIA

Enter Volumnia and Virgilia, mother and wife to Marcius. They set them down on two low stools and sew.

This note of puritan simplicity is struck at once by nothing more elaborate than the two low stools and the sewing. For these are great ladies, and live in state, as the attendant Gentlewoman announcing the Lady Valeria, and the Usher and the Gentlewoman to show her in, will help show us within another minute or so.[12] We remark too the formality of their manners to each other in the "sweet madam," "good madam," "my ladies both," "your ladyship." Volumnia dominates the household. It is to her that Valeria's visit is announced, and Virgilia asks her for permission to retire. Valeria, by contrast, will seem a very frivol; yet it is for a no wilder gaiety she would have Virgilia lay aside her "stitchery" than to "go visit the good lady that lies in."

The scene gives us Volumnia's Spartan temper, harsh at its kindliest, her son's tones—his very words—echoing through hers; Virgilia's gentler spirit, her tremulous courage, her soft stubbornness; Valeria, witty and merry, primed with her news of the war. The opening prose is austere; it paints Volumnia. For the picturing of Marcius in the field comes colored and moving verse. Valeria's chatter about the child brings prose again, easy and decorative, in which medium the scene ends. By reference, Valeria's news:

------

[12] For the implicit contrast with the scene between Charmian, Iras, Alexas and the Soothsayer in *Antony and Cleopatra*, see p. 94.

the Volsces have an army forth; against whom Cominius the
general is gone, with one part of our Roman power: your lord
and Titus Lartius are set down before their city Corioles. . . .

advances us several steps in the war; and the next scene's opening:

Enter Marcius, Titus Lartius, with drum and colours, with
Captains and Soldiers, as before the city Corioles.

with the later

Enter two Senators with others on the walls of Corioles.

THE WAR WITH THE VOLSCIANS:
BEFORE CORIOLES

—the walls being simply the upper stage—asks no further
explanation.

The earlier scene has ended with a gentle little tussle between
Valeria and Virgilia, and the gentler of the two has won. Now
begins, under every form of contrast, the man's war. Marcius and
Titus Lartius are in the highest spirits, the old soldier as youthful
as the young, and laying bets—an English trait if not a Roman!—
upon the news the Messenger, just sighted, will be bringing:

> A wager they have met.
> My horse to yours, no?
> 'Tis done.
> Agreed.
> Say, has our general met the enemy?

and, the horse so sportingly lost and won, the bet is then, as
between comrades, generously discounted.

This scene, and the three which follow, are to be predominantly
scenes of action. Marcius is above all a fighting hero, and, most
effectively to warrant him his title, Shakespeare lets us see him
fight. Henry V, Antony, Othello, Macbeth, they also are soldiers;
but—even with Henry V—that is not the aspect of them most
vividly lighted. With Coriolanus, it is his personal prowess in war
and its unlucky linking to as trenchant a pugnacity in peace that
make and mar him. We have heard him for a start at his worst.
We are now to see him at his best, winning valiantly to the
summit of his fortunes. He will thus hold our regard the better
along the descent to his tragic end.

For the battle without its walls, a Roman reverse and recovery, and the taking of Corioles; for a second wavering battle, Marcius to the rescue, and final victory, Shakespeare's material resources are little other than those of the old inn-yard, although doubtless the Globe Theatre at the height of its fame can enrich their quality and be more lavish with them. But *drum and colours* still sufficiently betoken an army on the march, and a recognized code of alarums, trumpet flourishes and the sounding of parleys and retreats illustrate the course of a battle or a siege. It is indeed only by the use of such tokens that the extension and swaying confusions of a battle can be made clear. For with hand-to-hand combat realism's limits are reached.

Shakespeare, using both speech and action, sets his board and makes his moves on it, with exactitude and economy. Marcius and Titus Lartius before Corioles learn that Cominius with his army facing the army of the Volsces are

> Within this mile and half.

Marcius' comment is that

> Then shall we hear their 'larum, and they ours.

When, therefore, a little later we hear the *Alarum afar off*, its meaning is at once plain to us, and distracting explanations are saved. For by then the Senators of Corioles are upon the walls, defying the Romans, and—as drums from within the city help inform us—about to anticipate their assault by a sortie. That Aufidius is not in the city we have at once been told. To the noise of the distant fight is added word that he is a captain in it. Marcius here, then, he there; they are not to meet yet.

> *Enter the army of the Volsces. . . . Alarum. The Romans*
> *are beat back to their trenches.*

The hiatus is filled by a seven-line speech from Marcius, both indicating and interpreting the accompanying action:

> They fear us not, but issue forth their city.
> Now put your shields before your hearts, and fight
> With hearts more proof than shields. . . .

That allows, if barely, the symbolic army time to enter and form line, the Romans to start to face them:

> Advance, brave Titus:
> They do disdain us much beyond our thoughts,
> Which makes me sweat with wrath. . . .

—impetuous, impatient!—

> Come on, my fellows:
> He that retires, I'll take him for a Volsce,
> And he shall feel mine edge.

rating them for cowards too, even by anticipation. Fighter but no leader! Then battle is joined and the Romans are beaten back.[13] After which

Enter Marcius, cursing.

~~~~~~~~~~

[13] The ordering of the action upon Shakespeare's stage must be gathered by piecing together text, stage directions and our yet imperfect and disputed knowledge of the mechanics of the Globe.

The stage directions are for the most part figurative and recommendatory, not set down by the book-holder or in his fashion (see p. 238ff.). The curtains to the inner stage could no doubt be made to serve, but it looks as if this Corioles had solid gates.

Enter the army of the Volsces.

might, by convention, mean that these opened to discover the dozen men or less who made the army standing there; and this, for the short time the text allows, would be convenient. It fits, too, the First Senator's

> our gates,
> Which yet seem shut, we have but pinn'd with rushes;
> They'll open of themselves.

They could—wide enough to let the men through, and close behind them. This looks likely, and that they reopen later to accommodate the retreat—

The Volsces retire into Corioles and Marcius follows them to the gates.

—and then stay open, to suit Marcius'

> So, *now* the gates are ope: now prove good seconds:
> 'Tis for the followers fortune widens them,
> Not for the fliers. . . .

until they shut on him.

The Romans are beat back to their trenches apparently through one of the side doors, the Volsces following them. It would need to be of some width to allow for the melee of men, swords and shields, and they might more conveniently be fought to a standstill on the stage. But *Enter Marcius, cursing,* contradicts this possibility. He has been beaten off too, the last of the Romans to go. Further, Titus Lartius is absent when he is shut in the city.

A textual note. In the line

> we'll beat them to their wives,
> As they us to our trenches follows.

(some editors preferring "follow," others "followed"). The "follows" has probably slipped in by some accident from the neighboring stage direction, *Marcius follows them to the gates.* Neither sense nor verse accommodates its speaking.

and the Romans rally; whether thanks to his magnificent vitu-
peration we are free to judge. What is made plain, however, is
that when he calls on them to follow him into the city in pursuit
of the flying enemy—

> mark me, and do the like.

—none of them do. His is no way to win just such devotion from
his soldiers.

> Fool-hardiness; not I!
> Nor I!

And when the gates close on him, for all comment comes a

> See, they have shut him in.

with the grim humor of

> To the pot, I warrant him.

added. Then, Titus Lartius reappearing, Shakespeare stages his
great "effect." The gates open, and there stands Marcius

> *bleeding, assaulted by the enemy.*

alone, at cut and thrust with the whole Volscian "army"; and
the amazing sight, and Titus Lartius' call to them, shame the
recalcitrant Romans—honest fighters enough—into rescuing him,
and so to taking the city..

The stage stays empty for a breathing-space. Then

> *Enter certain Romans, with spoils.*

and we have a three-line tokening of the customary sack of a town:

> This will I carry to Rome.
> And I this.
> A murrain on 't! I took this for silver.

while the

> *Alarum continues still afar off.*

to remind us that Cominius and Aufidius, a "mile and half"
away, are battling still. Marcius and Titus Lartius return,
Marcius fuller than ever of angry scorn for the common soldier,
"these movers . . . these base slaves" that

> Ere yet the fight be done, pack up. Down with them!

he cries, down with these paltry prizes they are pilfering.[14] The distant alarums continue.

> And hark, what noise the general makes! To him!
> There is the man of my soul's hate, Aufidius,
> Piercing our Romans: then, valiant Titus, take
> Convenient numbers to make good the city;
> Whilst I, with those that have the spirit, will haste
> To help Cominius.

His wounds still bleed. The veteran Titus counsels prudence, some respite. He will have none of that. He is off. Titus returns to the city.

The stage is again empty. Then

COMINIUS' PART OF THE BATTLE

Enter Cominius, as it were in retire, with soldiers.[15]

to a very different tempo.

> Breathe you, my friends; well fought! We are come off
> Like Romans, neither foolish in our stands,
> Nor cowardly in retire. . . .

Cominius is Consul and General in Chief, a steady, responsible soldier; and this has indeed quite the tone of an official bulletin, issued in mid-battle. For

> believe me, sirs,
> We shall be charged again. . . .

And news of Titus Lartius and Marcius is lacking, and when, long delayed, it comes, is bad. With clarity and economy Shakespeare connects the one fight and the other. Cominius has heard the alarums of the besiegers even as they have heard his. It is "above an hour" since the Messenger left the Romans "to

---

14 The *exeunt* occasionally marked for the spoilers after "I took this for silver" is an editorial interpolation and not in the Folio.

15 How, in the terms of Shakespeare's theater, is this vacating of the stage, which marks the end of a scene and change of place, differentiated from that of a few lines earlier, before the entry of the soldiers with their spoils, which indicated neither? In the first instance, probably, the open gates still confront us; in the second, after Titus Lartius and his attendants have passed through them, not only will they be closed, but the curtain masking the inner stage will be drawn too.

their trenches driven"; and *we* know what has happened since then, and that Marcius himself is now upon his way here.[16] And when he arrives, so masked in blood that Cominius does not recognize him, we appreciate the effect to the full, since we have already seen him so, and it is as if we had a share ourselves in astonishing Cominius.

No more waiting now, with Marcius here, to be "charged again," if he has aught to say in the matter.

> Where is the enemy? are you lords o' the field?
> If not, why cease you till you are so?

He has left Titus Lartius to do the "mopping-up" in Corioles, is too impatient to be at it again to tell the story of the fight that is over, can scarce spare breath for further railing at "the common file" he so detests. He begs to be set against Aufidius without more delay, and appeals for volunteers to follow him into what must prove a desperate struggle in nobler tones than have sounded from him yet:

> If any such be here,
> As it were sin to doubt, that love this painting
> Wherein you see me smeared; if any fear
> Lesser his person than an ill report;
> If any think brave death outweighs bad life
> And that his country's dearer than himself . . .

and—though momentarily touched by doubt of it when it comes— wins as generous a response.[17] Cominius, we note, without

---

[16] Time, as usual with Shakespeare in such cases, is elastic. We are to picture the Messenger and Marcius dashing across country; so they are allowed likely time for this. As to Titus Lartius' work of making good the city, issuing decrees and the rest of it, that, like the unquestioned minutes of a meeting, we "take as read."

[17] There is corruption of the text hereabouts. When the soldiers take him up in their arms:

> Oh, me alone, make you a sword of me?

has found (to my mind) no very satisfactory interpretation or amendment.

> If these shows be not outward . . .

marks the touch of doubt; and there may be some connection of thought between this and the corrupt line.

Another corruption must be in the line

> Please you to march;
> And four shall quickly draw out my command. . . .

Why "four"? The "Please you to march" is worth noting too, with its unusual suavity.

throwing more doubt upon its zeal, adds solid inducement:

> Make good this ostentation, and you shall
> Divide in all with us.

And so they march—thanks to Marcius, with fresh spirit—to renew the fight.

BACK TO CORIOLES

Titus Lartius, having set a guard upon Corioles, going with Drum and Trumpet toward Cominius and Caius Martius, enters with a Lieutenant, other Soldiers and a Scout.

The scene's action and its seven spoken lines help—and most economically—both to space out and knit together the movements of the siege and the battle as a whole, do so in time and place too. Titus Lartius gives final orders to the Lieutenant for the holding of the town and the sending of reinforcements for the battle still in progress if they are needed. The Lieutenant retires within the gates, which are finally closed; and Titus Lartius with his symbolic Drummer and Trumpeter, the Scout for "guider," and a selection of soldiers takes the road that Marcius more hastily took a while before. The stage is empty again. The curtains before the inner stage (and the gates of Corioles) can now close.

BACK AGAIN TO COMINIUS' SIDE OF THE BATTLE: CAIUS MARCIUS AND AUFIDIUS MEET

Alarum as in battle.

—much such a sound as that which went with the fighting under the walls, the Alarum afar off brought close, and to its most startling and insistent. After which preparation·

Enter Marcius and Aufidius at several doors.

It is for each the peculiarly critical moment of the day. But before they come to blows they go to it with words, the one outscorning and outbragging the other. There is something of convention in this, doubtless; but it follows not so much Shakespeare's accustomed "high Roman fashion" as that of Trojan and Greek in the scurril *Troilus and Cressida*. And it again gives us Marcius at his crudest, excusable by a certain boyishness in him, of character if not of years, of the unlicked cub in the man. Yet it is a flaw of character, which future subtler fighting than this will fatally widen. Nor is the outcome of this duel to prove lucky. Clean conquest of his enemy might serve him well. But

certain Volsces come in the aid of Aufidius.

Marcius has little choice but to turn on them, and he

fights till they be driven in breathless.

But for Aufidius to be left (since he can hardly make yet another in such a melee) to stand there a looker-on, or to follow after while Marcius so magnificently drives the fellows before him—

> Officious, and not valiant, you have shamed me
> In your condemned seconds.

—will he ever forgive that?[18]

THE VICTORIOUS ROMAN FORCES
REASSEMBLE

Flourish. Alarum. A Retreat is sounded. Enter at one door Cominius with the Romans: at another door Marcius with his arm in a scarf.[19]

The battle is over. The strenuous beat of the action relaxes to

---

[18] Once more Shakespeare, by an incidental stroke, regulates the clock of the action.

> Within these three hours, Tullus,
> Alone I fought in your Corioles walls. . . .

The echo from *Troilus and Cressida* is in

> Wert thou the Hector
> That was the whip of your bragged progeny. . . .

It may even perhaps echo Hector's own

> You wisest Grecians, pardon me this brag. . . .

[19] So, but for amended spelling, the Folio. Capell, it seems, added . . . *and other Romans*, and some editors have copied him. But Shakespeare evidently wishes—be it by an arbitrary effect only—to contrast Cominius and his officers and men, with the solitary figure of Marcius, once more wounded.

The stage directions hereabouts tend to be emblematic. How precise a meaning Shakespeare's audience would read into *Flourishes and Alarums. A Retreat is sounded*, and the like, it is hard for us to estimate. A few lines later, moreover, we have *Enter Titus with his Power from the Pursuit*. Could there have been any means of illustrating . . . *from the Pursuit*? I fancy this is simple narrative.

the soberer measure of Cominius' stately praise. The threads of the play's other themes begin at once to be woven back into the fabric. Cominius, addressing Marcius, speaks of

> the dull Tribunes
> That, with the fusty plebians, hate thine honours . . .

Marcius, in deprecating response, of

> my mother,
> Who has a charter to extol her blood . . .

And here we have him at his best; not too mock-modestly belittling his own feats, genuinely generous to his comrades:

> I have done
> As you have done; that's what I can; induced
> As you have been; that's for my country:
> He that has but effected his good will
> Hath overta'en mine act.

rejecting reward without a second thought; acknowledging the supreme honor of

> For what he did before Corioles, call him,
> With all the applause and clamour of the host,
> Caius Marcius Coriolanus! Bear
> The addition nobly ever!

with humorous, becoming simplicity:

> I will go wash;
> And when my face is fair, you shall perceive
> Whether I blush or no: howbeit, I thank you.

Still more attractive is his plea amidst this triumph for the poor Volscian, some time his host, whose name he only finds himself too weary now to remember. He wants a drink of wine. And so we part from him, happy and magnanimous in victory; free too for the moment—or all but—from that self-conscious egotism which so besets him.

But the war is not to finish upon this note.

THE STANDPOINT OF THE VANQUISHED

A flourish. Cornets. Enter Tullus Aufidius, bloody, with two or three soldiers.[20]

Here are the defeated Volscians, and the shamed Aufidius. Cominius the Consul in the scene just past had ordered Titus Lartius back to Corioles, and from there to

>   send us to Rome
> The best, with whom we may articulate,
> For their own good and ours.

But Aufidius scoffs at confidence in such a peace, in Rome's surrender of the conquered city:

>   Condition!
> What good condition can a treaty find
> I' the part that is at mercy? Five times, Marcius . . .

—There it is!—

> I have fought with thee; so often hast thou beat me,
> And wouldst do so, I think, should we encounter
> As often as we eat.

From this sense that he will never now by fair means prove himself the better man springs the mistrust, and hatred, and will the treachery at last to come.

>   My valour's poisoned
> With only suffering stain by him. . . .

—the keynote to Aufidius' spiritual tragedy, which time and the event are to work out.

ROME REJOICES

The entry of Menenius and the Tribunes, Sicinius and Brutus, shows that we are back in Rome. Their acrimonious banter— Menenius an expert at it, the other two doing their humorless best—opens a prospect of the civic war, which is to be rekindled now that the Volscian war is won. But the factors will differ, and

---

[20] It is likelier that *A flourish. Cornets.* rightly belongs to the end of the scene before rather than to the beginning of this, which certainly seems not to call for any sort of "flourish."

the people, with the Tribunes to lead them, prove tougher combatants than before. We have a revaluing of the forces to be engaged, a fresh adjustment of sympathy. Menenius lures the two on. Marcius is blamed for his pride. But

> do you two know how you are censured here in the city, I mean of us o' the right hand file? do you? . . . You talk of pride: O! that you could turn your eyes toward the napes of your necks, and make but an interior survey of your good selves. O! that you could. . . . Why, then you should discover a brace of unmeriting, proud, violent, testy magistrates, alias fools, as any in Rome.

and then, before they can retort on him, he paints his own faults to his liking; an old trick in debate:

> I am known to be a humorous patrician, and one that loves a cup of hot wine with not a drop of allaying Tiber in 't. . . . What I think I utter, and spend my malice in my breath. . . .

with which excuse he goes on to tell them in comically colored terms just what he thinks of them, of their exploiting of the people, and their pretentious folly in general:

> When you speak best unto the purpose, it is not worth the wagging of your beards; and your beards deserve not so honourable a grave as to stuff a botcher's cushion, or to be entombed in an ass's pack-saddle. Yet you must be saying Marcius is proud. . . . God-den to your worships: more of your conversation would infect my brain. . . .

And he turns from them, leaving them glowering, to accost Volumnia, Virgilia, Valeria—a high contrast, in dignity and beauty both—who are hastening across the stage. The news due tonight has come already (Shakespeare's habitual device for sharpening our expectation): the victorious army is approaching, with Marcius, who·

> comes the third time home with the oaken garland . . .

Acrid old Menenius transformed to a cheering schoolboy, his cap flung in the air; he and Volumnia, the two elders, competing in extravagant glee; Virgilia and Valeria the staider in joy, Virgilia shrinking from the thought of the wounds

> I' the shoulder and i' the left arm: there will be large cicatrices to show the people when he shall stand for his place. . . .

—this hint of what is to come another habitual device for the sharpening of our expectation. The Tribunes stay glowering in the background; Menenius cannot forbear a passing gibe at them. But suddenly from the distance comes a shout and the sound of trumpets, cutting sharply into the ferment of their jubilation. Volumnia, in a flash, responds; the Roman matron, and inspired:

> Hark the trumpets!
> These are the ushers of Marcius: before him he carries noise, and behind him he leaves tears:
> Death, that dark spirit, in's nervy arm doth lie;
> Which, being advanced, declines, and then men die.

A bold and masterly transition; from the familiar and excited prose of the exchanges with Menenius to the portentous trumpet-echoing

> These are the ushers of Marcius. . . .

and the measured music of the conventional "sentence."[21]

> *A sennet. Trumpets sound. Enter Cominius the general, and Titus Lartius; between them Coriolanus, crowned with an oaken garland, with Captains and Soldiers, and a Herald.*[22]

—with all possible pomp and circumstance, that is to say; and dialogue and stage direction now combine to make a notable and most eloquent effect. Nor is it eloquence of words alone;

---

[21] Shakespeare has been by no means sparing of space in this scene so far. In particular he could have lessened the passage between Menenius and the Tribunes by half and kept all its substance. Is there any reason for this? He may, one suspects, have been sure of an exceptionally good actor for Menenius. Throughout the play he indulges the character and spaciously—in incidental opportunities. Unfounded surmise, no more; but it is somewhat as if he felt he safely could. Another and more technical reason here, if any at all be needed, is at least worth canvassing. We have left Marcius bloody and unkempt after his fighting. The actor must have time to put himself in proper array for his triumphal entry. Will the speaking of 190 lines allow him more than enough? And here the question of act-division—between I and II—is also involved. Is this Shakespeare's, or an editor's? And if Shakespeare's, and to be marked in performance, was an appreciable interval allowed or no? Speculative questions, and of no capital importance; pertaining to the play's study, nevertheless. For the main question of act-division, see p. 237ff.

[22] *Titus Lartius?* A slip, apparently, on Shakespeare's part. Menenius tells us later that he has been sent for, and, a scene later still, he arrives, to be questioned by Coriolanus about Tullus Aufidius and the Volscian preparation for revenge.

Shakespeare's stagecraft has outpassed that. Ringing speech
pertains to the Herald:

> Know, Rome, that all alone Marcius did fight
> Within Corioles gates. . . .
> Welcome to Rome, renowned Coriolanus!

and to the response, in unison, of the nameless onlookers:

> Welcome to Rome, renowned Coriolanus!

The flow of sound—trumpets, the Herald's trenchant tones, the
volume of voices—suddenly ceasing, creates, so to speak, a silence
in which Coriolanus' or Volumnia's simplest phrase, spoken in all
simplicity, will tell to the height of its value.

> No more of this; it does offend my heart:
> Pray now, no more.

he begs them. The distaste is again genuine, barely tainted by
mock-modesty. But the self-consciousness which sets him so
continually insisting on it shows a crack in character, if a slight
one.

The three women, becomingly, do not press forward; this, to
the end, is soldiers' business. Cominius himself must intervene
with a

> Look, sir, your mother!

And Marcius steps from his place of honor to kneel to her. For
once her sterner self dissolves in emotion. There is tenderness in
the pride of the

> Nay, my good soldier, up . . .

and thereupon he is her "gentle" Marcius, her "worthy" Caius,
the pride returning almost shyly in the

> What is't? Coriolanus must I call thee?

as if she scarce dare trust the gloriously earned title on her tongue.
Then she yields her mother's claim to the wife's.

Virgilia stands quietly, happily, crying. Marcius, to mask his
own emotion at their reuniting, rallies her with a loving, but
half-humorous

> My gracious silence, hail!

with the gentle irony of

> Wouldst thou have laughed had I come coffin'd home,
> That weep'st to see me triumph? . . .

The thought follows:

> Ah, my dear,
> Such eyes the widows in Corioles wear,
> And mothers that lack sons.

none better befitting the poignant gravity of such a triumph. It is Marcius' noblest moment.

Menenius recalls them to their rejoicings. These center on this group of the people of consequence in Rome, exchanging greetings, so content with themselves and their world. Says Marcius:

> Ere in our own house I do shade my head
> The good patricians must be visited. . . .

He ignores, that is to say, the Tribunes, although Menenius, with another merry gibe, points them out to him. Volumnia voices more positively now her high hopes of the consulship for him. His response is cold. Then *Flourish. Cornets. . .* , and the procession, Volumnia and Virgilia joined to it, passes on its way, leaving the neglected Brutus and Sicinius to discuss the situation.[23]

First, Brutus must vent his spleen. And if the coloring of his picture of Rome's greeting to her hero is dyed deep in jealousy of Marcius, it reflects contempt too for the people whose champion he is, as little kindness for "the kitchen malkin" who

---

[23] There is an inconsistency in the stage directions here to be noted. The Folio marks an *Enter Brutus and Sicinius*, having accorded them no certain *exeunt*. Nothing very out of the way in this; both Folio and Quartos abound in such apparent slips. But it opens up a question of the movements and the placing of the two during the interchange between Menenius and Volumnia, and next while Marcius dominates the scene. They are still there, of course, when Menenius addresses them with his

> God save your good worships! Marcius is coming home.

But are they when he cites them to Marcius for the

> old crab-trees here at home that will not
> Be grafted to your relish. . . .

If not, but for a responsive shrug or the like, Marcius' neglect of them will be purely negative. It looks, however, as if they were intended still, at this moment, to be thereabouts, glowering in the background. And probably they go off with the procession, hang back from it, and immediately return. This will at least justify the Folio's stage direction and give point to Brutus' sequent speech, his description of the hero's greeting by the crowd.

> pins
> Her richest lockram 'bout her reechy neck,
> Clambering the walls to eye him . . .

as for the "seld-shown flamens" who "press among the popular throngs" and "our veiled dames" with "their nicely-gawded cheeks." A man of no rose-tinted illusions, Brutus, except, possibly, about himself!

Sicinius has his mind on realities. In a dry seven words he states them:

> On the sudden
> I warrant him Consul.

and Brutus, rancor indulged, is as shrewd:

> Then our office may,
> During his power, go sleep.

Very coolly the two then canvass the prospect: Marcius' failings,

> He cannot temperately transport his honours. . . .

—the unstable temper of the commoners, which, in his pride, he is sure soon to provoke again. So

> At some time when his soaring insolence
> Shall touch the people—which time shall not want,
> If he be put upon't; and that's as easy
> As to set dogs on sheep—will be his fire
> To kindle their dry stubble; and their blaze
> Shall darken him for ever.

They themselves have but meanwhile to "suggest" to the people—the word is twice used—

> in what hatred
> He still hath held them . . .

and wait, not for long.

The scene ends upon a Messenger's summoning them to the Capitol, for

> 'Tis thought
> That Marcius shall be Consul. . . .

and he breaks, his commission done, into a rapturous

> I have seen the dumb men throng to see him, and
> The blind to hear him speak: matrons flung gloves,

Ladies and maids their scarfs and handkerchers,
Upon him as he passed; the nobles bended,
As to Jove's statue, and the commons made
A shower and thunder with their caps and shouts:
I never saw the like.

It is Brutus' tale again, but by this young hero-worshiper how differently told; its enthusiasm gall to the hearers, who, bracing themselves for the coming struggle, depart.

MARCIUS' FIRST STEP IN POLITICS

So much for the hero's greeting by his patrician equals and by the populace. Shakespeare now provides a passing comment on him from a third standpoint.

Enter two Officers, to lay cushions, as it were, in the Capitol.[24]

Here is—to modernize it somewhat—the permanent official's detached view of the politician, with its somewhat cynically critical discrimination. Coriolanus is

a brave fellow; but he's vengeance proud, and loves not the common people.

Who, then, in Rome will not say that of him? Detached analysis follows:

there hath been many great men that have flattered the people, who ne'er loved them; and there be many that they have loved, they know not wherefore: so that if they love they know not why, they hate upon no better a ground. Therefore, for Coriolanus neither to care whether they love or hate him manifests the true knowledge he has in their disposition; and out of his noble carelessness lets them plainly see it.

True enough, and "noble carelessness" no doubt becomes a hero. But, comes the answer, is it only that?

---

[24] *To lay cushions, as it were* . . . is one among the play's "suggestive" stage directions. A cushion can mean "the seat of a judge or ruler" (though the reference for this definition in the O.E.D. is dated 1659). Presumably the officers have a couple of actual cushions, or more, to lay. But the phrase has, I fancy, a further implication; it tells us—even as the subsequent dialogue shows—the sort of persons they are, not menials, but men of a definite dignity, the equivalent, possibly, in Shakespeare's mind, to officers of Parliament, who may bring to their covenanted respect for its members, Lords or Commons, a very critical private view of their individual worth.

he seeks their hate with greater devotion than they can render in him, and leaves nothing undone that may fully discover him their opposite. Now, to seem to affect the malice and displeasure of the people is as bad as that which he dislikes, to flatter them for their love.

"He seeks their hate. . . ." Shrewd comment! And it is the seamy side of this aspect of the man, the impulse which sets him upon his road to disaster. For his defense:

> He hath deserved worthily of his country. . . .

and not to let such deeds excuse his faults were gross ingratitude. Finally, "He's a worthy man"; on that they agree. Again—and here upon the verge of the action's chief struggle—Shakespeare has trimmed the balance of its sympathies.

> *Sennet. Enter, with Lictors before them, Cominius the consul, Menenius, Coriolanus, Senators, Sicinius and Brutus. The Senators take their places; the Tribunes take theirs by themselves. Coriolanus stands.*

The Lictors before the Consul, the Senators and Tribunes in their respective places, Coriolanus standing facing them, as one about to be harangued—this paints the occasion accurately enough; and Menenius' opening

> Having determined of the Volsces, and
> To send for Titus Lartius, it remains,
> As the main point of this our after-meeting . . .

enlarges the circumstances, and, by suggestion, lengthens the apparent time events have been taking, lending them more reality.[25]

Marcius is to be publicly thanked for his "noble service" to the State. The question of the consulship, which is in everyone's

---

[25] At Cominius' command the procession moved "on to the Capitol." Brutus and Sicinius, after a fifty-five-line talk, are summoned there also, because

> 'Tis thought
> That Marcius shall be Consul.

and the thirty-five-line talk between the Officers lets them arrive in time for the business. Menenius' "This our after-meeting . . ." implies that more has been happening, and associates the public thanks to Coriolanus and his proposal as Consul with the general business of the State, and lends them verisimilitude and importance thereby.

mind, will be canvassed later, and with no voice to the contrary, supposedly, and so hard upon the praise with which Cominius will crown his triumph. Wherefore the Senators' confident request to the Tribunes, as "Masters o' the people," for their "kindest care," and their

> loving motion toward the common body,
> To yield what passes here.

But parliamentary courtesy between the parties is even now at a strain. Note Sicinius' canting

> We are convented
> Upon a pleasing treaty, and have hearts
> Inclinable to honour and advance
> The theme of our assembly.

continued smoothly into Brutus' sarcastic

> Which the rather
> We shall be blest to do, if he remember
> A kinder value of the people than
> He hath hereto prized them at.

and Menenius' temper tetchily shortening with these "Masters o' the people" ("*your* people"—he cannot disguise his contempt). And while Cominius, ready with his Consular speech, is thus kept waiting, Coriolanus himself, hero of the occasion, declaring that

> I had rather have one scratch my head i' the sun
> When the alarum were struck than idly sit
> To hear my nothings monstered.

hardly improves it by abruptly departing. Altogether, an unpromising beginning to a political career!

But Cominius' speech, its recalling of what this man has done for Rome, must surely obliterate all petty differences about him. Says the chief Senator:

> He cannot but with measure fit the honours
> Which we devise him.

And when, brought back, Menenius announces to him without more ado:

> The Senate, Coriolanus, are well pleased
> To make thee Consul.

there is at least no dissentient voice. The business being on the crest of the wave, then, he adds at once—a monitory hint to Marcius, one fancies, in his tone:

> It then remains
> That you do speak to the people.

But—as is to be expected—without a moment's heed comes back the

> I do beseech you
> Let me o'erleap that custom. . . .[26]

and Sicinius is as quick with his

> Sir, the people
> Must have their voices; neither will they bate
> One jot of ceremony.

Menenius, however, all conciliation in success, would be closing the gap:

> Put them not to 't;
> Pray you, go fit you to the custom. . . .

And the self-conscious Marcius'

> It is a part
> That I shall blush in acting. . . .

is a yielding plea—were that all. But he must needs add:

> and might well
> Be taken from the people.

and play into the Tribunes' hands. Brutus'

> Mark you that!

is exultant. To cover the blunder and halt the dangerous argument, Menenius and the Senators, without more delay, in due form recommend him Consul to the Tribunes, through them to the people, themselves, moreover, positively acclaiming him:

[26] "Without a moment's heed . . .": this is sufficiently indicated in the continuity of the verse. Marcius' "I do beseech you . . ." completing Menenius' line. Besides which (the actor will remember) Brutus has

> heard him swear,
> Were he to stand for Consul, never would he
> Appear i' the market-place, nor on him put
> The napless vesture of humility . . .

> to our noble Consul
> Wish we all joy and honour.

—and every voice in the Senate answers

> To Coriolanus come all joy and honour!

It is one of the play's salient and most significant moments. Marcius has sworn (Brutus says he heard him, reiterates, "It was his word") that never, to be chosen Consul, will he stand in the market place, show his wounds and beg the people's voices. Yet plainly he now means, after a little persuasion, to do so. Shakespeare will not, in other words, bring him to grief upon a point of mere stubbornness and vanity. And the Tribunes would so far be facing defeat did he not in the very same breath—and how gratuitously!—open up the larger quarrel. Such a privilege

> might well
> Be taken from the people.

Thus jauntily he throws the gauntlet down. It is upon what grows from this, issues of statecraft, nothing petty and egotistic—however egotistically and arrogantly he may urge them—that he will take his stand, and will fail. Here is indeed the play's turning point, from which it develops into true tragedy, with Marcius' character, given that scope, itself rising to heroic stature.

The political war ahead, in which Coriolanus is to be worsted, asks for other qualities than those which so well served in him to beat the Volsces. Brutus and Sicinius will prove to be the successful generals now, and their tactics are to await for the while the adversary's errors. The Senators and their hero departed; says Brutus,

> You see how he intends to use the people.

And they set off themselves to anticipate Coriolanus in the market place and do what may seem wise to bias the proceedings there.[27]

---

[27] But here Shakespeare performs one of his occasionally convenient feats of sleight of hand. The Tribunes quit the stage with this intention; but immediately after the citizens enter, as in the market place, expecting Marcius, who shortly arrives. There has been no opportunity, then, for interference by the Tribunes—unless some break in the continuity of the action, some imaginary passage of time between the two scenes is to be conceded, and that can be counted out of

THE TROUBLES IN THE MARKET PLACE BEGIN

Enter seven or eight Citizens.

In the few lines spoken before Marcius appears we renew acquaintance with them, and sample their present mood.

> Once, if he do require our voices, we ought not to deny him.

—the First Citizen is quite positive about it.[28] The Second Citizen insists on their rights:

> We may, sir, if we will.

The Third Citizen enjoys arguing things out, and the sound of words, and, possibly, of his own voice:

> We have power in ourselves to do it, but it is a power that we have no power to do. . . . Ingratitude is monstrous, and for the

---

the question. Moreover, there is no sign in the talk of the citizens among themselves, or to Marcius, that Brutus and Sicinius have recently been at them. Yet, arriving later, when the ordeal is over and the "voices" have been accorded, the two pointedly refer to the good advice they gave, and scold their already disillusioned followers for neglecting it.

> Could you not have told him
> As you were lessoned . . . ?
> Thus to have said,
> As you were fore-advised . . .

We probably do not detect the trick. But what brings Shakespeare to playing it? Is it that, having dispatched the Tribunes (so to say) to the market place, he sees how much better it may be to let the citizens encounter Marcius in his "gown of humility" without their interference? Yet there is value in the present subsequent passage in which they expound and deplore the errors that, all against their advice, have been made, and undertake to relieve them. For it is in this that they give evidence of being "masters o' the people" indeed. It will then become important not to prejudice its effect by staging shortly beforehand a similar passage of the actual giving of the good advice. Very well; that can be omitted, advantageously from other points of view also. And if it is also important to have the Tribunes reproach the citizens for ignoring their advice, let them do so. We are unlikely to remark later that the advice was never given, nor, as the action ran, could have been.

[28] I doubt if any consistency of character can be established between the First or Second Citizens of the play's opening and of this scene, or between them in this and any of the later ones. Within the boundary of a single scene there will be consistency; they will be ineffectual figures otherwise. But to push the matter further would be to make each a character in his own right, so to speak, and to rob the populace of its collective strength. No matter how diverse the opinions and feelings to be vented, a crowd must remain dramatically a single if a multiple unit.

> multitude to be ingrateful were to make a monster of the multitude. . . .

They are not forgetful:

> for once we stood up about the corn, he himself stuck not to call us the many-headed multitude.

Yet they bear no malice; let bygones be bygones.

> if he would incline to the people, there was never a worthier man.

—upon which Marcius appears, as demanded, in the gown of humility, shepherded by a Menenius who is plainly most apprehensive of what may happen when in a moment his fatherly and restraining influence is withdrawn.

As with the scenes of battle, the passages which now follow between Coriolanus and the citizens are as eloquent, or all but, in their action as in their speech; and disposition and movement ask careful perceiving. Both parties at first shirk the encounter. The citizens, at the sight of the man who has heretofore never met with them but to abuse them, herd together for mutual support, until the sapient Third Citizen protests that

> We are not to stay all together, but to come to him where he stands, by ones, by twos and by threes. . . .

and stiffens their backs a bit. And Coriolanus, that bold fighter, at his most miserably self-conscious as he shows himself in the detested gown, would bolt, it seems, from these despised boors if he might, like a shy schoolboy. There is a generous measure of the comic in the scene, contributed by no means by its simpletons only. Shakespeare does not scruple now, should it suit him, to add to a tragic hero's diet a taste or two of the bitter sauce of ridicule.

Coriolanus takes his stand, to await assault. It is a queer caricature of the picture we so recently had of him, fighting "all alone . . . within Corioles gates." He now has instead of Volsces these kindly fumbling fellow Romans, offering him a victory which the arrogant demon in him does everything to spurn. Fatherly Menenius is in despair:

> You'll mar all:
> I'll leave you: pray you, speak to 'em, I pray you,
> In wholesome manner.

and Marcius' response is certainly not reassuring:

> Bid them wash their faces,
> And keep their teeth clean.

—let them hear it if they like; what does he care![29]

It looks, indeed, an embarrassing business enough: the hero, stripped of his martial trappings, his oaken garland, and appearing, it must be owned, a little ridiculous in this gown of humility. Not so ridiculous as he himself fears, and in the eyes of these simple, serious-minded citizens, not at all. But Marcius, his martial glory disregarded, has not—it is the fatal flaw—the humane and inward dignity which can outshine appearances.

It is distressing, also, to see him so smartly sparring at these simple folk, unable to resist the puzzling repartee, the adroit seizing of a vantage-point, the covert insolence. One gentle stroke pierces his harness. The Third Citizen has ventured the artlessly cunning, joke-in-earnest of

> You must think, if we give you anything, we hope to gain by you.

upon which Marcius pounces with

> Well then, I pray, your price o' th' consulship?

Says the First Citizen very quietly:

> The price is to ask it kindly.

That goes home. It does not soften him. He is no sentimentalist. But at least he next responds as one man allowably may to another—

> Kindly! Sir, I pray, let me ha't: I have wounds to show you, which shall be yours in private. Your good voice, sir; what say you?

—if, even so, he cannot keep derision from his tones, inverted arrogance from the concluding

> I have your alms. Adieu!

---

[29] A point obscured in most modern editions by their setting the entrance of the citizens after the line has been spoken, whereas the Folio has them enter just before. It does not follow that he definitely intends them to hear it; he does not see them until immediately after. But they were there a moment before; he knows they are about. The point is that he does not care.

They have not the wit nor the wish to retort on him in kind. But they are none the less conscious of his mockery, and resentment will secrete in them only the more abundantly.

These three are replaced by a Fourth Citizen and a Fifth, the Fourth plain-spoken:

> You have deserved nobly of your country, and you have not deserved nobly. . . . You have been a scourge to her enemies, you have been a rod to her friends; you have not indeed loved the common people.

The candidate counters with irony:

> You should account me the more virtuous that I have not been common in my love. . . .

But by all means, if they prefer it, he will flatter his

> sworn brother the people, to earn a dearer estimation of them . . . practise the insinuating nod . . . counterfeit the bewitchment of some popular man, and give it bountiful to the desirers. . . .

Could he—were they not such impervious clods!—do more positively to induce them to reject him? Nor will he frankly show these two his wounds; only, since he must, beg them for their "voices"—which they promise him "heartily." He is then left a breathing-space.

Marcius is no more given to reasoning coolly with himself than with others. Inward conviction is his only strength; and, erring against it, as he is erring now, he becomes like an animal caught in a net, frantic, struggling, self-strangled.

> Better it is to die, better to starve . . .

—by test of reason, certainly, a somewhat overcharged outburst. The protest against custom's tyranny,

> What custom wills, in all things should we do't,
> The dust on antique time would lie unswept,
> And mountainous error be too highly heaped
> For truth to o'erpeer. . . .

comes with unconscious irony from the conservative mind in rebellion. But, having brought himself thus far to "fool it so"—

> I am half through;
> The one part suffered, the other will I do.

—resentment would seemingly fade into shrugging self-contempt, did there not at this point

Enter three Citizens more.

The sight of them stirs him to a very self-scourging of mockery:

> Your voices! For your voices I have fought;
> Watched for your voices; for your voices bear
> Of wounds two dozen odd; battles thrice six
> I have seen and heard of. . . .

But, their own stolid simplicity unaffected, the scourge flags, the mockery peters out—

> for your voices have
> Done many things, some less, some more: your voices. . . .

—into the final surrender of

> Indeed, I would be Consul.

That he should come to this! They give him his reward:

> He has done nobly. . . . Therefore let him be Consul. . . . God save thee, noble Consul!

and as Menenius returns, the Tribunes with him, these simple folk inconspicuously depart; Marcius, released, venting an incorrigible

> Worthy voices![30]

Menenius is triumphant. His man wins; and the rest of the business can be pushed through without more delay. Sicinius stiffly assents. Marcius only demands: will it be decently done in the Senate House, not here in the vulgar market place; and

> May I change these garments?

—this ridiculous "gown of humility"? He may. Then all's well; and he and Menenius both are off in high feather. Diplomatic Menenius does not forget to ask their good colleagues the Tribunes to go along with them. No; they prefer to "stay here for the people"; their people. Sicinius' smooth "Fare you well" has an inauspicious ring.

Brutus thinks all is lost for the time being, and would dismiss

---

[30] For the technical treatment of this soliloquy, see the section upon the play's verse, p. 219ff.

the people. Sicinius will wait and see. And, sure enough, when
the plebeians reassemble, the tide of their favor towards Marcius
is already on the turn. Did he suppose, because they did not
retort then and there, that they were insensible to his sarcasm?

> To my poor unworthy notice,
> He mocked us when he begged our voices.

says the Second Citizen; and the Third, thus encouraged:

> Certainly.
> He flouted us downright.

But attack again brings defense. The First Citizen, in a minority
of one though he may be, stands out:

> No, 'tis his kind of speech; he did not mock us.

As in that old quarrel over the corn, Marcius must have fair play.
  Brutus and Sicinius know better than to join in the attack while
it is strong enough without them. There are better ways of
fomenting it. Surely he can never have refused—Sicinius won't
believe it—his fellow citizens their right to see

> His marks of merit, wounds received for 's country.

The Third Citizen is effectively roused:

> He said he had wounds, which he could show in private;
> And with his hat, thus waving it in scorn,
> "I would be consul," says he: "aged custom,
> But by your voices, will not so permit me;
> Your voices therefore."

Not a derisive phrase nor a scornful twist of the tongue did he
miss, it seems:

> When we granted that,
> Here was, "I thank you for your voices: thank you:
> Your most sweet voices: now you've left your voices
> I have no further with you." Was not this mockery?

The rest mutely agree. They have behaved like fools. The
Tribunes now read them—and not for the first time, upon this
very subject!—a sound political lesson.[31]
  Admitting that his recent "worthy deeds" gave him a claim

---

[31] "Not for the first time": see p. 154, note 27.

upon them, they should have reminded him of his ancient enmity
towards them. Clearly, they should have said, they could not
risk his remaining a "fast foe to the Plebeii." They should indeed have demanded from him a pledge for his future good
behavior—which, if he had given it, they could have held him to;
and if, as was more likely, the mere demand had "galled his
surly nature," then, "putting him to rage," they could have

> ta'en the advantage of his choler,
> And passed him unelected.

For do they suppose that a man who can treat them as he has now
done when he needs their votes will prove very considerate
when he no longer needs them? And are they, who have " 'ere
now denied the asker"—the candid, honest asker—to bestow their
"sued-for tongues" in thanks for such treatment as this? The
appeal is to sound sense and self-respect. And it needs but a
single evasive

> He's not confirmed; we may deny him yet.

to stampede the rest:

> And will deny him:
> I'll have five hundred voices of that sound.

And the rot will spread:

> I twice five hundred and their friends to piece 'em.

Brutus has the demagogue's sense of a crowd's mood and the
critical moment:

> Get you hence instantly, and tell those friends,
> That they have chosen a Consul that will from them take
> Their liberties. . . .

—rate them for fools as we are rating you. But Sicinius is for
putting a more temperate face on the affair:

> Let them assemble,
> And, on a safer judgment, all revoke
> Your ignorant election. . . .

—let them confess it to be so. Then he builds them up their
case; against Marcius' pride, and his old hatred of them, which
in the light of his great deeds they had been so ready to forget

as not to note the mocking scorn, sure sign that he hated them
still. Upon which draft Brutus is quick to improve:

> Lay
> A fault on us, your Tribunes, that we laboured—
> No impediment between—but that you must
> Cast your election on him.

A brilliant maneuver from the Tribunes' standpoint! The people
will save their faces, and they win credit for a patriotic effort to
heal this old unhappy quarrel. So excellent seems the notion that
they enlarge on it until they find themselves lauding, not Marcius
alone, but his ancestors also for their services to Rome and its
people; very practical, popular services; for

> Of the same house Publius and Quintus were,
> That our best water brought by conduits hither. . . .

So Sicinius must steer back to the point, that

> you have found . . .
> That he's your chief enemy, and revoke
> Your sudden approbation.

while Brutus encourages them again with another

> Say you ne'er had done it—
> Harp on that still—but by our putting on. . . .

for already the tide of their resentment has ebbed to the
uncertainty of an

> *almost* all
> Repent in their election.

But they depart to do the bidding of these political masters, who
linger a moment, themselves, before taking their shorter way to
the Capitol, to reflect that, mildly as it yet promises,

> This mutiny were better put in hazard
> Than stay, past doubt, for greater. . . .

and that, arriving "before the stream of the people," the threat of it
can be made to

> seem, as partly 'tis, their own,
> Which we have goaded onward.

THE BATTLEGROUND IS BEFORE THE CAPITOL NOW

Cornets. Enter Coriolanus, Menenius, all the Gentry, Cominius, Titus Lartius, and other Senators.

All the Gentry is to be noted, with the completeness of the contrast it indicates between this gathering and that of the home-spun group of citizens. The cornets, elaborately sounding, tell us that the ceremonies of the election are not yet over. Coriolanus is once more fitly attired for them. And he is already deferred to as Consul—Titus Lartius, back from Corioles, but still in fighting trim, calls him "my lord"; Cominius addresses him as "Lord Consul"—and spontaneously, confidently, so asserts himself. He nurses no illusions, as the more pacific Cominius does, that Rome has finished with the Volscians, points a prompt finger towards the source of trouble to come with his

> Saw you Aufidius?

is as boyishly himself as ever in the eager

> Spoke he of me? . . .
>   How? What?

Aufidius has retired to Antium, has he, there to bide his time? This by triple repetition is impressed on us. Then, says Marcius:

> I wish I had a cause to seek him there. . . .

—and the words will lodge in our memory.

So here is Coriolanus on the very crest of the wave, Rome's leader elect, and just such a leader as she may most need, with war, as is hinted, likely to threaten her again. Supported by the Senate and the gentry, he is now on his way back from the Capitol to the market place for the final act of the election, the people's confirmation of their acceptance of him. The Tribunes enter as from the market place. They do not speak at once; and Marcius apparently is not unwilling that, as they stand there, they should overhear his comments on them:

> Behold, these are the tribunes of the people,
> The tongues o' the common mouth: I do despise them;

> For they do prank themselves in authority,
> Against all noble sufferance.[32]

The Tribunes do not mean to be provoked into losing their tempers. They are come, on the contrary, to prevent disorder. Coriolanus must not proceed to the market place:

> The people are incensed against him.

Brutus confirming Sicinius with a solemn

> Stop,
> Or all will fall in broil.

Coriolanus, needless to say—and the Tribunes have counted on it—flares into anger at once, and first against the Tribunes themselves for failing to control their "herd":

> What are your offices?
> You being their mouths, why rule you not their teeth?

"Rule"—the first thought to his mind; and a minute later he is inveighing against

> such as cannot rule
> Nor ever will be ruled.

(Brutus and Sicinius could tell him if they would that while they get their own way with their "herd"—and better than he knows how to—it is not by rule.)

His tactic, in this sort of fight as in another, is at once to force the acutest issue:

> Have you not set them on?

—let them deny it if they can. Theirs is to lure him aside. The vexed, one-time question about the corn, Brutus neatly casts that into the arena. Marcius scoffs:

> Why, this was known before.

and—the quarrel then widening to admit Cominius and Menenius to a share in it—one hopes he may have the sense to drop the subject. But no!

> Tell me of corn!
> This was my speech, and I will speak 't again—

---

[32] If he is not at least willing for them to overhear, there is little or no point in the lines. But here is the schoolboy side of him, very similarly shown in the scene of the gown of humility.

and not Menenius nor the Senators can stay him.

Nor is this the worst. Though his friends beseech him not to, he must needs go on to raise the whole question of these privileges that have been granted to "the mutable, rank-scented meynie"— political disapproval and personal fastidiousness combined!—for

> I say again,
> In soothing them we nourish 'gainst our Senate
> The cockle of rebellion, insolence, sedition,
> Which we ourselves have ploughed for, sowed and scattered,
> By mingling them with us, the honoured number. . . .

Brutus' acid comment,

> You speak o' the people
> As if you were a god to punish, not
> A man of their infirmity.

is a not altogether surprising one.

Marcius had been ready with this protest, and was fended by but a little from making it, upon the verge of the prescribed appeal in the gown of humility on the market place. In hot blood he has, to their faces, denounced the people yet more fiercely; and Menenius urges the Tribunes not, in fairness, to take advantage of his choler now. Marcius consents to no such excuse:

> Choler!
> Were I as patient as the midnight sleep,
> By Jove, 't would be my mind.

And it is at this juncture that, a graver note sounding, we become aware of him grown to more heroic stature, to take his stand for a cause of greater import than his own:

> O good, but most unwise patricians! why,
> You grave but reckless Senators, have you thus
> Given Hydra here to choose an officer. . . ?

For of two things one: the hydra-headed people will rule, or he— this Sicinius or the like—in their name; and

> If he have power,
> Then veil your ignorance; if none, awake
> Your dangerous lenity. If you are learned,
> Be not as common fools; if you are not,
> Let them have cushions by you. You are plebeians,
> If they be Senators: and they are no less. . . .

> By Jove himself,
> It makes the Consuls base: and my soul aches
> To know, when two authorities are up,
> Neither supreme, how soon confusion
> May enter 'twixt the gap of both and take
> The one by the other.

—it is a note never sounded by Marcius before; the rare note of selfless intellectual passion.

This is the juncture too at which he begins to alienate his friends. Little do the Senators want less—they are as apt politicians as the Tribunes—than to have such an issue raised. Cominius would evade it with a

> Well, on to the market place.

But that only sets this incorrigible Consul-elect to prove his case by revising the well-worn quarrel about the corn—and, since he will, why, adroitly he argues it as could the most proficient politician of them all. And that brings him to lashing at the people yet once more for their wartime cowardice, and Menenius cannot stop him.

He finds himself at last upon the higher ground again, for him the highest. What can go well in a state

> where gentry, title, wisdom,
> Cannot conclude but by the yea and no
> Of general ignorance . . .

Even for the people's own sake

> at once pluck out
> The multitudinous tongue; let them not lick
> The sweet which is their poison. . . .

Dangerous ground! Brutus and Sicinius have no more need of their façade of indignation. It sputters from them:

> Has said enough.
> Has spoken like a traitor, and shall answer
> As traitors do.

But it is not in Marcius to retreat. Here, indeed, he is, in the sort of situation that most delights him, singlehanded against odds, reckless of consequence. And with the happy, schoolboy ribaldry of the question:

What should the people do with these bald Tribunes. . . ?

he is ready to

> throw their power i' the dust.

Not for this was he to be elected Consul. It is, as Brutus says, "Manifest treason." But revolutions do not always come from below.

Such a quarrel started, each must line up on his own side. And the summoning of the Aediles to apprehend Rome's hero

> as a traitorous innovator,
> A foe to the public weal . . .

—the Tribunes will carefully keep their law-abiding and conservative footing—rallies the troubled Senate round him.[33] Sicinius, violently excited, is for arresting Marcius with his own hands; Cominius, scandalized, protesting; Marcius, at his senile touch, with a

> Hence, rotten thing, or I shall shake thy bones
> Out of thy garments.

sending him yelping off in terror. Hullaballoo ensues; Coriolanus alone standing silent and unmoved.

The first thing is to quiet it; and this only the Tribunes, who have roused it, can well do. Menenius, outshouted, helpless, is reduced to begging "good Sicinius" to speak to the people. If he thinks he has a peacemaker in him he is much mistaken. Sicinius but repeats quietly and more clearly what he has already called aloud:

~~~~~~~~~

[33] There is significance in the two stage directions: first

Enter a rabble of Plebeians, with the Aediles.

The people were assembled in the market place ready to disavow their choice of Coriolanus, but prepared—neither they nor the Tribunes—for no such business as this. So, called upon for help, they appear as a "rabble." It will be a very different matter when, for the later encounter, they have been "collected . . . by tribes" and drilled in the required behavior.

Secondly, while the plebeians are mustering to the support of their Tribunes, the direction to the Senators is

They all bustle about Coriolanus.

It is one of the play's characteristically descriptive stage directions; and it suggests a certain embarrassment and fuss, the Senators little less perturbed than the Tribunes are.

> You are at point to lose your liberties:
> Marcius would have all from you; Marcius,
> Whom late you have named for Consul.

And to the shocked reproach from the Senate side that

> This is the way to kindle, not to quench.
> To unbuild the city and to lay all flat.

he launches at Marcius, who would throw the popular power "in the dust," the tit-for-tat

> What is the city but the people?

with its powerful chorus of popular response:

> True,
> The people are the city.

And thus can the political pendulum swing once it is started swinging.

For the Tribunes, cooler now and confident with their followers ranged behind them, this is a chance not to be missed, of pushing their power to its utmost. It marks them and their kind that they cannot resist the temptation. Their enemy, attacking them, has rashly talked treason too; and, says Sicinius:

> This deserves death.

Brutus adds categorically,

> Or let us stand to our authority
> Or let us lose it. We do here pronounce
> Upon the part o' the people, in whose power
> We were elected theirs, Marcius is worthy
> Of present death.

And, without more ado, the sentence ends, he is to be flung from the Tarpeian rock. Menenius—violence imminent, his side outnumbered—beseeches lenity. Marcius, silent till now, simply draws his sword, and says,

> No, I'll die here.

He adds, more sportingly,

> There's some among you have beheld me fighting:
> Come, try upon yourselves what you have seen me.

Urged by the Tribunes, they tumultuously do; and

In this mutiny, the Tribunes, the Aediles, and the People,
are beat in.

—as, with Marcius at the head of even a handful of men of good
fighting quality (Cominius is there, and Titus Lartius), such a
rabble might look to be.

But it is to be noted how the impromptu victory is taken:
Menenius' first thought is for Marcius to profit from it by
retreating to his house and leaving the reasonable rest of them to
patch up the best peace they can. One or two are left fighting
keen.[34] But

> Shall it be put to that?

—Romans at war with Romans—

> The gods forbid!

In affection for his hero the old man mitigates the effect of
Marcius' grimly vaunting

> On fair ground
> I could beat forty of them.

with the humor of his own

> I could myself
> Take up a brace o' the best of them; yea, the two Tribunes.

But it is a relief to have him gone.

Comment is practical:

> This man has marred his fortune.

—this is *not* the way to campaign for the consulship in Rome.[35]

~~~~~~~

[34] Cominius, apparently, one. But I fancy that the
> Stand fast:
> We have as many friends as enemies.

is misascribed to him. For if not, he changes his mind barely a moment later;
and, a little later still, a six-line speech conclusively puts him among the prudent
ones. Further, he and Coriolanus depart together.

[35] The Folio has marked an *exeunt* for Coriolanus and Cominius only; and the
minor speeches immediately following are given to *Patri*, translated by later
editors into First and Second Patrician, instead of to the Senators who have
fulfilled this need till now. One queries at first an (unrecorded) departure of the
Senators too; but at the end of the scene there still remains one Senator at least.
A possible explanation is that the Senators in their robes—whatever on
Shakespeare's stage these were—are meant to be withdrawn to the background,
the gathering to lose the last of its ceremonial aspect. This will add, by contrast,

And through Menenius' loyally laudatory

> His nature is too noble for the world:
> He would not flatter Neptune for his trident,
> Or Jove for 's power to thunder. . . .

can be heard, perhaps, the man of the world's sigh of exasperation
at being left to clear up if he can the mess this noble nature has
made of things. It issues in a final

> What the vengeance!
> Could he not speak 'em fair?

But a breathing-space at least has been gained, in which
Menenius himself can "speak 'em fair," can try, as he said,

> whether my old wit be in request
> with those that have but little . . .

and here we may recall our first sight of him at the play's
opening, and the skill with which he quieted the mutiny over the
corn. This is a harder task. Brutus and Sicinius are not to be so
cajoled. They possess authority, moreover, to which he takes care
to show deference, while Marcius has put himself indefensibly in
the wrong. And the people are for the moment—wherefore the
Tribunes are astutely demanding death without delay—authentically incensed against him, witness the full chorus of reiterated
"No, no . . ." which greets his mere tentative naming as "the
Consul Coriolanus." He must make for him, then, must Menenius,
such a place with the people as the Tribunes dare not, for shame—
will not, for policy—obstruct.

First, it is to a regard for Rome's good name:

> whose gratitude
> Towards her deserved children is enrolled
> In Jove's own book . . .

Then:

> What has he done to Rome that's worthy death?
> Killing our enemies, the blood he hath lost—
> Which, I dare vouch, is more than that he hath,
> By many an ounce—he dropped it for his country;

---

to the semblance of authority worn by Brutus and Sicinius, reappearing at the
head of their rabble.

> And what is left, to lose it by his country
> Were to us all, that do 't and suffer it,
> A brand to the end o' the world.

"Were to us all"—they are one in citizenship with him, and all are Rome.

The Tribunes see that they must put a stop to this, must let loose the pent wrath of the people, before, under such soothing, it abates altogether. But—each minute a gain—Menenius begs for

> One word more, one word.

And of full effect he makes it; with its warning whither "tiger-footed rage" may lead, his repicturing to the people of their soldier

> bred i' the wars
> Since he could draw a sword . . .

and his final promise to bring him back to them compliant in spirit. And the Senatorial

> Noble Tribunes,
> It is the humane way. . . .

solidly supports him.

They are practiced politicians, are the Tribunes, and can quickly tack and veer, and turn moderation to account as well as rage. If they do not now give Marcius another chance, they may well, under the effect of such appeals for him, split their own party. If they do, and he does not take it, he will probably split his own, and they will have him the more at their mercy. Besides, Menenius will almost certainly fail to bring him tamely to heel. So Sicinius generously consents; a touch of sardonic humor in his

> Noble Menenius,
> Be you, then, as the people's officer . . .

And the

> Masters, lay down your weapons.
> Go not home.
> Meet on the market place. . . .

is but a menace postponed. To Menenius and the Senators, indeed, Sicinius is coldly explicit:

> Where, if you bring not Marcius, we'll proceed
> In our first way.

Menenius' "old wit" has won him somewhat; but despite the jovially confident

> I'll bring him to you.

he knows how precariously little yet. And the scene ends upon the ominous muted note of his

> He must come,
> Or what is worst will follow.

as he and the Senators depart to fulfill the no easier second half of their task—if they can!

Coriolanus absent, and his violent stimulus to the action lacking, its pulse has kept a steadier beat. There is no slackening, the tension is sustained; and we are stirred to question: will he once more yield to persuasion, or no?

VOLUMNIA'S SHARE IN THE QUARREL

Finding him at his house, the young nobility around him, high-mettled and willful as he, truly it does not seem likely.[36] He is at the highest pitch of indignant wrath:

> Let them pull all about mine ears; present me
> Death on the wheel, or at wild horses' heels;
> Or pile ten hills on the Tarpeian rock
> That the precipitation might down stretch
> Below the beam of sight; yet will I still
> Be thus to them.

flattered in it by these young supporters of his own breed and mind whom conflict begins to gather to him—one of them exclaiming,

> You do the nobler.

------

[36] The Folio's stage direction speaks here only of his entering *with Nobles*; actually it is later, on his way to banishment, that he is said to be accompanied to the city gate by *the young Nobility of Rome*. But the distinction implied at both points between them (whether called *Nobles* or *young Nobility*) and the rest of his party is the same, and its meaning is, I think, clear. At first he has, of course, the Senate on his side; and among the variously termed Patricians, Gentry, Nobles, some will be Senators, some not. Step by step, in his intransigence, he alienates the Senators, and—if it can be shown, if the theater company can muster sufficient numbers—possibly some of the elders among the mere gentry too. But the young nobility—men more or less of his own age—side with him to the last. And it is at this point in the action that—though not much is made of it—they begin to be distinguished from the rest.

—pricked the more to it by a most unexpected crossing just
encountered:

> I muse my mother
> Does not approve me further. . . .

We may note how Shakespeare here concentrates his action,
dovetails it, coils it like a spring to give it strength. Marcius left
the Capitol with Cominius, who has now, apparently, gone
elsewhere; we shall learn where and why later. He himself has
been at home long enough for a first encounter with Volumnia,
the result of it shown in the outburst with which the scene opens,
the violent recoil from her sober counsel; and that this *is* the result
of it to be surmised from the sight of her as she slowly follows him
and stands, disapproval in her attitude, until he turns to discover
and ask,

> Why did you wish me milder?[37]

Here too the depicting of Marcius takes a more intimate turn.
Man of action, of impulse, and of quick response to his fellows
whether in anger or affection, we do not find him reflecting in
solitude. Shakespeare allots him but one short soliloquy, and that
to mark his loneliness and defeat.[38] He is brought nearest
to consciousness of himself—the boyish self-consciousness that
plagues him a very different thing!—when he looks, as now, in
the glass of his mother's opinion of him. This has been satisfyingly
flattering so far; he "muses" the more that she should now wish
him to be false to himself. And the tragedy of character gains
shape.

He yielded to persuasion and was false to himself when he put
on the gown of humility and stood begging for votes in the
market place. But at least he did it ill; and he atoned to himself,
moreover, when the chance came, by giving Tribunes and people
a fuller taste of his true mind than otherwise he would have done
—gave it to his own prejudice too. This new temptation to go back
upon himself finds him at first more violent in resistance, yet the
less able to resist.

[37] A simple effect, lost in the modern editorial delaying of her entrance by
nine lines.

[38] The exclamatory "Better it is to die, better to starve . . ." in the scene in
the market place is hardly a soliloquy.

Having vented in defiance his astonishment that Volumnia should so rebuke him, he listens to her respectfully, lovingly; to Menenius and the Senators, coming in hope and doubt from their parley with the Tribunes; to Cominius, who later reports from the market place that the issue must be faced—to all their politic advice. But it is a chilling change from his mother's accustomed fervors to the biting

> You might have been enough the man you are
> With striving less to be so. . . .

apt and deserved though this may be. That he is right in what he has said, but that he should wait, should he, to say it until those that hold him wrong are in his power?—it is foxy doctrine. He has been, protests genial old Menenius, "too rough, something too rough. . . ." From Volumnia, again, who claims for herself

> a brain that leads my use of anger
> To better vantage.

(not that, tested so little later, this appears) he faces a

> You are too absolute.

He, then, their hero, if he is to be their Consul, has some most unheroic lessons to learn. To return to the Tribunes and publicly repent what he has spoken—which he would not do to the gods! But he listens still. He has no taste for argument. Strange that it should be his mother cleverly proving to him, his friends applauding, that a lie told to his fellow Romans here to gain his ends no more dishonors him than it would in war thus

> to take in a town with gentle words,
> Which else would put you to your fortune and
> The hazard of much blood . . .

But a good argument doubtless. Not a very admirable picture, though, that she sketches of him for his copying:

> with this bonnet in thy hand . . .
> Thy knee bussing the stones—for in such business
> Action is eloquence, and the eyes of the ignorant
> More learned than the ears—waving thy head,
> (Which often) thus correcting thy stout heart,
> Now humble as the ripest mulberry
> That will not hold the handling. . . .

And, even more than in his donning of the gown of humility, does it put him to a part which, he protests, he never can "discharge to the life." But, waging this sort of war, his friends have him at their mercy as never had his enemies when he faced *them* sword in hand. For his wife's sake, his son's, in the Senators' cause and the nobles', it is his duty, so it seems, to forswear himself. And Volumnia, argument unavailing, coaxes and chides him like a child, and, as a last resource, treats him to a hot fit of the very temper she has so disastrously bred in him.

He is swung from a baited

> Well, I must do 't.

and from his own yet sorrier filling-in of her sorry picture of him—

> Away, my disposition, and possess me
> Some harlot's spirit! my throat of war be turned,
> Which quired with my drum, into a pipe
> Small as an eunuch . . .
>   a beggar's tongue
> Make motion through my lips, and my armed knees,
> Who bowed but in my stirrup, bend like his
> That hath received an alms! . . .

—to the violent revolt of

>   I will *not* do 't
> Lest I surcease to honour mine own truth,
> And by my body's action teach my mind
> A most inherent baseness.

but, finally, as she rounds on him, to a boylike

>   Pray, be content,
> Mother, I am going to the market place;
> Chide me no more. . . .

It is the endearing side of him.

>   I'll mountebank their loves,
> Cog their hearts from them, and come home beloved
> Of all the trades in Rome. Look, I am going:
> Commend me to my wife. . . .

The invincible soldier! Vulnerable in the simplicity of his affections, as son, husband, father, friend! Pure patriot, by his unquestioning lights; his life his country's! As a politician, a fool!

He is foredoomed to fail in this coming test, with which the long strain of his campaign for the consulship is to end. It does not lie in him to be cynically false to his nature. He knows only how to be true even to its faults. Still, he will please them if he can; to have his mother turn her back on him in anger distresses him. So, with "Mildly" for his watchword—a wry irony evolving from the sound of it as he and Menenius pass it between them— he sets out again at the head of his party.

BANISHMENT

Sicinius and Brutus (the appointment was for the market place; when we see them enter, then, we shall presume them there) have not wasted time. While Senators and nobles have been at odds with their candidate and leader, they, by contrast, have been drilling their followers and developing their tactics. Coriolanus can still be best accused of aiming at tyrannical power; and, says Brutus,

> In this point charge him home. . . .

But "if he evade us there. . . ," if, that is to say, Menenius has succeeded in making him see reason, why, to tax him with having, in his hatred for the people, deprived them of their share of the spoil "got on the Antiates," will certainly rouse his wrath again. He is coming, they hear; accompanied, of course, by old Menenius

>   and those Senators
> That always favoured him.

There are others, then; and his party can be divided. Then come their last-minute instructions to the Aedile. The people have been organized in their legal groups? Good. Let them listen for their leaders' voices; and, says Sicinius,

> when they hear me say "It shall be so
> I' the right and strength o' the Commons," be it either
> For death, for fine, or banishment, then let them
> If I say fine, cry "fine," if death, cry "death". . . .

—for only with such docile followers can a democratic leader do himself full credit, reap the moment's maximum harvest. But there are, besides, the opposite uses to which a crowd can be put:

> And when such time they have begun to cry,
> Let them not cease, but with a din confused
> Enforce the present execution. . . .

Then Brutus, kindling to the opportunity:

> Put him to choler straight.

and the rest will follow. The unhappy Coriolanus is no better than a child in their hands. Sicinius, beneath the surface, is as excited:

> Well, here he comes.

It is a tense and a pregnant moment.

Menenius, on the way here, has been harping, seemingly, on the single string, its note varied only from the parting "Mildly" to this

> Calmly, I do beseech you.

—Marcius' muttered answer not reassuring! The opponents face each other like duelists with a ceremonious salute; and what could be more exemplary than Marcius'

> The honoured gods
> Keep Rome in safety, and the chairs of justice
> Supplied with worthy men! plant love among's!
> Throng our large temples with the shows of peace,
> And not our streets with war!

Menenius applauds, as might a proud tutor his pupil:

> A noble wish!

The Tribunes duly proceed:

> Draw near, ye people.

And the Aedile sustains their dignity:

> List to your Tribunes! Audience! Peace, I say!

Now comes maneuvering for position. Is this to be the end of the dispute? Marcius demands; Sicinius in turn:

> If you submit you to the people's voices,
> Allow their officers, and are content
> To suffer lawful censure for such faults
> As shall be proved upon you?

"Submit ... censure ... faults ..."; it is a bitter pill. The Tribunes hope, the Senators fear, that he will never swallow it. With a Spartan

> I am content.

he does. Upon which, his friends cannot in prudence but see, the business had best be brought to a quick finish. Yet Menenius, though he himself sees it—

> Lo! citizens, he says he is content. . . .

—cannot resist pleading once more the cause that is already won, so well has he pleaded it; the advocate's common fault! "War-like service" and "wounds" must again be commended; and Marcius himself, as before, must mock-modestly protest,

> Scratches with briers;
> Scars to move laughter only.

And the fresh tribute to his soldiership stirs him, despite Cominius' caution, to reopen the quarrel:

> What is the matter
> That being passed for Consul with full voice,
> I am so dishonoured that the very hour
> You take it off again?

—then he sees his error, and checks himself. But, if the Tribunes have failed so far to "put him to choler," they will not now:

> We charge you, that you have contrived to take
> From Rome all seasoned office, and to wind
> Yourself into a power tyrannical;
> For which you are a traitor to the people.

A two-edged thrust!

> The fires i' the lowest hell fold in the people!
> Call me *their* traitor! . . .

—no holding him after that!

The people are ahead of their leaders here. Spontaneously the cry rises:

> To the rock, to the rock with him!

So now the supple demagogue can play the moderate man, gain credit with the moderate men of the other side, and insure himself

against reaction, should that come. The people are right. Marcius'
treachery to them

> Deserves the extremest death. . . .
> But since he hath
> Served well for Rome—

(Brutus is more than a little patronizing) sentence on him
shall mercifully be commuted to banishment for life. Neither
Menenius' comically frantic

> Is this the promise that you made your mother?

nor Cominius' noble plea, can turn Coriolanus from his defiant
wrath, the Tribunes from their triumph. And in their lessoned
unison the people echo once and again:

> It shall be so! It shall be so!
> Let him away!
> He's banished, and it shall be so.

Against such a chorus the single voice sounds nobly:

> You common cry of curs! whose breath I hate
> As reek o' the rotten fens, whose love I prize
> As the dead carcasses of unburied men
> That do corrupt my air . . .

and the superlative pride is warranted of the

> I banish you.

To his grim presage of what must be in store for such a mob
and for their Rome the Tribunes listen in complacent silence, the
people heedlessly, awaiting but the sight of his departure—

> Despising,
> For you, the city, thus I turn my back:
> There is a world elsewhere.[39]

~~~~~~~~~~

[39] It is just possible, I think, that F's quaintly corrupted stage direction:
Exeunt Coriolanus, Cominius, with Cumaligs (due to a muddled deletion in the
MS evidently) has to do with the several other stage directions and hints in
the text meant to indicate the growing division among Coriolanus' supporters (see
p. 172, note 36, and page 182, note 40). Was the *with* to have been followed
by particulars of those that accompanied him and those that did not, and did
Shakespeare, for lack of room or any other likely reason, content himself rather
with the *cum aliis*, leaving the fact that some went one way, some another to be
deduced (and implemented by the actors) from the opening stage direction of
the next scene: *Enter Coriolanus . . . with the young Nobility of Rome*; the

—to take their time once more from the fugleman-Aedile with a jubilant

> Our enemy is banished! He is gone! Hoo! hoo!

though its ending is mere wolfish clamor.

"Despising, for you, the city . . ."; there is the first faint sound— if the actor can accent it, and we are quick to hear—of the deeper and more tragic discord to come.

Brutus and Sicinius meanwhile will lose nothing of a popular triumph, nor of their revenge. The hero, cheered but a few hours since, shall now be hooted through those same streets:

> Go, see him out at gates, and follow him,
> As he hath followed you, with all despite;
> Give him deserved vexation. . . .

—it is the mob's part. For the assertion of their own inflated dignity:

> Let a guard
> Attend us through the city.

THE DEPARTURE

Marcius is at once more likable in adversity than in triumph. Of the cheering crowds that greeted, so short a while back, his conqueror's entry, of the gathered Senate praising and honoring him, out of all Rome nothing friendly seems left him as he takes his way to exile, but his mother, his wife, two tried friends, and this silent, useless handful of the young nobility, reluctant though they are to see their hero depart; and these he will leave behind. But he makes no complaint, has no word against the Tribunes— in that omission the perfectest contempt!—and, for the people, only the humorously bitter

> the beast
> With many heads butts me away.

He can rally his mother's spirits by retorting on her a choice few of the precepts with which she was wont to load him, and with a bantering

---

elders, but for Cominius and Menenius, having definitely deserted him? Mere conjecture, and the point a small one; but the very smallest may have its worth in a reconstructing of the play's intended staging.

What, what, what!

when anger breaks from her—

> Now the red pestilence strike all trades in Rome
> And occupations perish!

even as his own, to her reproving, was so apt to do. His harsher

> Nay, I prithee, woman!

vented upon his wife, is rather curb to himself lest he give way
to grief as she is doing. Menenius—

> Thou old and true Menenius . . .

—already in tears, he comforts with kindly affection. Cominius,
of sterner mettle, he calls on to

> tell these sad women
> 'Tis fond to wail inevitable strokes
> As 'tis to laugh at them.

To the wreck of his own fortunes there is no more reference than
the boyishly simple

> I'll do well yet.

But this is the Marcius passingly glimpsed, who remembered,
amid the acclaiming shouts, the poor man in Corioles who had
once used him kindly, and, after victory, the widows there, and
the "mothers that lack sons."

But beneath the cheerful courage, the buoyancy of

> I shall be loved when I am lacked.

we become conscious of a dark, of a sinister sorrow, its shadow
apparent in the

> I go alone,
> Like to a lonely dragon, that his fen
> Makes feared and talked of more than seen. . . .

of a suffering repressed, but up-welling in that single

> O, the gods!

He will go to his exile alone, as befits his pride; and whatever
they hear of him it shall be

> never of me aught
> But what is like me formerly.

No regrets, therefore, no compunction! He is the same Marcius still; and what cannot soften will but harden him the more.[40]

THOSE LEFT BEHIND

Brutus and Sicinius follow at his heels, the Aedile attending them. Their amiable plan to have a mob hoot him "out at gates" is thwarted. He has gone. The sooner, therefore, their violence having served its turn, the people are quieted and sent home the better. This is the Aedile's task. Besides, a change of policy is called for now.

> The nobility are vexed. . . .

—and doubtless will repent their weakness in letting Coriolanus go.[41] Therefore, says the sagacious Brutus,

> Now we have shown our power
> Let us seem humbler after it is done
> Than when it was a-doing.

Neither do they fancy an encounter with Volumnia as she now returns—a lowering thundercloud!—with Virgilia and Menenius from the farewell at the gate. But they dodge unavailingly. For the cruel strain of that parting asks fuller relief than in tears—and here they are, very much to the purpose.

Marcius has gone, ominously self-controlled, to nurse his

---

[40] The young nobility, "my friends of noble touch," here also left behind, are evidently closely related to the "three or foure of his friends only" who, in North's Plutarch, did accompany him. The main point of the change is, of course, to bring Marcius, without more complication, to Antium all alone. A lesser dramatist might, then, have rid himself of the young nobility altogether. But to Shakespeare the enrichment of Marcius' character, slight as it is, by his dismissal of them at the gate, is worth while. And it costs him but half a line of text.

[41] It is likely, I should say, that the sight of the young nobility returning from their farewell to Coriolanus at the city gate (to be followed in a minute by Volumnia, Virgilia and Menenius) and their demeanor when they see the Tribunes suggests this

> The nobility are vexed. . . .

to Sicinius. They would merely cross the stage. Cominius would presumably be with them. There is nothing, of course, either in text or stage direction to indicate this; but it fits with the rest of the scene's business. Clearly they should have appeared to follow Marcius to the gate, for he has said to them

> *when I am forth,*
> Bid me farewell, and smile.

wrongs and breed them into—we shall see what monstrous shape.
With Menenius what's done is done. Why waste more words on
the fellows? So he finds himself pleading to Volumnia—and as
fruitlessly as to her son. For the touch of the unexpected with
which Shakespeare is wont to reinforce such eddies in the action
as this: Virgilia too, foregoing her "gracious silence," sets about
Sicinius, seconds Volumnia valiantly. The wretched Tribunes
take refuge from the volleying words, at first in scandalized
astonishment:

> Are you mankind? . . . O blessed heavens!

then in cant; their answer to Volumnia's

> I would my son
> Were in Arabia, and thy tribe before him,
> His good sword in his hand.

to Virgilia's

> He 'ld make an end of thy posterity.

to Volumnia's

> Bastards and all!
> Good man, the wounds that he does bear for Rome!

a smooth, white-of-the-eye,

> I would he had continued to his country
> As he began, and not unknit himself
> The noble knot he made.
> I would he had.

To which her retort comes plumply:

> "I would he had!" 'Twas you incensed the rabble:
> Cats . . .

Only a dignified departure is left them:

> Pray, let us go.

appropriately tinged with malice:

> Why stay we to be baited
> With one that wants her wits?

They gone, and the storm past, he trusts, Menenius essays for
solace:

> You have told them home;
> And, by my troth, you have cause. You'll sup with me?

—old age's comfort in the commonplace! Virgilia, spent by unwonted wrath, is in tears again. But Volumnia:

> Anger's my meat; I sup upon myself,
> And so shall starve with feeding. Come, let's go:
> Leave this faint puling and lament as I do,
> In anger, Juno-like. . . .

These are the natures—like mother, like son—to be broken, never bent; born to catastrophe.

TRADERS IN THE IGNOBLE

Enter a Roman and a Volsce.

Before we see the noble and heroic fallen, infatuate, into infamy, Marcius, amazingly, a traitor to his country, we are given—for edification!—this marginal passage of cheerful trading in the ignoble. The Roman is a Fifth Column fighter, a Volscian spy, on his way to his masters to tell them that, Coriolanus banished, now is the time for them to take their revenge on Rome. His name, it appears, is Nicanor. He luckily encounters a Volscian comrade, one Adrian, who, being in something the same line of business, has been sent to discover him in Rome. He knows Adrian at once, who does not recognize him in his present guise— or disguise:

> You had more beard when I last saw you. . . .

his quizzical apology. The Roman bringing good news, the couple warm to each other:

> the nobles receive so to heart the banishment of that worthy
> Coriolanus, that they are in a ripe aptness to take all power from
> the people, and to pluck from them their Tribunes for ever. . . .

—which is not true, we shall learn later; but no matter, since it is good news, not necessarily the truth, that curries favor for your Nicanors.

> I shall, between this and supper, tell you most strange things
> from Rome, all tending to the good of their adversaries. . . .

continues this pleasant specimen of them, preening himself on the sensation he will make. Coriolanus banished, Aufidius and his Volscians ready to strike:

I am joyful to hear of their readiness, and am the man, I think, that shall set them in present action. So, sir, heartily well met, and most glad of your company.

And renegade Roman and Volscian go their way together, arm in arm, and as merry as grigs.

The scene forms a bridge between Coriolanus' departure from Rome and his appearance in Antium, suggests some likely period of time passing between the two. Also it shows us a seamier side to the magnificent and tragic treason he is about to commit. He will at least not draw sordid profit from it, and be merry over it.

ANTIUM

Enter Coriolanus, in mean apparel, disguised and muffled.

From now to its end the tone of the play is changed. Marcius is changed, or rather—since men do not change—he seems no longer himself. The vengeance incarnate he becomes is but an empty simulacrum of himself; "a kind of nothing," Cominius calls him later. His troubles until now have come upon him because he could not learn to be false to his proudly faulty nature. But he has at least been honestly himself in struggling with them —and with the tricky Tribunes—however faultily. Now, under defeat, his untried soul will abjure the spontaneous loyalty, the faith, that had chiefly made him what he was; and he will be the mere tool of his vengeance, until, abjuring this, he is himself again. Meanwhile the passionate and unstable, temptation-tossed Aufidius will be covertly compassing his destruction. By such twisted and blind paths is it that the action now proceeds.

Marcius appears alone. It is the first such solitary appearance in the play, and will be the more striking because of that.[42] Till

---

[42] The first and the last for that matter, even as the scene thus begun contains the play's sole soliloquy. A play of action, not reflection; by its nature it does not run to soliloquies.

One may note, in passing, the baldness of the introductory

A goodly city is this Antium.

Shakespeare, in his maturity, is master of a dozen or more different ways of indirectly locating his scenes, as vaguely or as exactly as he may choose. But he will still use means as plain and direct as Sir Philip Sidney's notorious (and possibly apocryphal) placard, if they happen to be dramatically effective also.

now, too, we have seen him only either in fighting trim or in the
panoply of his triumph and his consulship, except for the
grotesque interlude of the *gown of humility*; his present *mean
apparel* is a grimmer variation of it. Outcast, destitute, unarmed,
in this city where—pride bitterly reminds him—discovery could
mean death, he is seeking his chief enemy Aufidius.[43] And from
a soliloquy—short, and the only one allotted to him—we learn
why.

He is here to enlist with the Volscians against Rome. It has
come to that with him. Neither now nor later are we told of any
process of debate within him, any struggle or yielding to temptation. He simply comments now—coldly, cynically—upon the fact
that such spiritual revolutions do occur, from hate to love, and
love to hate; and

> So with me:
> My birth-place hate I, and my love's upon
> This enemy town.[44]

---

[43]   At Antium lives he? . . .
          I would I had a cause to seek him there. . . .
—the unconsciously ironic words, spoken at the very height of his good fortune,
may well have lodged in our minds.

Destitute, unarmed: Shakespeare does not stress the point of poverty, "my
misery" covering much more than that, if that; but the "meanness" of his
apparel, superfluous to mere disguise, seems meant loosely to suggest it. And it is
evident that, in the encounter with Aufidius' servants, he at least wears no sword.

[44] The phrase

          Some trick not worth an egg . . .

recalls Hamlet's

                    delicate and tender prince,
          Whose spirit with divine ambition puffed
          Makes mouths at the invisible event,
          Exposing what is mortal and unsure
          To all that fortune, death and danger dare,
          Even for an egg-shell . . .

It is not to say that there was, as he wrote, any constructive connection between
the two in Shakespeare's mind, but the parallel is there; between Fortinbras the
happy and Coriolanus the unhappy man of action, the one that (says Hamlet
enviously) is ready

                    greatly to find quarrel in a straw,
          When honour's at the stake . . .

his sense of honor exalting him, the other coming to see men and friends

          On a dissension of a doit, break out
          To bitterest enmity . . .

while his extravagant sense of his honorable duty to himself only betrays him to
deep dishonor.

But it is of a piece with the rest of him that there should have been no such debate or struggle. Of the faculty of introspection he most certainly has none. Not once do we hear him question himself. He acts upon conviction, and is never less than fully convinced. That has helped to make him a fine fighter. Moreover, he must act; inaction is against nature with him, and exile has condemned him to it. And in what he does there will be no compromise, no middle course taken. His soldier's genius and his love of country have inspired him to the doing of great deeds, and the thwarting of these forces in him deprives him of all purpose in life. It is no argument that has turned him traitor. But the present sight of him—so altered and worn that Aufidius, who has five times fought him foot to foot, does not know him—speaks eloquently enough of the lonely misery endured, until, in some dark moment, natural love dead in him, he sought salvation in hate.

Of this sight of him so altered Shakespeare makes much. Deferential enquiry for "great Aufidius'" house takes him to its hall-fire, to stand there, a gaunt, muffled, forbidding figure, while, contrastingly, cheerful music plays within and the liveried servants pass to and fro on the business of the feast. Ironically submissive to his first rebuff,

> I have deserved no better entertainment,
> In being Coriolanus.

it is the old Marcius that answers with an ominous

> Away!

to the temerity of the Second Servant coming to oust him. What to make of him and that humbly dignified

> Let me but stand; I will not hurt your hearth.

A third servant, with the first two to back him, will deal with the fellow:

> What are you?
> A gentleman.
> A marvellous poor one!
> True, so I am.

But another rash move to oust him brings the Third Servant within reach of that formidable arm, to be sent spinning by a

touch from it. These are matters for their master. But awaiting
Aufidius, the Third Servant holds his jack-in-office course:

> Where dwell'st thou?
> Under the canopy.
> Under the canopy?
> Ay.
> Where's that?
> I' the city of kites and crows.

while Marcius, the fateful moment nearing, finds a sardonically
trivial satisfaction in mystifying these blockheads, a solider one
when, turning on the unlucky Third Servant with a

> Thou prat'st; serve with thy trencher: hence!

he whacks him over the head with it.

Aufidius appears; he also, in his feasting finery, little like the
man we saw last, bloody with his wounds, savagely sullen in
defeat. Genial, flushed with wine, he surveys the uncouth
stranger. He has drunk enough to allow for an obstinate repeating
of

> What's thy name?

a petulantly willful

> I know thee not.

while the haggard gaze is leveled at him. And when at last the
steeled voice says,

> My name is Caius Marcius. . . .

he sobers to very dumbness, listens at first stupent. Nor is
Marcius, nor are we, to know until the whole tale has been
rigorously told, how he will take it, what he will do.

Marcius is as absolute as ever, and as proud, still prouder in
ill fortune than in good. He does not excuse, nor condescend to
justify, nor find fine phrases for what he is ready to do; "in
mere spite" to fight against his "thankless country," his

> cankered country, with the spleen
> Of all the under fiends . . .

and with as fierce a hate for the "dastard nobles," his own party,
who have suffered him

> by the voice of slaves to be
> Hooped out of Rome.

as for the slaves themselves.

He stoops to no flattery of Aufidius, pretends to no more thought for him and his Volscians than as mere instruments of revenge. A callous bargain; scornfully provokes Aufidius if he will not strike it:

> if so be
> Thou dar'st not this, and that to prove more fortunes
> Thou'rt tired, then, in a word, I also am
> Longer to live most weary, and present
> My throat to thee and to thy ancient malice,
> Which not to cut would show thee but a fool. . . .

Not in mercy then, but as callously, and to his own profit and content, let Aufidius end an enemy's misery here and now. This, in Marcius, is no bravado, but a sober measuring of the worth of revenge to him. He clinches his argument—

> Since I have ever followed thee with hate,
> Drawn tons of blood out of thy country's breast,
> And cannot live but to thy shame, unless
> It be to do thee service.

—and awaits, as uncertain as are we, the issue.

Aufidius, come to credit eyes and ears, has heard dumbfounded these amazing things unfolding, while within him one responsive impulse ousts another; until at last:

> O, Marcius, Marcius!
> Each word thou hast spoke hath weeded from my heart
> A root of ancient envy. . . .

—the generous emotion gushes forth, playing like a warm stream upon the ice, this ice that is Marcius. But he, for his part, yields, nevertheless, with little grace to the rhapsodies and embraces of his so suddenly converted foe, nor responds at all to such flowery rhetoric as the

> Know thou first,
> I loved the maid I married; never man
> Sighed truer breath; but that I see thee here,
> Thou noble thing, more dances my rapt heart
> Than when I first my wedded mistress saw
> Bestride my threshold. Why, thou Mars! . . .

Only when he hears of the "power on foot," of the Volscian plan already made for

> pouring war
> Into the bowels of ungrateful Rome . . .

does he tardily, sternly, utter that

> You bless me, gods!

—and the thankfulness must sound strange in his own ears. For the rest: the leadership proffered, the welcome from the "friendly Senators" awaiting him, Aufidius' superlative

> A thousand welcomes!
> And more a friend than e'er an enemy . . .

—he accepts it all in silence, passing in to the feast, little like a man so lavishly granted his desire. He goes—already—as to his doom.[45]

Withdrawn to a respectful distance, First and Second Servant have been listening prick-eared:

> Here's a strange alteration!

---

[45] "Such flowery rhetoric": to Marcius, at any rate, in such a mood as he is, it will seem so. The contrast between the dry, angular phrasing of his speech to Aufidius and the rich, decorative and flowing melody of Aufidius' response is marked. A distinguished critic has connected—and somewhat carpingly—the dry angularity with the fact that Shakespeare took entire phrases for the speech from North's Plutarch, and used them unaltered. But this effect of a man speaking not spontaneously, as Aufidius does, but after long and bitter brooding with painful thought given to what he should say, speaking moreover not out of the fullness but the very emptiness of his heart, is, I suggest, precisely the effect meant to be made. And if Shakespeare found he could best make it by tacking together phrases from Plutarch he would certainly do so.

Marcius, at the thrilling moment of joining forces with Cominius on the battlefield before Corioles, had launched into something the same imagery that Aufidius uses now. But he was happily himself then as he will never be again. And, even so, that

> O, let me clip you
> In arms as sound as when I wooed, in heart
> As merry as when our nuptial day was done,
> And tapers turned to bedward.

denoted a harder temper than sounds from Aufidius'

> never man
> Sighed truer breath; but that I see thee here,
> Thou noble thing, more dances my rapt heart . . .

Shakespeare, in writing them, may or may not have had the likeness between the two passages in mind. It is unlikely that an audience will remark it.

—and readily do they adapt their artlessly servile minds to it. A great man; they might have known that, of course, despite his rags, from his high-minded way with them. And if great, if, in the next breath "the rarest man i' the world," why, another must be the lesser. Promptly begins the comically pitiful little shuffle of loyalties, their servile version of the tragic treason upon which they have been eavesdropping.

> a greater soldier than he, you wot on.
> Who? my master?
> Nay, it's no matter for that.
> Worth six on him? Nay, not so neither: but I take him to be the better soldier.
> Faith, look you, one cannot tell how to say that. . . .

—for in prudence we must both commit ourselves, or neither. And to Third Servant strutting excitedly in—happy to have been knocked over the pate with his own trencher by so great a man— and to his reckless

> here's he that was wont to thwack our general. . . .

First Servant makes shocked protest:

> Why do you say "thwack our general"?

reducing him to double-quick recanting:

> I do not say "thwack our general. . . ."

But, with a wink and a wag of the head from Second Servant,

> Come, we are fellows and friends. . . .

the three are in a tale together.
The consummation of Coriolanus' welcome, the sight of him

> set at upper end o' the table; no question asked him by any of the Senators, but they stand bald before him. . . .

while

> Our general himself makes a mistress of him; sanctifies himself with's hand, and turns up the white o' the eye to his discourse. . . .

—this we see through the simpleton eyes of Third Servant, puffed with the pride of coming fresh from the very sight of it. The comic coloring of the picture heightens, by irony of contrast, its tragic import. The blundering parroting of the talk at table over the noble renegade's prospects—

> for, look you, sir, he has as many friends as enemies; which friends, sir, as it were, durst not, look you, sir, show themselves, as we term it, his friends, whilst he's in directitude. . . . But when they shall see, sir, his crest up again, and the man in blood, they will out of their burrows like conies after rain, and revel all with him.

—embellishes its cynical shrewdness. And already, while Aufidius is still erecting his fragile fane of devotion to his late enemy, this belittling of him by these faithful followers is providing for its wreck.

The scene ends with a noncombatants' chorus in praise of war, coming from Volscians too, who have just been soundly beaten and accorded by their conquerors a merciful peace.

ROME ONCE MORE

The Tribunes Sicinius and Brutus reappear; we are in Rome again. They are pluming themselves·upon

> the present peace
> And quietness o' the people . . .

upon—at this most appropriate moment!—having heard no more of Coriolanus, while

> Here do we make his friends
> Blush that the world goes well, who rather had,
> Though they themselves did suffer by 't, behold
> Dissentious numbers pestering streets than see
> Our tradesmen singing in their shops and going
> About their functions friendly.

It may be so. But there are men—politicians and others—who learn, whether by experience or from the book of their own natures, to think the worst of everyone. Menenius, passing by, outfaces their complacency—

> Your Coriolanus is not much missed
> But with his friends: the Commonwealth doth stand.
> And so would do, were he more angry at it.

—with a glum, blunt

> All's well, and might have been much better if
> He could have temporised.

After which they take the opportunity that offers of edifyingly patronizing a group of humbly grateful citizens—who beseech the gods preserve them, who for

> Ourselves, our wives and children, on our knees,
> Are bound to pray for you both.

to be unctuously repaid by a showering of

> Good den our neighbours.
> Good den to you all, good den to you all. . . .
> Live and thrive!
> Farewell, kind neighbours. . . .

with—a sting for Menenius!—a

> we wished Coriolanus
> Had loved you as we did.

It is for a beginning to the play's ending that we are given this passage of sharp contrast with its beginning; the genial bullying of the citizens by Menenius, their brutal rating by Marcius, here replaced by the soft smiles of their Tribunes—from which official fool's paradise they are very quickly to be expelled.

From its beginning to the moment of Marcius' banishment the play has abounded in physical action, in battles and rioting. From now to the verge of its concluding catastrophe we shall have only the increasing tension of the threat of his reprisals; then, suddenly, their frustration. The battle to be fought now is one of moral forces, culminating in the struggle between Marcius and Volumnia, in which, silently at the last, he accepts defeat. The two sections of the play stand in nearly every respect contrasted. The scene with Aufidius in Antium may be called a bridge between the two; that of Marcius' death is in the nature of an epilogue.

The drama of Coriolanus' approach to his revenge begins at a very zero point, that of Brutus' fatuous

> Rome
> Sits safe and still without him.

Promptly an Aedile appears, to convey, with due official dignity,

the news, brought by "a slave, whom we have put in prison . . ."
that

> the Volsces with two several powers
> Are entered in the Roman territories. . . .

For Menenius, it is Marcius' banishing that has brought them,
Aufidius, doubtless, at their head. For Brutus, such an unpleasant
thing simply "cannot be" and the slave must be whipped for
saying so. "Cannot?"; but it has been, thrice within Menenius'
memory. Sicinius is as blandly confident:

> Tell not me;
> I know this cannot be.

Whereupon

> *Enter a Messenger.*

Shakespeare gives a hundred lines more to the completing of
this scene of the Tribunes' discomfiture, and the whole is a
minor masterpiece of treatment. He employs the economical
convention of the Messenger, which gives drama the continuity
of narrative. But, to vary and enrich it, the story to be told is put
into four mouths instead of one, differing in temper and quality,
each supplementing or revising the other. The Aedile is un-
hurried and correct. He has taken order with the slave; he reports
the matter; his duty is done. The first Messenger is precipitate
and perturbed; wide-eyed. Is it to be believed, this rumor

> that Marcius,
> Joined with Aufidius, leads a power 'gainst Rome,
> And vows revenge . . .

Menenius, for a moment, is at one with the Tribunes in disbelief.
But the pendulum is swung violently back by the coming of a
second Messenger in all haste to summon the pair without
ceremony to the Senate, the ill news cumulated into worse:

> A fearful army, led by Caius Marcius,
> Associated with Aufidius, rages
> Upon our territories; and have already
> O'erborne their way, consumed with fire, and took
> What lay before them.

And, before they can take breath to protest, comes finally Co-

minius, not only to confirm it but, with grimly humorous satisfaction, to point them out as the culprits:

> O, you have made good work.

Trouble not to be mended by the whipping of a slave! The
Tribunes are struck dumb.

Cominius does not spare them, keeps Menenius impatiently
demanding his news while he loads them with terrors:

> You have holp to ravish your own daughters, and
> To melt the city leads upon your pates,
> To see your wives dishonoured to your noses—

and—this is the fruit of their rule in Rome—

> *Your* temples burned in their cement, and
> *Your* franchises, whereon you stood . . .

Menenius—his still incredulous

> If Marcius should be joined with Volscians—

extinguished by the sardonic acclaim of

> If!
> He is their god; he leads them like a thing
> Made by some other deity than Nature,
> That shapes man better; and they follow him
> Against us brats. . . .

—takes up the refrain too:

> You have made good work,
> You, and your apron men . . .
> You have made fair work!

until Brutus at last finds a meek and fearful tongue:

> But is this true, sir?

Satisfaction with the vengeance to fall on the Tribunes—capable
themselves now of little but agonized grimaces—mingles in
Cominius and Menenius with genuine alarm for Rome.[46] This is
shot through with renewed pride in Marcius—one of themselves—

[46] Brutus and Sicinius are semi-comic characters, and the actors of them were,
I think, expected to make their conspicuous silence here even more conspicuous
by facial play.

and the power of his name, this again with the shameful memory
that they, his friends, abandoned him.

> We loved him; but, like beasts
> And cowardly nobles, gave way unto your clusters,
> Who did hoot him out o' the city.

The theme of betrayal and self-betrayal permeates the play.
Some "clusters" gathering round—

> *Enter a troop of Citizens.*

—Menenius can relieve his mind with a little of his old frank
abuse of them. Echoing from past clashes,

> Now he's coming. . . .
>   as many coxcombs
> As you threw caps up will he tumble down,
> And pay you for your voices. . . .

Cominius echoing him with a

> Ye're goodly things, you voices!

they leave the poor citizens to their pitiful excuses—

> That we did we did for the best; and though we willingly
> consented to his banishment, yet it was against our will.

—and the Tribunes, freed from their daunting presence, to the
flattering futility of

> Go, masters, get you home, be not dismayed:
> These are a side that would be glad to have
> This true which they so seem to fear. . . .

Spiritless all, they go their several ways. Menenius and Cominius:

> Shall's to the Capitol?
> O, ay; what else!

The Second Citizen to the rest:

> But come, let's home.

Sicinius to his fellow:

> Pray, let's go.

While as to Brutus, his rueful

> Would half my wealth
> Would buy this for a lie!

reminds us, incidentally, that politics and the leadership of the poor can be made to pay.

AUFIDIUS DISILLUSIONED;
MARCIUS SCANNED

The scene between Aufidius and his Lieutenant prepares the play's final stroke without discounting this by telling us too clearly what it is to be. The impulsive generosity to a fallen enemy has soon burned out in him, and Aufidius, recovered from the experience and ready to treat Marcius as an enemy again, can estimate his virtues and failings the more fairly, even though he is now but the more set to "potch" at his prodigious rival by

> some way
> Or wrath or craft may get him.

For generosity repented has hardened him.

> I do not know what witchcraft's in him. . . .

says the Lieutenant. Well, Aufidius himself has been its victim, and, beside him, will doubtless be

> darkened in this action . . .

—which, however, since there's to be Volscian profit in it, must be carried through. It is only too true that

> All places yield to him ere he sits down;
> And the nobility of Rome are his;
> The Senators and Patricians love him too:
> The Tribunes are no soldiers, and their people
> Will be as rash in the repeal as hasty
> To expel him thence. I think he'll be to Rome
> As is the osprey to the fish, who takes it
> By sovereignty of nature. . . .

But—! Now follows the coldly, carefully, qualified verdict of second-rate success upon first-rate failure:

> First he was
> A noble servant to them, but he could not
> Carry his honours even. Whether 'twas pride . . .
> whether defect of judgment . . .
> or whether nature,

Not to be other than one thing . . .
                    but one of these,
As he has spices of them all—not all,
For I dare so far free him—made him feared,
So hated, and so banished. . . .

Let the greatly gifted man remember, then, that

                    So our virtues
        Lie in the interpretation of the time. . . .

and, their turn served, are apt to be canceled out. It will be so
with Coriolanus:

One fire drives out one fire; one nail, one nail;
Rights by rights founder, strengths by strengths do fail.

Aufidius, nursing his plans, his last lethal stroke conceived, is
oracular:

                When, Caius, Rome is thine,
Thou are poor'st of all; then shortly are thou mine.[47]

The scene allows incidentally for the time taken by Cominius'
intercessory visit to Coriolanus, now encamped before Rome. This
is over when the next opens, with the tension notably increased by
its failure.

NEMESIS NEARS

*Enter Menenius, Cominius, Sicinius, Brutus, the two
Tribunes, with others.*

—*with others*, listeners and onlookers; a token of the general
anxiety.

Grave as they saw it to be, their enjoyment in saddling the

---

[47] Such now unusual phrases as "not moving from the casque to the cushion"
and "even with the same austerity and garb as he controlled the war" increase
for us the difficulty of following Aufidius' analysis of Coriolanus' virtues and
defects, its repeated "whether . . . s" making it already difficult enough. (The
trick of the speech, one notes, is much that of Hamlet's "So oft it chances in
particular men. . . .") And in quoting it here I have had, so as to isolate the
continuity of thought, to reduce it to an ugly skeleton. Then, when it comes to
the more general comments on success and failure, we meet with a corruption of
the text—"hath not a tomb so evident as a chair . . ."—which no one yet, as far
as I know, has been able satisfactorily to clarify. Altogether, it is a troublesome
speech to the modern actor; and Aufidius, as a whole, may be called a troublesome character in the acting. Shakespeare, it seems, found him interesting, but
would not afford space for his expansion. (Cf. p. 116.)

Tribunes with the blame for it was some sign that Cominius and
Menenius had not, despite all, thought the situation quite hopeless, had underlyingly felt, rather, that even though they had
deserved Marcius' hate, "and therein showed like enemies," yet
they were the men to redeem it. But Cominius has been on his
mission since: and

> He would not seem to know me.

Once, indeed, he did call him by his name. But thereafter,

> Coriolanus
> He would not answer to, forbad all names;
> He was a kind of nothing, titleless,
> Till he had forged himself a name o' the fire
> Of burning Rome.

Plea following plea, none moved him, nor will; Cominius is
hopelessly sure of it.

Menenius, on the other hand, protesting that he never can
succeed if Cominius has failed—

> He called me father,
> But what o' that? . . .
> Nay, if he coyed
> To hear Cominius speak, I'll keep at home.

—is plainly "coying" himself, and only waiting to be pressed
harder to consent, in his turn, to go. He is cheerful enough still
to be mockingly reminding the now quite crestfallen Brutus and
Sicinius that they

> have made good work!
> A pair of Tribunes that have racked for Rome,
> To make coals cheap . . .

There is no spirit left in them. Sicinius, begging him to go, is
reduced to the pitiful

> if you refuse your aid
> In this so never-needed help, yet do not
> Upbraid's with our distress. . . .

An "instant army" will be all they can muster for Rome's
protection.[48] They fall to wheedling and flattering him. Even if

---

[48] It is implied in more than one passage that the Tribunes now rule Rome,
and Aufidius has just remarked of them that they "are no soldiers." Theirs is, in

he fails, Sicinius says:

> Yet your good will
> Must have that thanks from Rome, after the measure
> As you intended well.

—which puts him on his mettle. A final show of diffidence, for tribute to "good Cominius" and his failure, and he is the buoyant old Menenius still:

> He was not taken well; he had not dined.
> The veins unfilled, our blood is cold, and then
> We pout upon the morning, are unapt
> To give or to forgive; but when we have stuffed
> These pipes and these conveyances of our blood
> With wine and feeding, we have suppler souls
> Than in our priest-like fasts. . . .

—the imagery characteristically recalls our first hearing from him with the fable of the Belly and the Members—

> therefore I'll watch him
> Till he be dieted to my request,
> And then I'll set upon him.

And, cheerily confident, off he goes.

Cominius has listened in silence. He shakes his head, strikes the stern note again:

> He'll never hear him. . . .
> I tell you, he does sit in gold, his eye
> Red as 't would burn Rome, and his injury
> The gaoler to his pity. . . .

pictures and prepares us for the pitiless figure we are soon to see.

Then, to end the scene, the step beyond the next is forecast:

> So that all hope is vain,
> Unless his noble mother and his wife,
> Who, as I hear, mean to solicit him
> For mercy to his country. . . .

As the crisis nears the action is knit the closer, that our attention may be the more closely held.

---

fact, what would be called today a "pacifist" government, quite unprepared for war.

MENENIUS TRIES, AND FAILS

Enter Menenius to the Watch or Guard.

Yet another encounter between patrician and commoners, and a scene of ebb and flow of emotion and humor before—it will be a contrast—the powerfully sustained tension of the trial to come.

Menenius deploys his tact. He answers the sentry's sharp challenge with affable praise:

> You guard like men, 'tis well. . . .

asserts his own quality with accustomed ease:

> but, by your leave,
> I am an officer of state, and come
> To speak with Coriolanus.

—in vain. The sentries disappointingly deserve his praise.

> You may not pass, you must return. . . .
> You'll see your Rome embraced with fire before
> You'll speak with Coriolanus.

He tries the flattery of familiarity:

> Good my friends,
> If you have heard your general talk of Rome,
> And of his friends there, it is lots to blanks,
> My name hath touched your ears: it is Menenius.

is brought to vaunting his own with the great man—

> I tell thee, fellow,
> Thy general is my lover. . . .

—and, in euphemistic phrase, the unconscionable services he has done him:

> Therefore, fellow,
> I must have leave to pass.

Hectorings and wittiness alike get plain answer:

> Faith, sir, if you had told as many lies in his behalf as you
> have uttered words in your own, you should not pass here. . . .

But the old gentleman persists, to be given finally a sound and most disrespectful talking to:

> You are a Roman, are you?
> I am, as thy general is.

> Then you should hate Rome, as he does. Can you, when you
> have pushed out your gates the very defender of them . . . ?

Truly these Volscian sentries know their own minds and can
speak them; the dose no pleasanter to Menenius for its likeness
to his own recent medicining of the Tribunes. And if it is to
come to an issue between fretful dignity on one side and discipline
with cold steel to warrant it on the other—

> Sirrah, if thy captain knew I were here, he would use me with
> estimation.
> Come, my captain knows you not.
> I mean thy general.
> My general cares not for you. Back, I say, go: lest I let forth
> your half-pint of blood. Back; that's the utmost of your having:
> back.
> Nay, but fellow, fellow—!

At which moment Coriolanus and Aufidius pass.
  After a sharp, soldierly

> What's the matter?

Coriolanus waits in silence, fulfillment of Cominius' picture of
him. Menenius, tossed between emotions, lets the lightest first
possess him; tit-for-tat with impudent sentries will restore him his
confident good humor.

> Now, you companion . . . you shall perceive that a Jack
> guardant cannot office me from my son Coriolanus. . . .

He is himself again in the jaunty extravagance of

> guess but by my entertainment with him, if thou standest not
> i' the state of hanging, or of some death more long in spectator-
> ship, and crueller in suffering; behold now presently and swoon
> for what's to come upon thee.

It gives him time, too, in which to face this changed Marcius,
distant, mute, hostile, companioned there with Aufidius. But he
neither hesitates nor calculates. Eloquence overflows in affection
and tears:

> The glorious gods sit in hourly synod about thy particular
> prosperity, and love thee no worse than thy old father Menenius
> does! O my son! my son! thou art preparing fire for us: look
> thee, here's water to quench it. . . .

and, for a final fillip, into the familiar humor:

> The good gods assuage thy wrath, and turn the dregs of it
> upon this varlet here; this, who, like a block, hath denied my
> access to thee.

The one word of the answer, spanning the space between them—

> Away!

—falls like a blow. The old man staggers under it. Had he ears for
aught else he might note in the sequent

> Wife, mother, child, I know not. . . .

the flaw in the armor of which that too rigid figure is himself
aware, might even read in the strain of the

> Yet—for I loved thee—
> Take this along, I writ it for thy sake
> And would have sent it. . . .

in this letter with which he is dismissed, defense ready to crumble.
But pride, if not affection, is now too wounded for him to think
of aught else.

Coriolanus and Aufidius pass on their way:

> This man, Aufidius,
> Was my beloved in Rome; yet thou beholdst!

to which utterance of twisted, tortured pride Aufidius pays
sardonic tribute:

> You keep a constant temper.

But Menenius can take a blow gallantly still, and pay back
mockery with mockery. To the sentries' jubilant

> Now, sir, is your name Menenius?
> 'Tis a spell, you see, of much power. You know the way home
> again.
> Do you hear how we are shent for keeping your greatness
> back?
> What cause, do you think, I have to swoon?

he returns as good as he gets, and better:

> I neither care for the world, nor your general: for such things
> as you, I can scarce think there's any, y'are so slight. . . .

—but it is graver defiance than that—

> He that hath a will to die by himself, fears it not from
> another. Let your general do his worst. . . .

—no business of theirs though!

> For you, be that you are, long; and your misery increase with
> age! I say to you, as I was said to, Away!

They are left laughing; won, nevertheless, to the verdict of

> A noble fellow, I warrant him.

VOLUMNIA COMES, AND THE CONQUEROR
IS CONQUERED

Coriolanus and Aufidius were, it seems, on their way to a
council of war; they are taking their places at its table now.[49]
First, formally and for all to hear, the two exchange assurances
that so far in this strange business all has been frankly done.
Aufidius is most generous in his assurance. Coriolanus then falls
to confession; and—how changed!—it is of kindly, politic trickery. "With a cracked heart" it was, then, that he stood outfacing
Menenius there; and he had offered him in the letter, to make
things easier for them both, something to carry away that he yet
knew must be rejected. It was only

> A very little
> I have yielded to. . . .

but it is right they know it. That is all finished now. Then

> *Shout within.*

He asks what it may mean, knowing too well:

> Shall I be tempted to infringe my vow
> In the same time 'tis made? . . .

The dreaded trial has come. He steels himself:

> I will not.

---

[49] The Folio stage direction for the first scene is simply *Enter Coriolanus and
Aufidius.* Capell added *and others*; and pretty plainly Coriolanus is not speaking
to Aufidius alone. The council of war at a table set upon the inner stage is as
easily deduced. The curtains will be closed as the two pass across the outer stage,
finding Menenius there. They could be discovered when the curtains are drawn,
the fifteen lines or so spoken by the Watch and Menenius allowing them that
much time to take their places, or, having gone off by the side door, they can
wait and enter again upon the inner stage.

The pending struggle has been fully prepared. Cominius, Consul and General, revered as both, kneeling, repulsed, the loved Menenius dismissed—this the one aspect, completed by the sentry's admiring view of the traitor-hero as

> the rock, the oak not to be wind-shaken.

For another; he has armored himself with an oath offered to Aufidius, a vow solemnly taken. The closer our sight of him, the plainer it is that nevertheless he feels not so sure of the issue. He has a fight still to win. And the play is not over yet.

When he sees the figures of the women approaching the scene's tension rises instantly to high pitch. It is to be a long scene, of a struggle the deadlier for its quiet; even as wrestlers in a lock strain silently, motionless, until one is exhausted and as silently loosens grasp, and the match is over. The tension will hardly relax; a moment's relief, and it tightens again. The action is clearly articulated, deliberate, sparse; the speech indicates it and allows for it. Marcius is its firm and sensitive center. The argument ranges round him, widely, closely; touches him as husband, lover, father, son, Roman, uses his wife's tears, his boy's gallantly shrill defiance, Volumnia's desperate barring of the end to this road on which—it was she that set him. Silence is his ultimate answer; and the whole, with its passion, in its intimacies and simplicities, is keyed to the tenor of a great event.

Note the dramatic generalship with which Shakespeare employs his forces. First is the duel effect made by the mute, anonymous approach of the women, their speech, even for a moment their identity, held in reserve, while Marcius, describing them, at once interprets besides the effect made on him.[50] The battle begins and ends with a struggle within himself. It will end in silence; it

---

[50] The *in mourning habits* of the stage direction for this entrance is owed, apparently, to Capell. It implies veils, and is, I think, justified. The stage picture intended is not hard to reconstruct. Coriolanus will be seated at the council table on the inner stage surrounded by the contrastingly uniformed Volscian generals. The *Shout within* heralds the entry by a side door of the little group of veiled women and their attendants, who stand facing him and more or less with their backs to the audience, so that the "curtsy," and, upon Virgilia's unveiling, the "doves' eyes" and Volumnia's "bow" take effect more directly upon him than upon us. "Describing them"; I do not, of course, mean to imply to the Volscian generals, but to himself and to us, as the convention of that stage allowed.

begins articulately. Back and forth he is swayed; by the very sight, the first since his exile, of those three that he loves.[51]

> But out, affection!
> All bond and privilege of nature break!
> Let it be virtuous to be obstinate! . . .

Then, his wife's "doves' eyes" turned on him:

> I melt, and am not
> Of stronger earth than others. . . .

Lastly, to break the spell of Volumnia's grave obeisance, and against his boy's

> aspect of intercession, which
> Great nature cries, "Deny not." . . .

he violently flings away with

> Let the Volsces
> Plough Rome and harrow Italy; I'll never
> Be such a gosling to obey instinct, but stand
> As if a man were author of himself
> And knew no other kin.

But he is drawn to face Virgilia and her gentle

> My lord and husband.

to invite, with his repelling

> These eyes are not the same I wore in Rome.

her as gently keen

> The sorrow that delivers *us* thus changed
> Makes you think so.

He owns to the effect of the thrust:

> Like a dull actor now,
> I have forgot my part, and I am out,
> Even to a full disgrace. . . .

and, the next instant, she is in his arms.

---

[51] "Long as my exile. . . ," he says later. Actually how long Shakespeare leaves indeterminate; but while the suggestion, when he comes to Aufidius in Antium, is that he has lost little time in doing so, here and hereabouts the implication is that, at any rate, much has changed in his absence. There is no need at either juncture to be exact, so that—open inconsistency avoided—the dramatic best can be made of each calendar.

> Best of my flesh,
> Forgive my tyranny; but do not say
> For that "Forgive our Romans." O, a kiss,
> Long as my exile, sweet as my revenge!
> Now, by the jealous queen of heaven, that kiss
> I carried from thee, dear, and my true lip
> Hath virgined it e'er since. You gods! I prate. . . .

Much of Marcius is lit up in this. In his love for his wife a quality of nature rarer than that bred of the exchange of pride between him and his mother. From it had sprung at his triumphal entry into Rome the thought of the Volscian widows left desolate; the kindling touch of her lips might free him to sudden forgiveness now. Love and hate are near akin in him, are but the two sides of the one shield; and each he justifies by what he does, and that by what he is. To spend more words on either is to "prate."

He turns to

> the most noble mother of the world . . .

and with a

> Sink, my knee, i' the earth. . . .

gives her full due. She bids him

> stand up blest!

then kneels herself, thus "unproperly," she says, to

> Show duty, as mistaken all this while,
> Between the child and parent.

She shocks him, and means to. But the irony is rather in the event; and when he raises her she unconsciously gives it voice again:

> Thou art my warrior;
> I holp to frame thee.

She did indeed! As well her teaching as his learning has brought them to this pass.[52]

---

[52] This kneeling of each to other recalls Cordelia and King Lear. Shakespeare had found that in the old play about King Lear and his daughters. It clearly makes an affecting picture. Whether it was a favorite one with other dramatists of the time I am not well enough read to say. Whether or no, ceremonial kneeling was then in habitual use, and widely by comparison with the few occasions on which it is called for now.

Valeria, dignified, beautiful, silent—

> The noble sister of Publicola,
> The moon of Rome, chaste as the icicle
> That's curded by the frost from purest snow,
> And hangs on Dian's temple . . .

—follows in her place. Is she also to find her fate in the sack of a city?[53] Lastly the boy is put forward, sturdily stubborn, even against this great man his father's thrilling exhortation, until Volumnia takes order with a stern

> Your knee, sirrah!

and Marcius, delighting in him:

> That's my brave boy!

He, who has never counted the odds at which he fought, has never had to fight, surely, at such odds as this.

Volumnia, with due dignity, opens her plea. Upon its very threshold he stops her, the more petitionary himself in his denials:

> Do not bid me
> Dismiss my soldiers. . . .
>   tell me not
> Wherein I seem unnatural, desire not
> To allay my rages and revenges. . . .

But she answers with an insistence matching his own:

> O, no more, no more!
> You have said you will not grant us any thing,
> For we have nothing else to ask but that
> Which you deny already. . . .

an obstinacy too:

> Yet we will ask. . . .

So he turns back to Aufidius and the Volsces, returns to their

---

[53] To suggest this, by her mere appearance in the scene, with, for aid, the gem-like phrase describing her put into Coriolanus' mouth, seems to be her only use to it. But it is an incidental use of some little value; and since Shakespeare had her available, why not bring her on? One may even speculate whether the part itself does not chiefly owe its existence to such a fact as that the King's Men had, at this juncture, a boy in the company, who could both look and act it well. Even in these, their well-furnished days, they were unlikely to be overburdened with that sort of thing.

council table, seats himself there again, as in judgment with them.[54]

Her speech before this strange tribunal comes from a Volumnia compelled at last to see Coriolanus' valor from the standpoint of the vanquished. The exulting fierceness of her once-triumphant

> Death, that dark spirit, in 's nervy arm doth lie. . . .

has melted to the grief of

> Think with thyself
> How more unfortunate than all living women
> Are we come hither. . . .
>   the mother, wife and child to see
> The son, the husband and the father tearing
> His country's bowels out. . . .

grief highly argued:

>   thou barr'st us
> Our prayers to the gods. . . .
>   for how can we,
> Alas! how can we for our country pray,
> Whereto we are bound, together with thy victory,
> Whereto we are bound? . . .

Yet out of the deadlock and division to which pride and wrath—his fostering of it, and hers—have brought them, out of the fatal dilemma—

>   for either thou
> Must, as a foreign recreant, be led
> With manacles through our streets, or else
> Triumphantly tread on thy country's ruin. . . .

—she sees one way. But—Volumnia still!—her passion bids fair to swamp her very plea for following it

>   For myself, son . . .
>   if I cannot persuade thee
> Rather to show a noble grace to both parts
> Than seek the end of one, thou shalt no sooner
> March to assault thy country than to tread—
> Trust to 't, thou shalt not—on thy mother's womb,
> That brought thee to this world.

[54] Note (once more) the visual effect of this, the contrast in the dress they wear, he the single Roman among these Volsces.

Virgilia echoing her with

> Ay, and mine,
>> That brought you forth this boy, to keep your name
>> Living to time.

even the child, ridiculously, gallantly defiant:

>>> A' shall not tread on me;
>>> I'll run away till I am bigger, but then I'll fight.

Thus does this breed set about making peace.[55]

Marcius sits silent until the effect of the triply unanswerable challenge has died away. Then, quietly, reflectively, to the foiled self in him:

>> Not of a woman's tenderness to be,
>> Requires nor child nor woman's face to see.

And he rises and moves mechanically away, defeated and avoiding defeat. Volumnia's pursuing arguments sound strange to him; from her to him they well may! "Our suit is, that you reconcile . . ."! The Volsces are to say,

>> "This mercy we have showed"; the Romans
>> "This we received"; and each in either side
>> Give the all-hail to thee, and cry "Be blest
>> For making up this peace!"

She to be telling him:

>>> The end of war's uncertain. . . .

asking him:

>> Thinkst thou it honourable for a noble man
>> Still to remember wrongs?

Is this Volumnia?

~~~~~~~~~

[55] Were Shakespeare a didactic dramatist how well he might from this point build up his play to a moral and a happy ending: Marcius and his family reunited, Romans and Volsces clasping hands, peace over all! But he has the historic story to deal with (Plutarch is not to be lightly treated) and the tragedy it involves—which, however, we must remark, is a tragedy, not wholly of character, but of character and circumstance combined.

Volumnia (of all people) urges reconciliation. Coriolanus is not the man to sponsor that; he can at best, he feels, stand aside and "make convenient peace." But Aufidius also has to be reckoned with, and the Volscians who, for their part, want loot. It is in the fresh circumstances of the squabble over this that "character" once more plays Coriolanus false, and Aufidius can seize the chance to kill him.

It is here that his silence comes to be stressed by the baffled recurrence of her

> Speak to me, son. . . .
> Why dost not speak? . . .
> yet here he lets me prate

Like one i' the stocks. . . .

> He turns away.

And the technique of the scene is in itself remarkable. Usually such a speech as this will concentrate our attention on the speaker; and, the more strongly, the less of even a side-glance from us can surrounding characters claim. But Volumnia makes Virgilia's tears, the child's high spirit, Valeria's quiet dignity a living part of the action, adding their eloquence in its kind to her own, to wield it all against the opposing silence of Marcius' last stand.

His silence counterbalances, and by a little will outbalance, her share in the encounter. For she ceases her attack, unbeaten but munition spent—

> I am husht until our city be a-fire,
> And then I'll speak a little.

—and still he has not answered.

> *Holds her by the hand, silent.*

is the stage direction, Shakespeare's own certainly. In the silence is his answer, and he spares her all other. She has won. And for him

> the heavens do ope,
> The gods look down, and this unnatural scene
> They laugh at. . . .

—unnatural, since pride and her pride in him have brought him to this, and she that helped make him is bidding him remake himself now. And that he can no longer do. Mercy and forgiveness are not for him. And it is she that has vanquished him. Only she could.

He gently warns her of what may follow:

> O, my mother, mother! O!
> You have won a happy victory to Rome;
> But for your son, believe it, O, believe it,

> Most dangerously you have with him prevailed
> If not most mortal to him. . . .

But, the great strain relaxed, she seemingly thinks but of her victory and does not heed. He braces himself again—as at the beginning of the struggle, so now to what must follow—with a

> But let it come.

next, pride abated, turns to Aufidius—out of all the world—for sympathy:

> Now, good Aufidius,
> Were you in my stead, would you have heard
> A mother less, or granted less, Aufidius?

—who, coldly observant, commits himself to no more than a

> I was moved withal.

and then comes to the decision that is to be his death:

> for my part,
> I'll not to Rome. I'll back with you; and pray you,
> Stand to me in this cause. . . .

Aufidius felt sure (we heard him say) that even those in Rome who feared Marcius most

> Will be as rash in the repeal, as hasty
> To expel him thence . . .

But if the traitor prefers conflict in Corioles, so much the worse for him—and the better for Aufidius!

It is not in Marcius to enter Rome again. For the last time—he knows to what he may be going—he lets himself be stirred to his depths:

> O, mother! wife!

After which, lest they should now catch up with his thoughts, should try, as it seems they will, to keep him there, he plays the man of affairs with them, the game loser:

> Ay, by and by;
> But we will drink together, and you shall bear
> A better witness back than words. . . .

Gallantly courteous, he addresses the whole train:

Ladies, you deserve
To have a temple built to you: all the swords
In Italy, and her confederate arms,
Could not have made this peace.

ROME DELIVERED

Rome fearfully awaits news of her fate. *We* already know it, so the suspense must not be spun out. Menenius returning meets Sicinius, while the issue is still, he supposes, in doubt, and he can avenge on him his own repulse by assurance that Volumnia will do no better. The old Tribune is in despair:

He loved his mother dearly.

and Menenius finds satisfaction of the perverser sort in:

So did he me; and he no more remembers his mother now than an eight-year-old horse. The tartness of his face sours ripe grapes. . . . Mark what mercy his mother shall bring from him: there is no more mercy in him than there is milk in a male tiger; that shall our poor city find. . . .

and so falls back upon

all this is long of you.

There comes yet more for him in a messenger's tidings that the Plebeians have now seized upon the wretched Brutus,

And hale him up and down; all swearing, if
The Roman ladies bring not comfort home,
They'll give him death by inches.

So when the good news arrives that

the ladies have prevailed,
The Volscians are dislodged, and Marcius gone. . . .

he can but be at first a trifle disappointed. Sicinius, for his part, who would not credit the bad news when it came, is wary of the good news now.

Friend,
Art thou certain this is true? is it most certain?

But the rejoicing sounds without are evidence enough:

Trumpets, hoboyes, drums beate altogether.

Shakespeare's theater can do no more. From Menenius, then, breaks a generously happy

> This is good news:
> I will go meet the ladies. This Volumnia
> Is worth of consuls, senators, patricians,
> A city full . . .

with, for a last humorous gibe,

> of Tribunes, such as you,
> A sea and land full.

and he is away.[56]

Sicinius, so barely saved, must reassert his dignity:

> First, the gods bless you for your tidings; next,
> Accept *my* thankfulness.

The Messenger, afflicted by no such pomposity:

> Sir, we have all
> Great cause to give great thanks.

Rome's saviors near the city; at point to enter! A Tribune's benign presence is called for:

> We will meet them,
> And help the joy.

VOLUMNIA'S TRIUMPH

Enter two Senators, with Ladies, passing over the stage, with other Lords.

Thus this short stretch of the action ends, with such a procession, so acclaimed, as that which once brought Coriolanus back in triumph from his wars. And the people are to

> Unshout the noise that banished Marcius,
> Repeal him with the welcome of his mother. . . .

—but too late.

THE END

Enter Tullus Aufidius with Attendants.

—the *Attendants* an opening suggestion of authority.

---

[56] The Folio's stage directions leave him, by default, included in the general *Exeunt* a few lines later. But clearly he does not wait for Sicinius.

Aufidius gives the tone to this, the play's last scene. Its doings
are to win him success, and he promptly assumes control of them:

> Go tell the lords o' the city I am here;
> Deliver them this paper: having read it,
> Bid them repair to the market place. . . .
> > Him I accuse
> The city ports by this hath entered, and
> Intends to appear before the people, hoping
> To purge himself with words. Dispatch.

Of all men, Coriolanus, "to appear before the people" that he may
"purge himself with words"! The attendants go about the
business given them, and are replaced by

> *3 or 4 Conspirators of Aufidius' Faction.*

and he and they proceed to make the case against Coriolanus.
  Aufidius is an injured man, and although

> We must proceed as we do find the people.

—as troublesome in Corioles as in Rome apparently—it should
not be hard to show him a wronged man. Such generosity as he
has shown, with such advantage taken of it! For the "witch-
craft," we may note, which once made men "fly to the Roman"—
Aufidius among them!—has now become the

> > dews of flattery,
> Seducing so my friends . . .

And, above all,

> When he had carried Rome, and that we looked
> For no less spoil than glory—

for this, at least, Aufidius promises,

> > my sinews shall be stretched upon him. . . .
> > he sold the blood and labour
> Of our great action; therefore he shall die,
> And I'll renew me in his fall. . . .

—at which moment

> *Drums and trumpets sound, with great shouts of the people.*

So Marcius comes in triumph, if not back to Rome, into
Corioles. His rival stands to listen. And, were more provocation
needed, friends provide it in their low reminder that

> Your native town you entered like a post,
> And had no welcomes home; but he returns
> Splitting the air with noise.
>   And patient fools,
> Whose children he hath slain, their base throats tear
> With giving him glory.

The lords of the city, now arriving, offer their welcome, none the less—which Aufidius, with a certain sulky modesty, disclaims. More to the purpose, they have digested his charges against Marcius, the last that he should

>   give away
> The benefit of our levies, answering us
> With our own charge: making a treaty where
> There was a yielding; this admits no excuse.

and Aufidius can afford to stand aside; with an

> He approaches: you shall hear him.

Note now the stage direction:

> *Enter Coriolanus marching with drum and colours; the*
> *Commoners being with him.*

He is in full panoply of war, an impressive, a commanding figure. This is he to whose side Aufidius' soldiers flocked. Aufidius himself looks and will feel nothing beside him. Moreover, the commoners are with him, to cheer or hoot him, as the Roman commoners did. They are cheering him now. And whatever the Volscian case against him, he means to make a good one for himself. But it is a hardened Marcius that makes it:

> Hail, lords! I am returned your soldier,
> No more infected with my country's love
> Than when I parted hence, but still subsisting
> Under your great command. . . .

a Marcius brought to claiming that

>   Our spoils we have brought home
> Doth more than counterpoise a full third part
> The charges of the action. . . .

—the man of whom it could be said in Rome that

> Our spoils he kicked at,
> And looked upon things precious as they were
> The common muck of the world. . . .

Not that a third of the cost of the war is matter of great account either! But he means to make himself a place here too. He must. He has no other left.

Aufidius sees this, and that he must strike hard, and without delay. "Traitor" is a sharp blow; and the derisive "Marcius" added—

> Ay, Marcius, Caius Marcius. Dost thou think
> I'll grace thee with that robbery, thy stolen name
> Coriolanus in Corioles?

—will draw his enemy towards tricky ground. He says no word of his own wrongs; only that:

> You lords and heads o' the state, perfidiously
> He has betrayed your business, and given up,
> For certain drops of salt, your city Rome,
> I say "your city". . . .

The commoners are listening too, the conspirators are on the watch. Aufidius drives on:

> Breaking his oath and resolution like
> A twist of rotten silk . . .
> He whined and roared away your victory. . . .

To all of which Coriolanus has reasonable answer. But the insults to his soldiership, his manhood, blot out all else:

> Hear'st thou, Mars?

Aufidius ends with a contemptuous

> Name not the god, thou boy of tears. . . .
> No more.

Marcius, incandescent with anger:

> Measureless liar, thou hast made my heart
> Too great for what contains it. . . .

yet it is the "boy" that has pricked deepest, and the more intolerably for the truth of it. Of the lies let these "grave lords" judge; but for the liar himself:

> Who wears my stripes impressed upon him, that
> Must bear my beating to his grave . . .

Here is the old exultant—that boyishly exultant—Marcius. Let his enemies take vengeance on him if they will:

> Cut me to pieces, Volsces; men and lads,
> Stain all your edges on me. . . .

for

> If you have writ your annals true, 'tis there,
> That, like an eagle in a dove-cote, I
> Fluttered your Volscians in Corioles:
> Alone I did it. Boy!

One of Shakespeare's master-moments this, in which he brings the tragic figure to the very edge of the ridiculous, but stays him there.

Even as his friends in Rome were wont to check and save him, so might the Volscian lords, would he but let them:

> The man is noble, and his fame folds in
> This orb o' the earth. His last offence to us
> Shall have judicious hearing. . . .

But Aufidius, who while he rages can still calculate, in appealing to them is appealing over their heads to the commoners, those commoners that, in Corioles as in Rome, Coriolanus will so obligingly provoke for him:

> Why, noble lords,
> Will you be put in mind of his blind fortune,
> Which was your shame, by this unholy braggart,
> 'Fore your own eyes and ears?

It is the conspirators' cue for a fomenting

> Let him die for 't.

and, as once before, the mob howls for his blood. As once before too he draws his sword, disdaining aid:

> O! that I had him,
> With six Aufidiuses, or more, his tribe,
> To use my lawful sword.

An "Insolent villain!" from Aufidius gives the conspirators their cue again; and, with vociferous "Kills" to drown the cries of "Hold!", they crowd in on him, daggers drawn. He falls, and

> *Aufidius stands on him.*

He stands on him! Could words say more?
  His first thought is to justify his deed—

      My noble masters, hear me speak.

—and not until he hears the shocked reproaches does he realize
what he is shamefully doing now.

      O, Tullus! . . .
      Tread not upon him. Masters, all be quiet.
      Put up your swords.

But it will not be so difficult to persuade moderate men that,
though it has been wrong to kill him, yet Coriolanus is better
dead. Therefore

           Bear from hence his body,
      And mourn you for him. Let him be regarded
      As the most noble corse that ever herald
      Did follow to his urn.

The Second Lord already sees clearly the other side of the matter:

           His own impatience
      Takes from Aufidius a great part of blame.
      Let's make the best of it.

and Aufidius adds in all sincerity:

           My rage is gone,
      And I am struck with sorrow.

The Verse

In listening to the play we shall be conscious of the verse as a
thing in itself only at certain intenser moments, which are thus—
by one metrical device or another—emphasized and made
memorable. For the rest it will impress us rather as powerful,
rounded speech, resonant somewhat above the ordinary, and, in
particular, borne forward by a most compelling rhythm. A
change from verse to prose, even, we may chiefly remark as a
change of temper, a lessening of emotional pressure, or merely
a timely contrast.

  Not for long now—by the measure of his swift development—
has Shakespeare habitually dealt in "set pieces" of verse, "Queen
Mab" speeches, pronouncements that "All the world's a stage" or

that "The quality of mercy is not strained"; and, even when he did, they would seldom lack some direct dramatic sanction. Portia's, for instance, is legitimate forensic eloquence, and Jaques has been cast, in the Arden pastoral, for the part of moralizer-in-chief to the banished Duke. Again, the speeches of the two Henrys upon sleeplessness, ceremony and kingship may, in method, be more rhetorical than reflective, but they suit both character and occasion. A little later, Brutus' ordered soliloquies come as the due expression of an ordered mind, and Mark Antony's oratory is directed first to his Roman hearers, and only through them upon us, the audience; and let actor or audience forget this and its dramatic purpose is warped. Then, with *Hamlet*—and in Hamlet's own speech particularly—we come within reach of a seeming spontaneity. Shakespeare allows him all possible scope of expression, both in prose and verse; and in the choice between them, and in the form and color of the verse as well as in its content, his every mood, of contemplation, irony or despair, will be sensitively reflected. It is, of course, only a "seeming spontaneity." People do not naturally speak verse, be it but blank verse; and even in prose, and for the simple speech of citizen or peasant, Shakespeare never lapses into an *imitated* spontaneity, so to forfeit all the aids of form and accepted convention.[57]

It is a consonant part—this reaching towards a seeming spontaneity—of Shakespeare's general development as a dramatist, and it necessarily tends to loosen and even break down the form of the verse. To begin with he is a poet writing plays—as Marlowe was, and Lyly—and his lengths of verse, often narrative or descriptive in their bent, will readily fall into regular form. And for long enough the form, a little eased or a little fortified, accommodates the direct expression of character and emotion very well, as, for instance, in the forthright Hotspur, less well for the subtler Richard II. It is when character and emotion gain complexity and extraordinary force that—as a stream in flood eats

---

[57] An earlier instance of this "seeming spontaneity" in verse can be found in the Nurse in *Romeo and Juliet*. Really, it sometimes seems as if Shakespeare must have had all the secrets of his art stored in him from the beginning, as if he had only to enlarge upon what he already knew.

its banks away—the verse breaks bounds; then Shakespeare himself has developed from the poet writing plays into the true dramatic poet.

This is not a quibbling distinction, it indicates a very fertile difference. Incidentally, it overrides the question of the medium used, prose or verse. *Macbeth* could have been written in prose without fundamental loss; it is poetically conceived. There is as much poetry in the prose of *As You Like It* as in its verse.[58] Convention and convenience, both to the dramatist and his actors, will commonly have recommended verse; but from the beginning Shakespeare seemingly tended to use whichever, that or prose, better suited his immediate purpose.[59] Shylock's supreme outburst is in prose; there is dramatic value in the mere contrast with the mellifluous verse surrounding it. *Richard II*'s exceptional uniformity of verse remains unbroken, though we might look for prose in the short gardeners' scene. Bottom and Weaver and his friends demand prose, if only because they have a play to rehearse and perform. Its medium must not be their own, and it will go best in doggerel. But who that could write verse would not write it for the rest of *A Midsummer Night's Dream*? Prose suits Falstaff to perfection; and Beatrice and Benedick, Rosalind and Orlando, leave the verse of the plays they animate sounding dull by comparison. But, comedy yielding to tragedy, verse comes to its own again; since it can excite emotion and sustain illusion as prose cannot.

The verse must not, in its new-won freedom, be let flow too freely, too slackly, or it will lose its power—as did so much of the verse of Shakespeare's immediate successors; and when Dryden and his school thought at last to come to the rescue the mischief had gone too far. With Shakespeare himself there will always be some recurrent check, in the shape of a line or a passage of stricter meter. Not mechanically inserted; if dramatic demand breaks the form of the verse, dramatic demand will also restore it. Hamlet is recalled from the overflowing emotion of

---

[58] Without *fundamental* loss: for some proof of this see Maeterlinck's translation of *Macbeth*. And Dover Wilson discovers in *As You Like It* the fossils of a verse version, of which Shakespeare presumably thought better.

[59] "Convention and convenience": Blank verse may well, with a little practice, prove easier to write than formal prose; it is certainly easier to learn.

> Bloody, bawdy villain!
> Remorseless, treacherous, lecherous, kindless villain!
> O, vengeance!

to the controlled thought of

> About my brain! I have heard
> That guilty creatures, sitting at a play,
> Have by the very cunning of the scene . . .

And the firm rhythm of Othello's

> Farewell the tranquil mind! farewell content!
> Farewell the plumed troop and the big wars. . . .

or of his

> It is the cause, it is the cause, my soul:
> Let me not name it to you, you chaste stars! . . .

—with other such counterbalancings to the succession of minor metrical liberties lodged (inconspicuously for the most part) in the general run of the verse—help to keep him heroically dominant over the commoner traffic of the play. The larger the liberties taken, the greater the need for this recurrent control. For drama is a disciplined art, hedged in by a hundred restrictions. It is akin to poetry and to verse in that, and the restrictions themselves are akin. And in the poetic play a loosening of the ties of verse only leaves it to depend the more upon a more essential order of character and idea, upon which—and not chiefly upon form—it must in fact be built. But this will be essentially poetic and dramatic too since it will deal with the metaphysical things with which poetry most properly deals, and with conflicts of the human will. Shakespeare evolves, then, for the major medium of his maturer plays, this enfranchised verse; a rhythmic and melodious speech, powerful and malleable at once. Of its form we shall often be but indefinitely aware; as much is kept as will keep the structure intact, now more, now less being needed. Little sense of artifice is left to intervene between us and the acted play; the medium grows transparent. Sacrificing none of them, he molds his diversity of means into a unity of dramatic expression; and he lifts us—we have only to surrender—to the level of it.

Not much is to be gained—in appreciation, that is to say, of its living qualities—by carrying such verse, cold and dead, to the dissecting table, there to demonstrate its spondees and dactyls, its overrun lines and feminine endings. Assuredly Shakespeare never planned it so; and, multiply rules as we may in trying to round his practice into some sort of system, the exceptions will outrun them. We do not think in terms of prosody at all of

> I am dying, Egypt, dying; only
> I here importune death awhile, until
> Of many thousand kisses the poor last
> I lay upon thy lips.

noting, as we speak the lines, that the first has—rather surprisingly—the orthodox ten syllables; nor do we remember Lear's

> Never, never, never, never, never!

as five successive trochees. Form and meaning are not to be separated.

But for all the freedom in the general run of the verse the later plays furnish us still with rhymed couplets enough, "sentences," lengths of octosyllabics, and such like conventional forms. There is the difference, however, that these things now owe their place to some particular dramatic use that can be made of them—to clinch an argument, stress a desperate moment or clarify a reflective one.[60] And the use is overt; the effect made will stand out like a patch of bright color, or, if the main speech-fabric hereabouts is already brightly colored, of contrasting shade. Shakespeare never abandons a well-tried dramatic device; let it still serve his purpose, that is the only test.

One freedom opens up another. Individual expression besides, the verse may now be molded to the character of particular scenes, or of the play itself. The fantastic rhyming of Edgar and the Fool, attuned to Lear's own lunacy, does much for the storm-scenes in *King Lear*. The verse of *Othello* combines energy and color and ease in a manner of its own. And contrast in color and in rhythm generally is to be added to the others between *Antony and Cleopatra* and *Coriolanus*. Imperial Rome and exotic Egypt

---

[60] And here, it may be added, at the very opening of *Coriolanus*, is a "set piece," in the story of the Belly and the Members. But it is put to direct dramatic use. The picture of Menenius cajoling the assembled citizens, to be contrasted immediately after with Marcius' swift hard way with them—the two passages together serve as a sort of opening statement of this aspect of the play.

and the searching minds and sweeping passions which inform
them—the magnificent many-faceted verse of the one reflects
these, even as concentration on a narrower strife finds fitting
voice in the closer woven, more angular, lines of *Coriolanus*.

There is little in subject or characters to carry Shakespeare off
his feet and set the verse of *Coriolanus* soaring. Egoism, rivalry,
cunning and pride (the more generous traits, making by comparison a poor show) leave the radiant passages few, incidental
usually and as likely as not to illuminate some minor figure.

>   Now the fair goddess Fortune
> Fall deep in love with thee: and her great charms
> Misguide thy opposers' swords! Bold gentleman,
> Prosperity be thy page!

—the old warrior, himself outdone, but lavish in admiration of
his heroically truculent young comrade; those few lines brighten
the whole scene. And it is to an anonymous messenger that is
given the brilliant little

>   'Tis thought
> That Marcius shall be Consul.
> I've seen the dumb men throng to see him, and
> The blind to hear him speak: matrons flung gloves,
> Ladies and maids their scarfs and handkerchers,
> Upon him as he passed: the nobles bended
> As to Jove's statue, and the commons made
> A shower and thunder with their caps and shouts:
> I never saw the like.[61]

DRAMATIC VERSE INDEED

The verse in the main is vigorous, and it drives hard and
exclusively at its dramatic purpose. The rhythm is apt to be of
more import than the melody. The words are often unmusical
in themselves, and they may be crushed into the lines like fuel to
stoke a furnace. It is a cast of speech well fitting the reason-
searching strife which pervades the play; and none in the canon

---

[61] It is evident, I think, that for the later plays Shakespeare had actors who
could be relied upon to make good effect with these small but striking parts.
There are several others in *Coriolanus*, some in *King Lear*, and a dozen or
more in *Antony and Cleopatra*. They were doubled no doubt.

is fuller of quarrel of one sort or another from beginning to end.

But if the verse—with nothing in the matter of it to stir the imagination—does not soar, neither does it ever sag. The play in this respect has not a single weak spot. One detects, in the frequent lack of clarity, a certain effort in the writing; but at least the effort is never shirked. The most patent instance comes, perhaps, in Aufidius' summary of his rival's failings:

> Whether 'twas pride,
> Which out of daily fortune ever taints
> The happy man; whether defect of judgment,
> To fail in the disposing of those chances
> Which he was lord of; or whether nature,
> Not to be other than one thing, not moving
> From th' casque to th' cushion, but commanding peace
> Even with the same austerity and garb
> As he controlled the war; but one of these,
> As he hath spices of them all—not all,
> For I dare so far free him—made him feared,
> So hated and so banished. . . .

—and so on, until the long succession of saving clauses is tied off in a complex aphorism.[62] If Shakespeare could not render down his thought into something clearer than this he might better, surely, have omitted the passage altogether. But no; Aufidius at this point, he feels, needs rationalizing, Coriolanus too. And if the idea involved will not distill and flow freely, it must just be wrung out. It cannot be omitted, and a flaw left in the fabric of thought.

Clarity yields to intensity. Witness Sicinius' malignly prescient

> Doubt not
> The commoners for whom we stand, but they
> Upon their ancient malice will forget
> With the least cause these his new honours; which
> That he will give them, make I as little question
> As he is proud to do't.

Put on paper, the last part of this may not parse well. But in speech, if the speaker be skillful, the thoughts themselves can be

---

[62] There is corruption in the text of the closing lines. But its elucidating would still leave the passage as a whole far from clear.

related—the "which" linked to the "least cause," the "proud"
given its proper prominence—and the very lack of clarity be made
to suggest their urgency.

Volumnia's disingenuous arguments, which send Marcius back
to the market place, are wound out smoothly:

> If it be honour in your wars to seem
> The same you are not . . .
>   now it lies on you to speak
> To the people; not by your own instruction,
> Nor by the matter which your heart prompts you,
> But with such words that are but roted in
> Your tongue, though but bastards and syllables
> Of no allowance to your bosom's truth.
> Now this no more dishonours you at all . . .

—the verse cold, sustained, regular, unmelodious, fitted to the
occasion and her temper, its sense aridly clear.

The man himself, if but a worse side of him, is alive both in the
matter and manner of Marcius' beginning:

>   What's the matter, you dissentious rogues,
> That, rubbing the poor itch of your opinion,
> Make yourselves scabs?

with its curt "What's the matter?", its veritably physical repug-
nance for the "rogues" set in the ugly images which follow, these
followed the next moment by

>   What would you have, you curs,
> That like not peace nor war? The one affrights you,
> The other makes you proud. He that trusts to you,
> When he should find you lions, finds you hares;
> Where foxes, geese: you are no surer, no,
> Than is the coal of fire upon the ice,
> Or hailstone in the sun.

with its banging-about of contraries, like so many boxes on the
ear; the scolding then carried on into the crowded, contemptuous

>   Hang 'em! They say!
> They'll sit by the fire, and presume to know
> What's done i' the Capitol; who's like to rise,
> Who thrives, and who declines; side factions, and give out
> Conjectural marriages. . . .

together with such tunelessness as is in "hunger broke stone walls," "horns o' the moon," "insurrection's arguing"—suitably, not a line of clear melody or smooth rhythm.

Further than which—one may at this point note—in the shaping and attuning of his verse to the expression of *individual* character, Shakespeare, here or elsewhere, in this play or another, hardly goes. For there must be some prevailing unity of form, or a play would fall in pieces; so, whatever the liberty given to the verse, its ten-syllable, five-stress foundation is left (as we have seen already) solidly underlying it still. And characters, even at their most individual, are still only emergent from type; this is true of Hamlet, of Falstaff even, Rosalind or Beatrice. Coriolanus himself is a variation of the soldier-hero, Aufidius of a villainous rival, while Menenius fills—if overfills—the place of the worldly-wise old counsellor, and Volumnia traces a little less theatrical descent as Roman matron. And the scope and individual character of all dramatic speech, be this remembered, since it must be instantly understood, has its limits there.

Dialogue and action are made to interpret one the other with exact economy. We actually see, first the failure, then the exciting success of the attack on Corioles, the city's capture and its token sacking; and with this goes no more dialogue than is needed—a bare line or two might at a pinch be omitted—for illustration. Cominius in six lines—

> Breathe you, my friends: well fought; we are come off
> Like Romans, neither foolish in our stands,
> Nor cowardly in retire: believe me, sirs,
> We shall be charged again. Whiles we have struck,
> By interims and conveying gusts we have heard
> The charges of our friends.

—is made to tell us what we need to know of his share in the battle and its further prospects, to paint us himself as general (just such a one as Marcius is not; the contrast striking), to tell us something besides of the lie of the battlefield, even of the weather! When Corioles has been taken, and Marcius is speeding Cominius' aid and the discomfiture of Aufidius, old Titus Lartius, with him his general's drummer and trumpeter, a scout also, distinguished by his light running gear, come from the inner to the outer stage, an officer and some more soldiers following:

> So, let the ports be guarded: keep your duties
> As I have set them down. If I do send, dispatch
> Those centuries to our aid; the rest will serve
> For a short holding; if we lose the field,
> We cannot keep the town. . . .
> Hence, and shut your gates upon us.
> Our guider, come; to the Roman camp conduct us.

Seven lines of speech, together with the significance of the figures and their movement—away from the city: back into it; the closing of the gates—suffice for this taste of Roman caution and cool judgment in warfare. The contrast is to come this time in the next scene's furious duel between Marcius and Aufidius.

The verse in general is meaty and lean; it contains few images and is all but free of extended metaphor. Its quality of direct attack is a strength to the actor. As an instance:

> Officious, and not valiant; you have shamed me
> In your condemned seconds.

—for Aufidius, left standing there while Marcius triumphantly pursues the unwelcome interlopers, the least wordiness would seem weakness; but that one spare sentence an actor can pack with spleen.

Marcius' magnanimity is given as direct and simple expression. The battle over:

> I sometime lay here in Corioles
> At a poor man's house; he used me kindly.
> He cried to me; I saw him prisoner.
> But then Aufidius was within my view,
> And wrath o'erwhelmed my pity. I request you
> To give my poor host freedom.

It makes part—with the immediate weary-minded forgetting of the man's name; has he not the right to be weary!—of the up-building of his character, is a counterpart to that scornful rating of the commoners. And the verse accommodates this; as it does his joking response to the army's acclaim of him:

> I will go wash;
> And when my face is fair you shall perceive
> Whether I blush or no.

as it will later his lovingly ironic reproof to his wife's tears of welcome:

> Wouldst thou have laughed had I come coffin'd home,
> That weep'st to see me triumph? ...

Surely the very perfection of such simplicity!

The play contains little or no superfluous matter. With the civic struggle at full pitch, the effect to be made one of riot and confusion, each character, either chorus of Senators and plebeians, contributes exactly to the scene's need.

BRUTUS.   Aediles, seize him!
CITIZENS.   Yield, Marcius, yield!
MENENIUS.   Hear me one word;
          Beseech you, Tribunes, hear me but one word.
AEDILES.   Peace, peace!
MENENIUS.   Be that you seem, truly your country's friend,
          And temperately proceed to what you would
          Thus violently redress.
BRUTUS.   Sir, these cold ways,
          That seem like prudent helps, are very poisonous
          Where the disease is violent. Lay hands upon
              him,
          And bear him to the rock.
MARCIUS.   No, ·I'll die here.
          There's some among you have beheld me
              fighting:
          Come, try upon yourselves what you have seen
              me.
MENENIUS.   Down with that sword! Tribunes, withdraw
              awhile.
BRUTUS.   Lay hands upon him.
MENENIUS.   Help Marcius! Help!
          You that be noble, help him, young and old!
CITIZENS.   Down with him! Down with him!

In this mutiny, the Tribunes, the Aediles, and the People
are beat in.

The passage is scored as it might be for an orchestra, each instrument given its task: Brutus' sharp order, reinforced by the plebeians' shout; Menenius' half-heard remonstrance; the Aediles' command for the silence in which Menenius and Brutus exchange their acid arguments; this sharply broken again by Brutus. And no shout follows now; since Marcius, mute and motionless so far, suddenly draws his sword and challenges combat. Circumspect old Menenius presses peace on both parties. It is Brutus who is reckless and hounds on his outnumbering mob. Then, for Menenius, if it is to come to fighting, each must stand to his own side. And the fit few prove too much for the many.

THE DYNAMIC PHRASE

Spare dialogue need not be poor dialogue. The little said can be made to suggest much left unsaid. Dramatic art matures to this. In the cruder sort of play the characters will often not be fully dramatized, the dramatist himself to be heard speaking through them too plainly. But when they are, and their speech is authentically their own, then, by planning and a close collaboration with the actor, it can be brought to the expression of the implicit too, of those confusions of thought that trouble men, of feelings that never, in life, find words. The expression must be kept seemingly lifelike, not translated into overexplicit—into explanatory—terms: this would falsify the effect of it. The art of the dramatist lies in the discovering of more covert means.

The dynamic phrase, into which the actor is to pack the effect of a cumulated mass of thought and feeling, is one means. Shakespeare early learned the use of it. When Romeo hears of Juliet's death:

Is it even so? Then I defy you, stars!

rhetoric will follow later; but nothing of such deep and suggestive feeling. Falstaff's

Master Shallow, I owe you a thousand pound.

is a line of the sort, with its comically generous divining of Master Shallow's feelings too. So, when he has watched Cressid dallying with Diomed, is Troilus' response to Ulysses' "All's done, my lord," his grim "It is."

The dynamic phrase can be used in more ways than one. And there is purer tragedy in Macduff's cold

He has no children.

than in all his throbbing grief for his loss of them. Macbeth's own response to what once his servants would hardly have dared tell him:

> The Queen, my lord, is dead.

is no more than a silence, to be followed—when that bitter emptiness, his loss of the very power to feel, has made itself felt— by the wearily impatient

> She should have died hereafter:
> There would have been a time for such a word. . . .

and some detached reflections upon the meaninglessness of life. The effect—as of spiritual impotence—is not simply in these. To gain it, the underlying tragedy has been the play's length in development.

In a play, text apart from context may lose most of its meaning. The story itself, with Shakespeare, will run directly and openly along; there is no plot (the term will be misleading) to be spun and unraveled.[63] The play's structure is built up by the inter-locking of character and event, and the opposition of character to character; this gives it body, balance and strength. In *Coriolanus* the main stresses are between Marcius and the Senate on the one side, the people on the other; this beside, between Marcius and Aufidius, Marcius and Volumnia, jolly Menenius and the sour Tribunes. These are plain to be seen, and they implement the action. But there is much of auxiliary consequence as well, not set out at length or very explicitly, left latent, rather, for the actors to develop or elucidate in their acting.

The dramatist plans the essentials of this auxiliary action. Directions for it will be implicit in those passages of thrifty dialogue and their context; but only as realized and expanded will its full significance be made clear. When, for instance, in the play's first scene Marcius and Cominius and the Senators come together, their conduct to each other, the friendly yielding of precedence, Marcius' show of respect for the Consul and "our best elders," his easy acceptance otherwise of his own heroic eminence, and (pointed omission telling too) the ignoring of the

---

[63] *Othello*, among the greater plays, really the single exception, nor fully an exception even so.

new Tribunes—twenty pregnant lines and their acting suffice to picture us men and party; and not even the anonymous among them are left lay figures.

So it is with the triumphal entry after the victory at Corioles. Action and speech are knit together, the one clarifying and enhancing the other. The shouts of welcome hushed, Martius' look is turned—ours too again—to the women modestly withdrawn there; Roman mother and wife, the harsh Volumnia shaken by emotion, Virgilia happily weeping. Then he, Rome's hero, kneels dutifully to his mother, dries his wife's tears with words of gentle, magnanimously grave irony, frees himself from that mood with a joke for Menenius, his courteous bow to Valeria. More telling too will be this second ignoring of the Tribunes (on a third occasion, Marcius, confident of his consulship, will openly voice his contempt for them). Again, it is a matter of thirty-five lines or less. Yet not only their own significance, their illustration and the interplay of the response they demand, brings every participant in the scene into helping to give it life.

Shakespeare has come to demanding more of his actors, and to giving them more—though it may be less ostensible—opportunity. He demands their imaginative collaboration, leaves much to their discretion, gives them outlines to color in lightly or heavily. How large a part, for instance, does wine-flushed stubbornness play in Aufidius' repeated refusal to recognize the unmuffled Marcius, waiting by his hearth in Antium? The actor may decide. The text leaves him latitude and discretion, Shakespeare providing neither comment nor response to clinch the matter.

When Menenius returns with Volumnia and Virgilia from parting with the banished Marcius at the city gate: the strain now relaxed, the day lost, old age in him suddenly gives way; and against their vituperatings he can only set a "Peace, peace! be not so loud," a "Come, come; peace!"; and finally, the triumphant Tribunes departing, a

> You have told them home;
> And, by my troth, you have cause. You'll sup with me?

With no more to be done, there's left at least the comfort of a meal! The mere words given their surface meaning do little more than somewhat superfluously help the action on. But as bits of material to be used for filling out the figure of Menenius a skillful actor can put them to lively use. And that final consolatory bidding to supper then becomes also the better springboard for the grim, indomitable

> Anger's my meat; I sup upon myself,
> And so shall starve with feeding.

by which—its immediate effect besides—we shall be helped to keep Volumnia vividly in mind during her coming absence from the action.

The actor thus potently collaborating, one scene can be made to feed others that follow, and repeated expounding be avoided. Aufidius' backsliding from Marcius as they march together upon Rome is fully set out in his talk with his Lieutenant. After this merely his watchful presence through successive scenes will be eloquent, and the few cold phrases with which he breaks its silence need no enlarging: for example, his dry approbation of Marcius' rebuffing of Menenius with that

> You keep a constant temper.

his ironic sympathy for the son's breaking at last under the mother's pleading:

> I was moved withal.

A moment later comes an aside as explicit as was the talk with the Lieutenant:

> I am glad thou hast set thy mercy and thy honour
> At difference in thee: out of that I'll work
> Myself a former fortune.

and this keeps the trend of the action incontestably clear. But his open share in the two scenes, those two dry sentences (and one other) which positively do little more than emphasize his continuing presence, these an Aufidius can discreetly color, can most effectively charge with the strange blend of hatred and admiration that we know possesses the man. Such acting it is that adds something of another dimension to the personified narrative of a play, a dimension of being.

A speech may have an auxiliary sense, to which the actor must give value by his own particular means. When Marcius has finally yielded Rome's fate to Volumnia's plea he knows—and we are aware—that he has also put his own in Aufidius' hands. He turns to him:

> Aufidius, though I cannot make true wars,
> I'll frame convenient peace. Now, good Aufidius,
> Were you in my stead, would you have heard
> A mother less, or granted less, Aufidius?

The expressed resolve beside, in the mere repetitions of that "Aufidius," as the actor can give them varying cadence, will sound all the pleading on his own behalf—it is little!—that Marcius' pride could ever let him make.

To hark back to his banishment: much of the preceding scene is but preparation for the promised self-control of the curt

> I am content.

with which on his return to the market place he answers the Tribunes' provocative demand:

> If you submit you to the people's voices,
> Allow their officers, and are content
> To suffer lawful censure for such faults
> As shall be proved upon you?

for the countering too, a little later, of a yet more insolently peremptory

> Answer to us.

with the measured

> Say then; 'tis true. I ought so.

Such effects of self-control can, it is obvious, only be convincingly made when the elements of something to control have already been as convincingly built into the character.

THE USE OF SILENCE

Shakespeare has learned to put silence to a variety of uses. Although, later in this same scene, intolerably stung by that "traitor to the people," Marcius finally forswears his promised temperance, yet he stands rigidly silent while Sicinius

> in the name o' the people,
> And in the power of us the Tribunes . . .

passes formal sentence of banishment upon him, while the people
ratify it with a chorused

> It shall be so.

Thus he multiplies many times—when anger finally does break
bounds—the effect of his

> You common cry of curs! whose breath I hate . . .

And there is the silence to which the unhappy Tribunes are
reduced when, while Cominius and Menenius mock them, the
news accumulates that this once banished Marcius is marching
with the Volscians upon Rome—one meek

> But is this true, sir?

from Brutus, put in to emphasize it. There is most particularly the

> *Holds her by the hand, silent.*

—Shakespeare's own direction, that rarity! It is no more than a
simple gesture, with which Marcius accepts the doom his
surrender to his mother brings on him; a mere silence, yet it is
the culminating moment of the play.

In the vivifying of such silences, the imaginative use of the
"dynamic phrase" with its pent emotions, expressing things left
latent, in the general demand now made upon the actor that he
altogether assimilate himself to the character he is presenting,
much is changed from the earlier illustrative declaiming of verse
or prose. Yet Shakespeare's is, and remains through all changes,
the drama of eloquence. And his art's chief achievement in this
kind has been to turn eloquence for its own sake into a *relative*
eloquence (so to call it) springing, seemingly spontaneously,
from character-enlivening occasion; the poetic form not broken,
set free rather to be as personal and malleable a medium of
expression as may be.

DRAMATICALLY LEGITIMATE ELOQUENCE

The story of *Coriolanus* is pre-eminently one of public life; and
throughout the play—from Menenius' persuasive tale of the Belly
and the Members to Marcius' last desperate haranguing of his
Volscian masters—scene after scene offers dramatically legitimate
occasion for eloquence. There is much variety of occasion too, as

of speaker and temper of speech; the mutiny of the citizens, so differently dealt with by Menenius and Marcius; the crisis on the battlefield, the thanks to Marcius for his great part in the victory, later the public address to him with its carefully sought phrases; the war of words between Marcius and the Tribunes; Volumnia's spitfire retorting on them, to find contrast later in her stern, measured defense of Rome; Marcius finally brought to bay, fatally unchanged—here are many sorts of eloquence validly provided for. But there will be—and as legitimately—more likeness than difference in the matter of it, and between the speakers. For Menenius, Cominius and the Tribunes, Marcius and his mother, even the Volscians and Aufidius look—if not always from one standpoint—all towards the same horizon. There is the difference, truly, that less bitterness goes to battling against Volscian neighbors without the gates than against enemy kindred within. And this likeness lends to the temper of the verse a consistency which Marcius' own inevitable domination of it will but confirm, since there is little to be expressed in him that outranges the scope of the rest. And here again the close woven pattern of event and character, the internecine in the struggle, is an element of the tragedy.

There is nothing profound in Marcius, nor anything to set him inwardly apart from friend or foe, and all introspection is foreign to him. Of his two brief soliloquies, one is little more than an outburst of febrile ill-temper, a climax to his infatuate protest against donning the gown of humility and asking the citizens for their votes:

> Better it is to die, better to starve,
> Than crave the hire which first we do deserve.
> Why in this woolvish gown should I stand here,
> To beg of Hob and Dick, that does appear,
> Their needless vouches? . . .

—and the exceptional succession of six rhymed couplets with their jangling iteration goes to painting this. The second is detached comment, hardly more. He is in Antium, the revolution within him already accomplished.

> O world, thy slippery turns! . . .

If we hear of no doubts or misgivings or struggles of conscience it is because there will have been none. Plunged in misery,

> Longer to live most weary . . .

by a sudden "slippery turn" he has become—so he supposes—another man:

> My birth-place hate I, and my love's upon
> This enemy town.

It is as simple as that. Of the workings of a troubled mind he knows no more than does a child. He is frank and direct with mother, wife or friend, eloquent in anger. Of the inward Marcius we have passing glimpses only; in his thought for his one-time host in Corioles, for the widows his valor has left grieving there; in his respect for his mother, his chaste love for his wife; finally in the resigned realization of

> Not of a woman's tenderness to be,
> Requires nor child nor woman's face to see.

—its reflective cadence throwing it gently into relief against the stronger rhythm of the current speech.

The Question of Act–Division

THE play's action falls dramatically into three main divisions. The first, after some preliminary excursions into the citizens' discontent, covers the Volscian war; the second begins with Marcius' triumphant return from it, develops the struggle around his consulship and finishes upon his banishment; the third runs from his surrender to Aufidius, through the threats and alarms of his return, the surrender to his mother and the catastrophe of the end. This, however, being among the plays first found in the Folio, is there submitted to the formal five-act division—which, lacking more than once any dramatic warrant, one doubts to be Shakespeare's. A tricky question to answer, this of act-division; since we do not very certainly know how, at performances—and with what consistency—the act-pause was used. As a ten-minute interval during which the audience could relax? As a more formal minute's breathing-space for the actors? The punctuating power of the act-division will differ greatly.

What dramatic value can there be in the Folio's division here that parts Act II from Act III? In the action itself there is continuity. In Marcius' own tones and in his friends' attitude towards him, their deference to him as "Lord Consul," his readiness for more war with the Volscians, one may perhaps distinguish a change of key; but nothing, one would say that needs an act-division—certainly not a long pause—for its emphasis. Again, a fresh dramatic chapter in the story certainly begins with Coriolanus' appearance at Antium, *in mean apparel, disguised and muffled.* Just before this comes the "bridge scene" between the Roman and Volscian spies; and, from a dramatic standpoint, the Folio could suitably either end its third act with this or begin its fourth. It does neither. And if the practical convenience of a Marcius who must doff his Consul's insignia to make himself all but unrecognizable in his mean apparel ought also to be considered—it is not. Nor does there seem to be any very patent dramatic reason for ending a fourth act where the Folio ends this, nor for beginning the fifth act with Menenius setting forth on his errand after refusing to.

We may feel certain, surely, that Shakespeare sought, first and last, to make his plays dramatically viable, although we may not be so certain as we begin to think we are of the effects made by his stage on his stagecraft. But when we can be fairly certain of this, it is good evidence that what offends against these effects is not from his hand.

The Stage Directions

SOME of these are among the play's most notable features. Incidentally, their dramatic value apart, they stand among the items of evidence of a retirement to Stratford and the writing of the latest plays in a semi-detachment from the theater. Such evidence is, of course, inferential, no better than guesswork if you will. But *Coriolanus* at least speaks in this respect pretty plainly of a manuscript to be sent to London, and of a staging which the author did not expect to supervise himself.

The directions are always expert, devised by someone who has visualized the action very clearly. They may be such a mere memorandum as a prompter might write in, as where, in the passage covering the battle for Corioles, after the customary indicative

> *The fight is renewed. The Volsces retire into Corioles, and Marcius follows them to the gates.*

comes for Marcius the mandatory

> *Enter the gates.*

One builds nothing on that. But

> *Enter Cominius, as it were in retire, with soldiers.*

and later

> *Enter two Officers, to lay cushions, as it were, in the Capitol.*

—these "as it weres" are, so to say, "advisory"; the actors must devise their expression for themselves. On the other hand, action of dramatic importance may be underlined, though the spoken text indicate it clearly enough:

> *Enter Coriolanus, in a gown of humility . . .*

and the next words spoken are

> Here he comes, and in the gown of humility. . . .

And later—though nothing will be plainer than the sight itself—

> *Enter Coriolanus, in mean apparel, disguised and muffled.*

Here is the author, stressing these effects upon the actors, for his own satisfaction, to make sure they miss none of them; for his own great satisfaction, one feels, when it comes to

> *Draw both the Conspirators and kils Martius, who falles, Auffidius stands on him.*

And

> *Enter Menenius to the Watch or Guard.*

"Watch or Guard"; whichever you please, it comes to the same thing.

But the direction to be valued most of all is that given to the actor of Marcius himself. Before he yields to Volumnia he

> *Holds her by the hand, silent.*

—for an appreciable moment, it must be. Had Shakespeare had his actors at hand to direct should we now ever have had that?

Did a foolishly rash Macbeth go speeding on after the sledge-hammer blow of

> The Queen, my lord, is dead.

Not if Shakespeare was there to stop him!

Corry-ols, Corry-o-les, or Corī-o-les; Corry-o-lanus or Corī-o-lanus?

It is related of John Philip Kemble that once, when making at the end of a performance the customary announcement of the next, he told the house that the company would present Shakespeare's play of Corry-o-lanus in which he himself would undertake the part of Corī-o-lanus.[64] Such disputes would occasionally enliven the already livelier theater of those days, resembling as it could—the "Pit" of it—rather an unruly club than a mere shop in which plays are so tamely bought and sold. And while, despite three centuries of searching out—and willfully creating!—Shakespearean problems, there remain more than enough to be solved, few, whether of greater or less import, offer us such a free choice as does this. Nor is it of such little dramatic import as the pronunciation of a word will commonly be. It proclaims the hero's glory; its refusal to him is the final insult which he will not brook; at a dozen moments it is made the keynote of eloquence and emotion. The cadence of the word, and its music; those, therefore, are, dramatically, the two important things about it. Whatever Shakespeare's intention, we may be certain that he meant it to sound well.

It is not first met with precisely in that form, but coming from a Volscian Senator in his jaunty

> Let us alone to guard Cor-ī-oles. . . .

which is as simple a decasyllable as the play contains. But when, two scenes later, a messenger enters with his news, this is that

> The citizens of Corry-ols have issued,
> And given to Lartius and to Marcius battle. . . .

---

[64] I have the story from that able, and now so deeply regretted, theatrical historian Harold Child.

and the minor actor who did anything but stress the "Corry . . ."
might count, surely, upon sharp correction. Yet only twenty-three
lines later Marcius will be all but bound to say that Titus Lartius is

> Holding Co-ri-o-les in the name of Rome . . .

—and would possibly not be so amenable to correction. And a
little later he tells Aufidius,

> Within these three hours, Tullus,
> Alone I fought in your Co-ri-o-les walls. . . .

And what other than the longest of long ī's can that Corioles
contain?

But here, of course, are sources only of the "Coriolanus" of our
question; and this, when it first appears a scene later, still is so
much a proclamation (with an exulting echo) that it can be
counted out of the verse and its demands altogether. One can
only say that as it is surrounded by "Corioles" (one before and
two after), with their long ī's indubitable, "Coriŏlanus" would
seem to be the most instinctive derivative.

It comes again in the verse of a proclamation; and the Herald
may have it either way he will—or both.

> Know, Rome, that all alone Marcius did fight
> Within Corioles gates, where he hath won . . .

(there is the long ī undoubtedly)

> With fame, a name to Caius Marcius: these
> In honour follows Corry-o-lanus.

with, to conclude, either a

> Welcome to Rome, renownèd Corry-o-lanus!

or a

> Welcome to Rome, renowned Cor-ī-olanus!

which you choose; Volumnia also having her choice between
a poor line in

> What is it? Corry-o-lanus must I call thee?

and a better one in

> What is't? Cor-ī-olanus must I call thee?

—being sure, in rehearsal at any rate, of loud ironic protests from the rest of the company when, with a wink, she poses the problem!

Thereafter, however, and on all hands, the pronunciation "Corry-o-lanus" slides more easily into the verse, though never stimulating it. Sicinius can even squeeze a certain mockery into the tunelessness of

> Your Corry-olanus is not much missed
> But with his friends. . . .

Again, Volumnia will do the better with

> To his surname Cor-ī-olanus longs more pride
> Than pity to our prayers.

though the verse does not force it on her, and fits the word ill at best. But "Cor-ī-o-les," a minute later, it must be.

With the play's closing moments we are nearing the name's most pointedly dramatic use. Aufidius'

> Ay, Marcius, Caius Marcius. Dost thou think
> I'll grace thee with that robbery, thy stolen name
> Coriolanus in Corioles?

"Corry-o-lanus in Corry-ols" or "Corry-o-les" it certainly cannot be; "Corry-o-lanus in Cor-i-o-les" it just may be. But how much finer "Cor-ī-olanus in Cor-ī-o-les"! And what Marcius will hesitate an instant over

> "Boy"! false hound!
> If you have writ your annals true, 'tis there,
> That, like an eagle in a dove-cote, I
> Fluttered your Volscians in Cor-ī-o-les. . . .

"Corry-o-lanus," then, it would seem has the majority of voices. But let there never be one for "Corry-ols" or "Corry-o-les"!

One is tempted towards what is, doubtless, an indefensible heresy. Were the Elizabethans as inconsistent in the pronouncing of some uncommon words as in the spelling of them? Was it as possible for an actor to say "Corry-o-lanus" at one moment and "Cor-ī-olanus" at another—whichever suited the verse the better —with none of the hearers finding the change objectionable as it would be for a dramatist to sign himself "Shakespeare" at one moment and "Shaxpeer" the next? It would need, of course, a braver man than the present writer to plead this.

Notes on the Illustrations

Fig. A   Barker regards the staging of the monument scenes on the "Elizabethan stage as we now think we know it to have been," as "disputable matter," (p. 38). He was prepared, in 1930, to consider "some change in staging, or in the stage itself" to help to an understanding of how it might have been originally managed (p. 40, fn. 32). Since then G. F. Reynolds in *The Staging of Elizabethan Plays at the Red Bull Theatre* (1940), and C. Walter Hodges in *The Globe Restored* (1953), backed by the readiness of E. K. Chambers to consider for the monument "some porch-like projection from the back wall," have put up a good case for a temporary projecting structure which they believe might have been used also in other plays. Had the ordinary upper-stage gallery been used (cf. Vol. I, 6), its balustrade would have complicated the hauling up of Antony by Cleopatra and her women—i.e. by three boys, with possibly two more as attendants—and unless we postulate an upper chamber to increase the available space, the scene of the parting between Antony and Cleopatra would have been very cramped. Mr. Hodges points out that it is necessary to make sense of the passage in Act IV where Antony is brought on dying. As Cleopatra enters above, Diomedes enters below, and tells her to:

> Look out o'the other side your monument;
> His guard have brought him thither.

This she could only do if the monument were constructed in some such manner as suggested in his drawing. The manoeuvre would, of course, be equally practicable on the Stratford Ontario upper stage (Vol. I, 9; II, 46; IV, 46).

2.   The drawing shows Tamora, the captive Queen of the Goths, pleading with Titus to spare her sons. We cannot prove that Peacham was reproducing the scene as he had watched it played upon the stage, but what he has drawn corresponds very closely with what we know about Elizabethan stage practice from other sources. The chief point of interest is the costumes, and the

mixture of contemporary, classical and theatrical styles which remained usual in the theatre until the end of the eighteenth century. At the left are two normally clad Elizabethan pikemen. Every detail is vouched for by contemporary representations of soldiers of the period—even the plus-fours and the feathered helmet: the former are not, as is sometimes said, "Turkish trousers"; the latter is not the theatrical helmet of the classical hero, nor is the scimitar-type sword of the left-hand soldier of eastern origin—it is simply the curtilace (i.e. cutlass) of the time, which is "a broad-sword or sabre of the falcion family." Titus, Aaron and the sons wear a stage version of classical costume, resembling the *costume à la romaine* of the sixteenth and seventeenth century masques and the eighteenth century stage. Its features are the *lorica* or cuirass worn by Titus, the two sons and Aaron; their buskins; the "bases" (skirts) of the cuirass overlaid with "labels" (thin strips of material); and the cloak worn by Titus. The shoulder-knots are contemporary military style. The long sleeves worn with the cuirass by Aaron and the bearded son are incorrect for classical costume, but are very usual in the masque adaptations of it, and persist throughout the eighteenth century, encouraged by the French stage, where long sleeves, fleshings and breeches were *de rigueur* with this costume for classical tragedy. Tamora wears the crown, the train and the flowing veil that characterise the stage heroine or tragedy queen until the end of the eighteenth century. There is nothing classical about her.

Dover Wilson re-examines the attribution of the drawing to Henry Peacham, author of *The Compleat Gentleman*, in *Shakespeare Survey*, Vol. I (1948), and deals with the various problems presented by it and by the forty lines of text which accompany it in the original manuscript.

3-5. The figures from Braun and Hohenberg's pictorial map of Rome in their world-atlas, *Civitates orbis terrarum*, (1572-1618) show that the sixteenth century understood the difference between genuine classical costume and the theatrical version of it. The men in armour are comparatively genuine: the gentleman in 5, bearing a close resemblance to King Charles I, is a masque figure, of which the Inigo Jones design for the masque of *Oberon*

(4) provides an extreme example. The lady in 3, who can indeed say "Cut my lace, Charmian," belongs neither to Rome nor to Elizabethan actuality, nor yet to the masque convention, but is closer to the artistic convention which determined the dresses of the two young women in the Veronese painting, except for her short sleeves with labels. The Inigo Jones designs for women's costumes can be studied in *Shakespeare's England* (Vol. II, Ch. xxv) and in *Designs by Inigo Jones for Masques and Plays at Court*, P. Simpson and C. F. Bell (1924). The style is perpetuated in a formalized manner in the Rowe frontispieces to *Love's Labour's Lost*, (Vol. IV 1), *A Midsummer Night's Dream, The Winter's Tale* and *Troilus and Cressida*, in all of which the masque treatment of the classical *lorica* is reflected in the labels on the sleeves and skirts. The tiered skirts are characteristic of Stuart masque design. Whether we can let Rowe vouch for this carry-over into the theatre of *costume à la romaine* for women, in the absence of further evidence, may be disputable, seeing that there are no classical touches in Tamora's earlier dress or in the later costumes illustrated here. What Rowe does establish, just as clearly as the Peacham drawing, is the mixture of classical and contemporary costume which was accepted in the eighteenth as in the sixteenth century in theatrical practice. The "forest of feathers," or Plumes for Personages, which were a feature of Hamlet's stage and were being laughed at by Addison in 1711, are genuinely theatrical, as is the Princess's train and the child-attendant who carries it.

6 and 13. For Stern's designs for the stage for *Julius Caesar* see Figs. C and D in Vol. II.

7. Thomas Sheridan (1719-88), father of the more famous Richard Brinsley, appeared twice in London as Brutus: at Covent Garden in 1755 and at the Haymarket in 1767 (Hogan: *Shakespeare in the Theatre*, 2). His dress is a good example of late eighteenth century costume *à la romaine*.

8-10, 14. Whether costume like Tamora's was worn on the public stage for the women's parts, and later, perhaps, rejected in favour of the masquing style, it is quite clear by the time we get to the eighteenth century *ad vivam* drawings that the actresses have abandoned any "classic" concessions that may have existed. Apart from the train, the flowing veil and the feathers of the tragedy queen, they wear the fashionable dress of the day. In 9 Cleopatra has added the fashionable turban to the feathers, but she still keeps her regial diadem and duplicates its effect with trimming. Both Cleopatra and Portia (11), with their masses of luxuriant curls and long hanging ringlets, illustrate the latest thing in hair styles in 1786.

8-9.   Elizabeth Younge (1744-97, Mrs. Pope, cf. Vol. IV, 35 and Note) first wife of the actor Alexander Pope, is not known to have played Cleopatra (cf. Note 11-12, 15), except in Dryden's *All for Love*. Possibly these two portraits as Shakespeare's Cleopatra may show the costumes she wore as Dryden's heroine. Both are in the fashionable contemporary style, and in the later one she is almost a twin to Miss Farren as Olivia, just as Mrs. Ward (14) is a twin portrait to Miss Phillips as Miranda in the same series of illustrations (Bell's British Library), all of which show, when compared with those from Bell's *Shakespeare* (8), how the costumes of the actresses became less theatrical and more contemporary in the ten years after Garrick's retirement. Elizabeth Younge was the principal all-round actress of her day, and has been described as one of Garrick's chief supports and torments. She had a wider range than either Mrs Siddons or Miss Farren, but could not rival them in their greatest parts.

10.   Priscilla Hopkins (1758-1845), widow of the actor William Brereton, married John Philip Kemble in 1787. Her mother had been an actress of repute in Garrick's company, which Priscilla also joined in 1775. This print from Bell's *Shakespeare*, dated 1776, is an imaginary portrait. There is no record of her having played Volumnia in the eighteenth century. Her costume, with the feathers and the flowing veil, is similar to that of other tragedy queens in distress.

14.   Mrs. Thomas Achurch Ward (née Sarah Hoare, 1757-1838)

was a member of the Drury Lane company in the seventeen-
eighties (see Hogan, *op.cit.*). There is no record of her having
appeared in *Julius Caesar* in London, but she played Valeria on
several occasions to the Volumnia of Mrs. Siddons.

11-12, 15.   *Antony and Cleopatra* was not acted at all in the first
half of the eighteenth century. In 1759 it was given six performances by Garrick, with Mrs. Yates as his Cleopatra, in an abridged
version arranged by himself and Edward Capell. It was presumably dressed in *costume à la romaine* for the male leads and
contemporary costume for the women. These six figures, from
two sheets of characters published by Jameson's Theatrical
Warehouse, represent the earliest nineteenth century London
production at Covent Garden, 15 Nov. 1813-13 Jan. 1814 (8 performances). They illustrate the beginning of historical or archaeological costume for this play, of which Parker records only eight
London productions in the century. Antony was played by Charles
Mayne Young, Octavius by William Abbott, Lepidus by Barry-
more and Enobarbus by Egerton. The text was a mixture of
Shakespeare and Dryden, concluding with a grand funeral
procession.
    Mr. Martin Holmes, who discovered these sheets in the Jona-
than Stone Collection in the London Museum, suggests that "this
sudden access of costume-consciousness may be attributed, in
some degree at any rate, to the publication of Hope's *Costume of
the Ancients* the year before, in a new and enlarged edition." He
points out the "unexpected consistency" in the dresses and their
recognizably Egyptian features, in spite of the survival of the
theatrical Turkish trousers, and short-sleeved, knee-length tunics
"dear to theatre-land and associated indiscriminately with any
historical period short of the Renaissance" which are used for
Alexas and the Messenger. (See "A Regency Cleopatra," *Theatre
Notebook*, VIII, 2, 1954). All subsequent productions took their
cue from this 1814 production, and made attempts at Egyptian
scenery and costumes.

15.   Harriet Faucit, (1789-1857), mother of the more famous
Helen Faucit, was the Cleopatra. The playbill lays great stress on

the Egyptian dresses, and the new scenery, with a representation of the Battle of Actium for spectacular appeal. This was the first production to attempt anything more definitely Egyptian than the theatre's usual oriental touches, such as turbans, scimitars and fur-edged robes, though apart from the diadem with hanging lappets Mrs. Faucit's costume differs very little from the semi-classical type of gown then fashionable both on the stage and off it. The line, as it so happened, was still the contemporary fashionable line.

16.   This print, from *Tallis's Drawing Room Table Book*, bears out the contemporary description of Isabella Glyn (1823-89)—"a fine commanding figure, powerful voice and distinctly masculine manner." It would not of itself, however, enable us to realise that contemporary opinion also considered that Cleopatra was her greatest part, rivalled only by her performance as the Duchess of Malfi. She was a pupil of Charles Kemble and played in the traditional Kemble style, with formal gestures and effective poses. She joined Phelps's company as leading lady at Sadler's Wells in 1848, making her *début* as Volumnia. Phelps mounted *Antony and Cleopatra* with "great splendour," surpassing all his previous productions at Sadler's Wells. It was a big success and was performed twenty-five times that season. The text was closer to the original than any version since Shakespeare's day. *The Times* found Miss Glyn "promising," and best in the more subdued passages; and though objecting to her very formal style of gesticulation, allowed that "it resolves itself into some very effective *poses* in the scenes of queenly distress." The line of her dress is completely contemporary. She has acquired a real Egyptian collar, and her head-tire has lappets; but no self-respecting actress of 1849 could for one moment even have contemplated Egyptian swathings, and when she played it in 1867 she wore a crinoline style.

17-18.   This production attracted a great deal of notice and played for an extra week, though the Old Vic's runs were then strictly limited. To Ivor Brown, Gielgud's Antony was "the Renaissance adventurer and the Renaissance exquisite"; in *The Weekend*

Review (30 November 1930) he described him as "a grizzled, bearded Elizabethan, who might have sailed with Drake or sonneteered with the Mermaid boys, valiant, melancholy, and yet marching as a Roman to his fall." He found it "a beautiful as well as a brisk production." "Mr. Harcourt Williams and Mr. Owen Smyth have worked finely to give us the peacock strut of a Renaissance Orient, with all the archaeology left out and all the romanticism left in." Dorothy Green was hailed by *The Times* as making the production memorable for her Cleopatra:

> The whole spirit is understood and revealed: the twisting of that variable mind is never for an instant obscured; and through it all the great verse is spoken, not with the empty boast of rhetoric but with cunning and with majesty, the meaning and the music running intertwined like the mingled currents of some deep and powerful stream.

It has not been professionally staged in London in this style since the Old Vic production, but it was followed by a similar "Paolo Veronese" production by Bridges-Adams at Stratford in 1931, and was successfully presented at the Maddermarket in Elizabethan costume, and in 1960 at the Colorado Shakespeare Festival in the University's Mary Rippon open air theatre with its spacious 35 x 55 ft. stage. Whether the public will ever take kindly to this style seems doubtful, in spite of Herbert Farjeon's insistence that "a Cleopatra who calls for her laces to be cut and does not wear laces is not merely un-Elizabethan but insane." (*The Shakespearean Scene*, p. 173)

19-22. Justice is not always done nowadays to Beerbohm Tree's genuine devotion to Shakespeare and to the way in which he kept a repertory of the plays in production from year to year, and in all produced seventeen of them at His Majesty's. He employed some of the best actors of the day, and his aim was to present the plays as magnificently as possible. To do this he cut the texts till in some instances nearly a third part of the play was lost, and the actors' opportunities thereby limited and subordinated to display. *Julius Caesar*, his first production, (see Vol. II) was one of his best: *Antony and Cleopatra* was perhaps, with

Henry VIII, the most lavish of them all, and the most typical of his methods. *The Illustrated London News* considered that in it he "eclipsed his own records of spectacular splendour." *The Sketch* objected that there was "hardly enough Shakespeare in it" and no acting of outstanding quality and envisaged Shakespeare turning in his grave at the mutilations and transpositions of the text, which involved, among other ruthless excisions, the loss of the opening scene. Tree concentrated, we are told, upon the passion of the lovers. *The Times* adopted a somewhat ironic tone, and referred to Constance Collier as "a tiger." The photographs, perhaps, do less than justice to this aspect of her performance, especially in the scene where she nearly chokes the messenger, in which she appears completely unmoved and has assumed a stance which makes her look like a lady golfer demonstrating the interlocking grip.

19. *The Telegraph* gives a most interesting account of how the problem of getting "man into monument" was solved:

> In the gloom of oncoming night the wounded hero, Mark Antony, is carried to the bottom of the walls, and above, at a window, Cleopatra is looking out, to answer the cry of her defeated lover. As the lights go out we see the body being hoisted upwards to the window; then, by a quick change, we are transported to the interior of the monument and once more see Antony being lifted inwards through the open window, and brought to the couch to receive Cleopatra's farewell. It was a clever bit of stage work, which gave a complete and satisfactory impression, without any lack of verisimilitude. (28/12/06)

23. Dorothy Green (1886-1961) acquired her Shakespearian training with the Benson company, and when the Memorial Theatre at Stratford came under the direction of Bridges-Adams in 1919, she came to her full powers in the great Shakespearean leads as "Stratford's best loved actress," playing Viola, Imogen, Desdemona, Beatrice, Rosalind, Portia, Ophelia, Hermione, Lady

Macbeth, Katharina in *The Shrew*, etc. She was undoubtedly *the* Cleopatra of her time, and in 1921 *The Times* critic wrote:

> This year's Festival will be memorable for Miss Dorothy Green's performance as Cleopatra. She realizes (as few in recent years) the infinite variety of the Queen's moods. Stately, sinuous, arrogant, seductive, pleading, passionate, Miss Green is everything in turn; but she rises to her greatest height in the scene of sheer fury wherein she learns from the messenger of Antony's marriage . . . and all but strangles him in her madness.

Her lovely voice and perfect diction, the warmth of emotion and the intelligence of her playing and her remarkable versatility were the theme of every notice. She had played it first in 1912 to Benson's Antony, and in 1921 "proved again that she was the best living Cleopatra." She "rose, as no one in Stratford memory had done, to the passionate ecstasy before death." J. C. Trewin quotes W. A. Darlington on her "majesty of style," and says, "In all her changing moods she never forgets that she is a queen, and what is more she always looks a queen." She played the part again in 1924 and 1927 at Stratford, before playing it at the Old Vic in 1930 (17 and 18).

24-27. Tree's was the first production of *Antony and Cleopatra* in London in the present century, if Benson's in 1900 is regarded as the last of the previous century. There are no photographs to record the next London production, at the Old Vic in 1925, with Wilfred Walter and Edith Evans. For information one turns to the written word, and the general inference to be gathered is that it was put on with the unrelenting economy which perforce characterized the Old Vic revivals of the 'twenties. The next production recorded by Parker was this of 1946, with Edith Evans and Godfrey Tearle. It was the boldest experiment in the new kind of staging for Shakespeare that London had seen since Gielgud's 1934 *Hamlet* and his 1935 *Romeo and Juliet*, in both of which the producer, Glen Byam Shaw, had acted and which had both been designed by Motley. The setting was a non-representational permanent structure, which did not aim at reproducing any particular architectural style but at providing the essential elements of the Elizabethan stage—main stage, upper stage, and a recess or inner stage—which could be shut off with curtains or a shutter to indicate the movement of the action from Egypt to Rome or elsewhere. The costumes represented a free treatment of the Renaissance style, with some Roman and Egyptian suggestions, bearing the same kind of relationship to 17th and 18th century theatrical practice as the setting bore to Shakespeare's stage. The recess was set to give indications of particular localities: e.g., a barred door for the monument. A few scenes were played in front of traverse curtains fixed just behind the act drop, and the action of the rapidly changing scenes was perfectly continuous. On the whole the critics and the public did not take kindly to this architectural severity nor to the costumes; but its importance was not overlooked by other producers and designers, intent upon solving this problem of a stage for Shakespeare by providing a pleasing and functional architectural background; and it may well be that this brave attempt helped its designers, Motley, as well as Loudon Sainthill, to provide in 1953 and 1957, for Stratford and the Old Vic respectively, the most beautiful and satisfactory settings which have been achieved for this play in England.

For further comments on the setting see *Introduction to the Illustrations*, Vol. II, pp. xxxii-xxxiii. For Barker's comments on the two scenes illustrated in 26 and 27 see pp. 37-41.

28-29.   In this production, staged in repertory with Shaw's *Caesar and Cleopatra*, with an adaptable setting which could be used for both plays, the problem presented by the many swiftly-changing scenes was solved by a revolving stage which was skilfully used to achieve the necessary pace and continuity throughout. The elements of the scenes were pillars, arches, steps and rostrums against a cyclorama. Plain dark Doric pillars indicated Rome, the slender Corinthian pillar stood for Egypt. The monument, surmounted by the Egyptian Sphinx which was essential for the opening scene of *Caesar and Cleopatra*, did duty for both plays. Romans and Egyptians, as Barker would have them, "stood in picturesque contrast," the former in brilliant blue cloaks, the

latter in scarlet; and "for variety and pace, for colour and vitality
the production was splendid and delightful; crowned with beauty
at the close and rewarded with popular success," as George
Rylands wrote in *Shakespeare Survey 6* (1933): It was generally
felt, as this same critic realized, that Olivier "sacrificed Antony
to Cleopatra"; and if he "did not burn the great sphere he moved
in but stood darkling, it was to lend light to the fleeting planet,
the more than moon, who drew up tears to drown us in her
sphere."

30-32. For all-round achievement there has been no other production recorded by theatre history to equal this. *The Times*
characterized Redgrave's Antony as "superb," "with the nobleness
of a first-class fighting animal suffering from the inner ravages
made by his dissoluteness, vanity and overworked charm"; and
praised Peggy Ashcroft's "rare stage Cleopatra" as never failing
in the great scenes "to set the blood stirring" and in the end to
"still the stage with its slow beauty." The magnificence of the
actual production consisted in avoiding mutilating cuts but "allowing the forty-two scenes to follow each other in rapid succession."
Richard Findlater pointed out how completely Redgrave's height,
physique and voice fitted this "triple pillar of the world," so that
"the full magnitude of that oversize power" was successfully pro-
jected to make us feel both the ruin and the nobility of the man.

> From the first decisive entrance, the *look* of him is so right—
> a careless, laughing and abandoned magnificence—and when
> he speaks, one sees his past and future. spread around him
> like his scarlet cloak. Here is a man in a life's fever of love,
> consumed with the need to touch, agonised by jealousy and
> self-reproach; a man of heroic stature and ferocious pride,
> bold, generous and great-hearted, a very world-sharer.
> (*Michael Redgrave, Actor*, 1956)

For T. C. Kemp's comment on the setting see *Introduction to
the Illustrations*, Vol. II, p. xxxiii.

33-34. "Nothing could have been better calculated to suggest
the spaciousness essential to this play than Loudon Sainthill's

impressive but simple setting, which not only gave the illusion of the very curve of this great globe and its limitless horizon, but had the great theatrical merit of converting itself instantly into a sombre and stately Roman background and of dealing equally quickly and effectively with the problem of the monument and its two levels. The seven Egyptian obelisks, sized and spaced to help the illusion of cycloramic vastness and distance, were reassembled for the monument; and with a change of lighting and the blacking-out of the whole of the rear stage, the four in front became Roman pillars. Above and alongside the right-hand proscenium entry were the emblems of Rome: to the left, royal Egypt. The photographs give a good idea of the basic simplicity of the design: what they do not show is the warm, glowing beauty of the lighting of the Egyptian scenes and the sense of space which it imparted. There were moments in the drama when the producer had placed either Antony or Cleopatra standing alone against this background which matched the very poetry for lyrical feeling." (Quoted by kind permission of the Editor from the present writer's review of the production in *Shakespeare Quarterly*: Autumn, 1957).

35-49. CORIOLANUS

Barker does not devote special sections to the staging and costuming, but his running comments, mainly prompted by the stage directions, will be found at pp. 98n., 129, 134-139, 141, 167n., 169n., 182n., 204n., 205n., 209n. They both present difficulties which he does not tackle, presumably because this was the last *Preface* he wrote and by that time felt that he had set down his views on the Renaissance-Roman costuming of the classical plays fully enough already. To escape from the Alma-Tadema classicism of the conventional *Julius Caesar* production, of which Kemble and Macready gave us a foretaste early last century in this play (35, 38, 39), designers seeking a more primitive garb turn to clumsy and uncouth garments with more than a hint of the folk-weave bedspread about them. In the most recent production (48) the swathings of Menenius and the Tribunes were so voluminous as to seem positive deterrents to normal movement. Then there is the problem of the Volsces. As Barker says, we may take it for granted that Volscians and Romans "were dressed distinctively." In this same Stratford production the Volscians were half-naked, hairy barbarians with Welsh accents, clad mainly in furry animal skins. The contrast was theatrically effective up to a point, but when they leapt or lurked or darted about the stage their resemblance to the inhabitants of the monkey-hill at the Zoo became slightly ludicrous. It became positively damaging to the author's intentions in the scene in the house of Aufidius. The servants are typical Elizabethan serving-men, such as we find in the Capulet household. Barker instinctively refers to them as "liveried servants" (p. 187), and anyone reading the text and his comments will realise how badly at odds the words and the appearance of the speakers seemed. Saucy knaves they may be, but they serve the chief warrior of the Volscians who is at the moment entertaining the "Lords of the City," the honourable enemies to whom Rome had given a "good" peace, men who are shocked at the murder of Coriolanus. Because we have seen so few examples, as yet, of the kind of costume advocated by Barker for the classical plays, it does not follow that it may not eventually prove one of the best methods. It would indeed be a notable event if Sir Laurence Olivier were to produce *Coriolanus* in this manner, with a suitably dignified yet sufficiently strong and simple a setting on the open Chichester stage.

It is certain that no "Elizabethan-stage set," upon a proscenium-arch stage, will suffice nowadays. But give it an open stage with a permanent background incorporating the Elizabethan "practicables," plus the simple and sturdy equivalents of the elegant and sophisticated decorative overlay of his basic structure that Olivier gave us for *The Broken Heart*, and one feels that, at last, something genuinely congruous to the author's intentions might be evolved for *Coriolanus*, in our time. Barker rightly insists on the importance in this play of "the idea of Rome" and the way "everything centres upon Rome" (p. 95). "It is the play's one sounding-board. The springs of the action are there." It is surely to this, and to what the present writer more than thirty years ago described as the resultant assertion and vindication of the *right* of Rome—that normal centripetal force of classical drama—that a designer might look for inspiration for his setting for "the finest classical play in the English language," and "so set it upon the stage as to reconcile its audience to its unfamiliar quality, and burn into our consciousness the full wonder of Shakespeare's intense perception of 'the power, the pride, the reach of perished Rome.' "[1]

35. Kemble, with his scholarly interest in historical costume, introduced Roman civil costume to the English theatre, after which it was used in conjunction with Roman military costume by Edmund Kean, Macready, Phelps and their successors. The garment in which he is enveloped in this painting, however, is probably not meant to be a toga but a large military cloak, as it is worn over armour. He first played Coriolanus at Drury Lane in 1789, where he staged his greatest revival of the play in 1806. He never played Shakespeare's tragedy, however, but a version arranged by himself, with borrowings from James Thomson's and Thomas Sheridan's adaptations. Though Kemble prided himself on his "correct" ideas about antique costume, Macready referred to his toga as "the cumbrous drapery in which he was enveloped"; and John Forster, the critic of *The Examiner*, was equally severe about his *mise-en-scène* for this play:

> The pictures . . . might be splendid, but they were utterly unreal—they clustered fine buildings together with equal disregard to the proprieties of place or time—the arch of Severus or Constantine, the Coliseum, the pillar of Trajan, all the grandeurs of Imperial Rome, flaunted away within three hundred years of the first birth of the city.

He admitted, however, that

> The effect of solid long lines and triumphant-looking arches is so very Roman, generally speaking, and the idea of Rome in the mind of posterity possesses so mighty and enduring a grandeur analogous to its stone and marble, that one of these Kemble misrepresentations might be almost hailed as even the just substitution of a general truth for a particular one— a moral and characteristic, if not a chronologic truth.

[1] "Classical Coriolanus." *The National Review*; March 1931 (No. 575).

Although the scene from West's theatrical prints (49) is nearly twenty years later in date, it probably gives some idea of the kind of setting used by Kemble for his 1806 production. It was in this part, generally considered his finest, that he took his farewell of the stage on 25 June 1817.

36.   Geneviève Ward was an American who began life as an opera singer but lost her singing voice through illness and overwork and became an actress, making her first appearance at Manchester in 1873 as Lady Macbeth. She had a wide range in tragic roles, and with her fine, commanding presence and strong features, was the most impressive Volumnia the theatre has seen since Mrs Siddons. She joined Irving's company at the Lyceum in 1891, but did not play frequently after 1900. She was seen at the Old Vic as Queen Margaret in *Richard III* shortly before her death, and Lady Benson in her memoirs writes that for many years she "always joined us to play Margaret in *Richard III* and Volumnia in *Coriolanus*." The year before her death she was created D.B.E. It is interesting to compare the line given by her simple flowing robes with the first tragedy queen in this volume, Tamora, in 2.

37.   It might be rash to assert that this scene from a performance of *Coriolanus* at Drury Lane is meant to represent Kemble's 1806 production, as Dr W. M. Merchant has pointed out that the grouping, poses and gestures of the women pleading with Coriolanus resemble the scene as painted by Nicholas Poussin a hundred years earlier:

> So closely is Poussin's composition followed that we must assume it to be the source of this drawing (unless we allow the still more intriguing possibility that Kemble—or his designer, Capon—used the Poussin painting as the basis for this scene). (*Shakespeare and the Artist*, Chap. 11; 1959)

The drawing, by Pugin and Rowlandson, is one of the twelve of London theatres which they drew for Ackerman's *Microcosm of London*, 1808.

38-39. In their time Macready's Shakespearian productions at Covent Garden were the most elaborate that London had yet seen. *John Bull* considered that his *Coriolanus* "stands alone in the annals of the stage," and, like all the critics and audiences, was immensely impressed by the scene of the Senate (39) in the temple of Jove, for which we are told, nearly a couple of hundred supers were used, the ranks of the senators in the perspective distance being taken by children so as to keep the figures in scale with the scenery. The triumphant return of Coriolanus after his victory at Corioli (38) is interesting for several reasons. This is, of course, the scene that was made memorable in Kemble's production by Mrs Siddons as Volumnia, and though there is no extant portrait of her in the role, it is a fair guess that Macready's Volumnia was doing her utmost, in appearance and gesture, to recall that great performance. She is wearing the chin-band favoured by Mrs Siddons in various parts, and her flowing draperies are also reminiscent. It is perhaps unwise to guess whether the artist means to depict Miss Huddart, who played the part when the play opened in March, or Mrs Warner who played it when the 1838-39 season opened with *Coriolanus* in September, when Phelps also joined the cast as Aufidius. Scharf's drawing shows the "correct" toga and tunica, as used by Macready, and a genuine attempt at correct costuming, even for women supers. It also vouches for practicable scenic units, and the Roman architecture echoes by implication Forster's censure of Kemble's mixed styles and periods and gives a very correct background.

40-41. This 1933 *Coriolanus* was the Birthday Play and was also Bridges-Adams' first opportunity in the new theatre at Stratford to show what he could do with one of the Roman plays in settings of his own design. *The Birmingham Post* (25/4/33) found them "somewhat sombre in colour" but praised the architectural quality which gave a dignified background for the action, and especially commended the way he used the resources of the new stage to best advantage. Both illustrations show clearly the effectiveness of the rising stage and the way in which his designs provided for the strong, down-stage movements he has sketched for the taking of Corioli and the triumphal entry into Rome. They remind us of the use of central entries on the Elizabethan stage, (see also 47). The producer's mind and the designer's hand went together, providing a striking contrast with the weaker, sideways movement for the triumphal entry in 48, necessitated by the structure of the set and the lack of sufficient stage depth. Mr. Alec Clunes, who saw the battering down of the gates of Corioli staged thus in an earlier production by Bridges-Adams, says that after well over thirty years he still remembers this moment as one of the most tremendous and exciting things he has ever witnessed in the theatre.

Coriolanus was played by Anew McMaster, with Stanley Lathbury as Menenius, and Laidman Browne as Aufidius. The crowd scenes were extremely effective and the pace and vigour of the production as a whole received great praise. *The Birmingham Post* noted that there was "no trickery of costume. So far as dressing was concerned it might have been produced at any time these fifty years."

42-43. Staged with the utmost simplicity, the two pillars shown in 42 were, quite literally, the set for this 1948 *Coriolanus*. John Clements had vigour and dignity and was a dominating figure, but the player and the production both suffered from the inevitable comparisons provoked by memories of Olivier's blazing performance ten years earlier.

44 and 46. This 1938 performance was generally hailed as Olivier's greatest Shakespearian achievement before the 1939 war. Agate called it the "best to date," praising among other things, "a pathos we have not before observed" and the "great tenderness" of his scene with his mother, wife and son. Laurence Kitchin writes of it as his "first grave and contained interpretation" of a heroic Shakespearian part, "though bursting with Olivier's explosive impatience":

> Where Tearle would have showed his contempt for the mob with a statuesque disdain, Olivier gave it nasty overtones of distaste. He enjoyed calling them a "common cry of curs,"

with a relish that almost brought him down to their level, and fleeting twitches of the nostrils hinted that physical revulsion had as big a part as aristocratic pride in his rejection of them. They had not washed. (*Mid-Century Drama*, 1962)

To the outstanding performances of Olivier and Sybil Thorndike Agate added Cecil Trouncer's Menenius, and wrote of the production that it

strictly denies that Rome at any time looked like the pictures of Alma-Tadema. The first act is even grubby. But there is fine lighting throughout, and when necessary a fine darkness, as that in which the red cloak of Coriolanus glows like sullen fire. Yes, this is good Shakespearian production, even if it does suggest that Rome was built in a day! (*Brief Chronicles*)

The production moved speedily, but the permanent architectural setting with its predominating dark colouring gave a somewhat cramped effect. As Audrey Williamson says,

It missed the "lift" and pictorial beauty of Iden Payne's later production at Stratford-on-Avon, where a spacious open sky, and steps up which the mob swept in massed and mobile fury, gave a surging freedom and impetus to the action. In its acting, however, the Old Vic production led all the time and Olivier's performance put him finally on the map as a Shakespearian actor of the highest eminence. (*Old Vic Drama*, 1948)

45. Although the costumes were Elizabethan, with *costume à la romaine* for the military characters, the setting for this 1939 *Coriolanus* was not Iden Payne's familiar "Elizabethan theatre" background, but a semi-permanent set by John Gower Parks (cf. Vol. II 31, 32), which provided well for continuity and swift playing. There was a permanent central arch with slender columns, and matching columns at either side of the stage. Behind them ran traverse curtains. These, or doorways, walls etc., were used to fill up the spaces between the columns when required, somewhat in the manner of Lewis Casson's Manchester setting for *Julius Caesar*

illustrated in Vol. II (37, 38 and *Notes*). Alex Clunes' performance as Coriolanus was one of the successes of the season. (See
also *Note* to 44-46)

47. Praised by *Time and Tide* as the "straight and sturdy" basic
type of production, and by Ivor Brown in *The Observer* as a
"beautifully schemed, mobile and unfussy production" with "a
fine Motley setting," this 1952 *Coriolanus* at Stratford showed
that its "Roman strength and solidity" is best served by simplicity
in the *décor*, as experience of this play in the theatre almost
invariably reaffirms. In Anthony Quayle it had a Coriolanus—
"now so rich an actor," as Ivor Brown said—who could give the
speeches so that "we *heard* the big lines and knew them for
that . . . The whole had a splendid, virile ring," (*Time and
Tide*). Kenneth Tynan wrote that he "played the part as a furious
and impatient young bull, but not a mad or treacherous one";
and of his flamboyant outburst—

> . . . like an eagle in a dovecote, I
> Flutter'd your Volscians in Corioli!
> Alone I did it—boy!

he says, "the lines rang, as someone once said of Dryden's poetry,
like a great brass coin flung down on marble." As handled by
Glen Byam Shaw the play, which Tynan regards as more of a
public meeting than a play, "turned out to be a startlingly modern
public meeting." (*Curtains*, 1961)

48. In contrast to this last, the setting for the 1959 Stratford
production, though compendiously contrived as a permanent set
to meet all scenic exigencies, was basically at odds with the play's
overriding demand for plenty of stage space for the many scenes
of violent fighting, impressive processions, and the manoeuvring
of large crowds. *The Observer* described it as "a contraption,"
blocking most of the stage with its "bodeful and semi-Incaic
splendour." T. C. Worsley called it "portentous, dull, static."
From the stalls level it seemed to overhang the action, heavy,
menacing and claustrophobic, shrinking the stage space between

its steps and rostrums and the audience into a mean, narrow strip, and dwarfing the figures of the actors. The risers of the steps appeared too high for easy, assured movement, and the fighting seemed cramped and confused; though as seen from the circle the general effect was presumably more like that shown in the photograph. The painted backcloth—a fine pictorial conception, extending right up to the flies—was all wrong theatrically, because by suggesting that it might be a very plausible and imaginative rendering of the appearance of the towering *insulae* or tenement blocks which housed the rabble of Augustan or imperial Rome, it immediately set us wondering why such an implausible housing scheme should have been offered to us for the mob of B.C. 500—thereby committing the sin against the play and its actors of distracting our attention from both.

The acceptability of siting an equivalent of the Elizabethan inner stage down left, as first suggested by Tanya Moiseiwitsch's *Henry VIII* design in 1948 (Vol. I, 8), depends upon the discretion with which it is used. Impeccably handled by Guthrie for small intimate scenes such as the King's closet, in *Coriolanus* its similar use for Volumnia's house and the Volscian tent scene was appropriate. But to use it also for the mob's first entry was insensitive and inept, because nothing whatever was thereby gained, except, perhaps, a pedantic reminder that crowds, soldiers, etc. frequently rushed on through the central entry in Shakespeare's time. But the difference between a downstage run of perhaps 29 feet (cf. Vol. I, Note 11), and one of five feet or less, turned what was presumably meant to be a wild terrifying rush into an immediate right-wheel, anticipated before it happened, thus deflating the mob-effects for the rest of the performance. Pictorially instead of dramatically imagined, the "contraption" drove home the lesson that an equivalent for the stage space of Shakespeare's theatre and a setting as unpretentious as possible, of formal, architectural simplicity, will always serve this play's purposes best.

The critics found many points of similarity in Olivier's earlier characterization of the part and this 1959 rendering. Kitchin finds in the later performance the same "unrivalled flair for projecting impatience" and notes the same "terrifying concentration of contempt" in the "cry of common curs" speech, but "less volume" than in 1938.

> The speech had an impact like jagged stones parcelled together and hurled in somebody's face. There was a bizarre impression of one man lynching a crowd. (*Mid-Century Drama*)

This finely perceptive, detailed appreciation is the best account of the performance I have read. Tynan, who rightly regarded his performance as "the heart of the production," sees his conception of the part as the professional soldier, not the aristocrat, serving the patricians but not of them.

> A cocky, jovial commander, he cannot bring himself to feign humility in order to become Consul, and his sulky refusal to apologise to the people takes on, in Olivier's hands, the aspect of high political comedy. We cannot applaud the man, but we like him, and thus the battle of the part is half-way won. What spurs him to betray Rome is not pride but a loathing of false servility. (*Curtains*)

49. This design has been reproduced from one of the eight specimens, out of the set of ten, in the possession of the London Museum.

THE HEADBAND USED ON THE TITLE PAGE
AND AT VARIOUS OTHER PLACES IN THIS BOOK
WAS TAKEN FROM THE FIRST FOLIO
OF SHAKESPEARE
PRINTED IN LONDON BY ISAAC JAGGARD
AND ED. BLOUNT, IN 1623

1 "A RENAISSANCE VIEW OF A CLASSIC SUBJECT"

"In the National Gallery hangs Paolo Veronese's 'Alexander and the wife and daughter of Darius'. This will be very much how Shakespeare saw his Roman figures habited. Antony would wear Alexander's mixture of doublet, breastplate, sandals and hose. Here too is something very like Octavia's costume; and though Cleopatra might be given some Egyptian stigmata, there would still be laces to cut. It is all grievously incorrect, but we do not like the picture the less for that."

(Antony and Cleopatra Preface, pp. 49–50)

2 "THE FIRST ILLUSTRATION TO SHAKESPEARE"

The Longleat drawing of *Titus Andronicus*, attributed to
Henry Peacham and endorsed 1595

3 "Cut my lace, Charmian"
Figures from *Civitates Orbis Terrarum:*
1572–1618

4 A Knight Masquer
by Inigo Jones, 1611

5   Three classical figures from *Civitates Orbis Terrarum*

6   The Battle of Philippi in *Julius Caesar*.   Design by Ernst Stern
for Barker's *Players' Shakespaere*, 1925

7 Thomas Sheridan as
Brutus in *Julius Caesar*.
1776

8 Elizabeth Younge as Cleopatra: 1776

9   The same, in 1786

COSTUME A LA ROMAINE
AND   CONTEMPORARY   DRESS
IN THE EIGHTEENTH CENTURY

10   Priscilla Hopkins as Volumnia: 1776

11–12 ARCHAEOLOGY TAKES OVER IN THE EARLY NINETEENTH CENTURY

Characters in *Antony and Cleopatra*, as performed at Covent Garden, 1813–14 (from two sheets published by Jameson's Theatrical Print Warehouse, 1814)

13 (*above*) Design for the Proscription Scene, by Ernst Stern; *The Players' Shakespeare*, 1925

ELIZABETHAN-ROMANISM IN MODERN DESIGN AND "MODERN DRESS" IN THE EIGHTEENTH CENTURY FOR JULIUS CAESAR

14 (*r.*) Mrs. Ward as Portia (Bell's British Library) 1786

15 HARRIET FAUCIT AS
CLEOPATRA AT COVENT
GARDEN, 1813–14
(Engraved from the painting
by De Wilde, 1814)

EARLY AND MID-NINETEENTH
CENTURY EGYPTIAN STYLES

16 (*below*) ISABELLA GLYN
AS CLEOPATRA,
SADLER'S WELLS, 1849

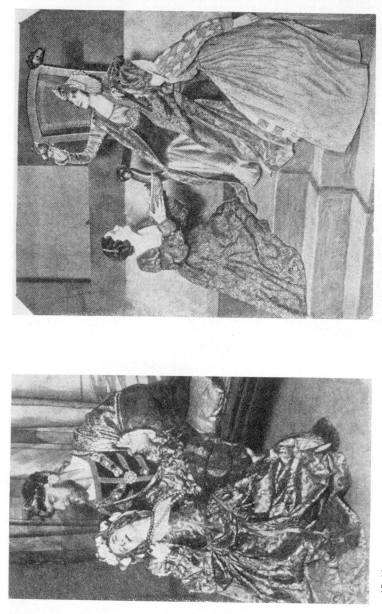

17–18 ANTONY AND CLEOPATRA AT THE OLD VIC IN 1930, STAGED IN THE RENAISSANCE MANNER SUGGESTED BY BARKER'S PREFACE WITH JOHN GIELGUD AND DOROTHY GREEN

Produced by Harcourt Williams, settings and costumes by Owen Smyth

19   ANTONY AND CLEOPATRA AT HIS MAJESTY'S: PRODUCED BY H. BEERBOHM TREE, 1906
Rome: the meeting of the Triumvirs
Enobarbus, Lyn Harding; Antony, H. B. Tree; Octavius, Basil Gill; Lepidus, Norman Forbes

20 EGYPT

BEERBOHM TREE AND CONSTANCE COLLIER AS ANTONY AND CLEOPATRA
Eros, H. C. Buckler; Charmian, Alice Crawford

20–22 TREE'S 1906 PRODUCTION AT THIS MAJESTY'S

Costumes and properties designed and scenery supervised by Percy Macquoid
scenes by Joseph Harker

21 POMPEY'S GALLEY

Enobarbus, Antony, Lepidus, Octavius, Pompey, Menas

22 THE MONUMENT
Tree's 1906 production

23 DOROTHY GREEN AS
CLEOPATRA AT STRATFORD
in the nineteen-twenties
(various seasons), under
the directorship of
W. Bridges-Adams

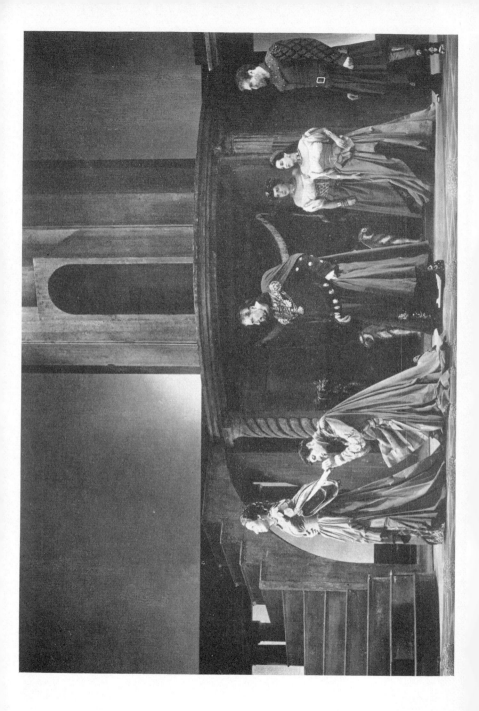

24 (*above*) Egypt: III xi Octavius Caesar's messenger kisses Cleopatra's hand
Cleopatra, Edith Evans; Thyreus; James Cairncross; Antony, Godfrey Tearle; Enobarbus, Anthony Quayle

24–27 ANTONY AND CLEOPATRA WITH EDITH EVANS AND GODFREY TEARLE, AT THE PICCADILLY, 1946
PRODUCED BY GLEN BYAM SHAW; SETTING AND COSTUMES BY MOTLEY

25 Misenum: II v
Antony (*centre*) greets
Pompey (David
Green);
(*r.*) Octavius Caesar,
Michael Goodliffe;
Lepidus, George
Howe

26 Alexandria: IV iii
(*Music of hautboys under
the stage*)
1st Soldier: What should
this mean?
2nd Sold: 'Tis the god Her-
cules whom Antony loved
Now leaves him.

27 (*r.*) Near Actium: III viii
Immediately after Antony's
decision to fight at sea
Octavius gives his orders to
his lieutenant, Taurus.
Oct. Strike not by land;
keep whole; provoke not
battle
Till we have done at sea.
Do not exceed
The prescript of this scroll:
our fortune lies
Upon this jump.
[*Exeunt.*

28   ANTONY AND CLEOPATRA AT THE ST. JAMES'S, 1951

Produced by Michael Benthall
Settings by Roger Furse, costumes by Audrey Cruddas

THE MONUMENT

ANTONY, LAURENCE OLIVIER; CLEOPATRA, VIVIEN LEIGH

29
ANTONY AND CLEOPATRA
AT THE ST. JAMES'S, 1951

Alexandria: VI iv
Antony: You that will
fight

Follow me close.

30 "HERE IS THE MOST SPACIOUS OF THE PLAYS"

ANTONY AND CLEOPATRA, PRODUCED BY GLEN BYAM SHAW; STRATFORD, 1953
Settings and costumes by Motley

ANTONY, MICHAEL REDGRAVE; CLEOPATRA, PEGGY ASHCROFT

(Transferred to Prince's Theatre, London, November 1953)

31

ANTONY AND CLEOPATRA
STRATFORD AND LONDON,
1953

Rome: the meeting of
the Triumvirs: II iii
Antony accepts Octavius
Caesar's offer of his
sister Octavia in marriage

Ant. Let me have thy
hand.
Further this act of grace,
and from this hour
The hearts of brothers
govern in our loves
And sway our great
designs

(*l.-r. centre*) Lepidus,
Donald Pleasance; Oc-
tavius, Marius Goring;
Antony, Michael Red-
grave; (*r.*) Enobarbus,
Harry Andrews

32 Alexandria: IV viii
Antony returns vic-
torious
Cleo. Lord of lords!
O infinite virtue! com'st
thou smiling from
The world's great snare
uncaught?

Antony,
Michael Redgrave;
Cleopatra,
Peggy Ashcroft

33 ANTONY AND CLEO-
PATRA AT THE OLD
VIC, 1957

PRODUCED BY ROBERT
HELPMANN. SETTINGS
AND COSTUMES BY
LOUDON SAINTHILL

Rome: the meeting
of the Triumvirs
(l.-r.) Octavius, Leon
Gluckman; Lepidus,
Derek Francis; An-
tony, Keith Michell;
Enobarbus, Derek
Godfrey

34 Egypt: the Interior of the Monument. The death of Cleopatra

(l.-r.) Dolabella. Richard Gale: Cleopatra, Margaret Whiting; Iras and Charmian, Ingrid Hafner and Rosemary Webster; Octavius Caesar, Leon Gluckman *Caes.* She looks like sleep,
As she would catch another Antony
In her strong toil of grace.

(engraved by Meadows, after the life-size
painting by Sir Thomas Lawrence)

36 GENEVIEVE WARD (1838–1922) AS VOLUMNIA

She first appeared in the part with F. R. Benson at the
Comedy in 1901, and was still playing it with him on tour
until the year before her death

37
CORIO-
LANUS
AT
DRURY
LANE,
1808

38 Coriolanus enters Rome in triumph

MACREADY'S COVENT GARDEN PRODUCTION OF CORIOLANUS, 1838
(drawings by George Scharf)

39 The Capitol: Coriolanus is made Consul by the Senate

40   The Attack on Corioli

CORIOLANUS AT STRATFORD, PRODUCED BY W. BRIDGES-ADAMS, 1933
"Inner proscenium and built sets on rolling stages; sunk forestage."

W. B.–A.

41   The Triumph of Coriolanus

42   "You common cry of curs . . . I banish you." (III iii)
The Tribunes, Mark Dignam and Peter Copley; Menenius, Alec Guinness;
Coriolanus, John Clements; Cominius, Cecil Winter

CORIOLANUS AT THE OLD VIC (NEW THEATRE) PRODUCED BY MARTIN BROWNE, 1948
Settings by Stella Mary Pearce; costumes, Kathleen Ankers

43   "O! a kiss Long as my exile, sweet as my revenge!" (V iii)
His mother, wife and son plead with Coriolanus for Rome
Volumnia, Rosalind Atkinson; Valeria, Pauline Jameson; Virgilia, Eileen Vine

45 At Stratford, 1939.
Produced by Iden Payne

Coriolanus, Alec Clunes; Volumnia, Dorothy Green;
Virgilia, Lesly Brook

CORIOLANUS

44 and 46 At the Old Vic, 1938.
Produced by Lewis Casson

Coriolanus, Laurence Olivier; Volumnia, Sybil Thorndike
46 (below) Virgilia, Vivienne Bennett

47 CORIOLANUS AT STRATFORD, 1952 PRODUCED BY GLEN BYAM SHAW. Settings and costumes by Motley

Coriolanus returns in triumph to Rome

(l.-r. up centre) Cominius, Raymond Westwell: Coriolanus, Anthony Quayle; (down l.) Valeria, Margaret Chisholm; Virgilia, Siobhan McKenna; Volumnia, Mary Ellis; (r.) Menenius, Michael Hordern

48 CORIOLANUS AT STRATFORD, 1959. PRODUCED BY PETER HALL

Setting by Boris Aronson: costumes by Riette Sturge Moore.

The triumphal return to Rome

(*l.-r.*) Virgilia, Mary Ure; Titus Lartius, Donald Eccles; the Tribunes, Peter Woodthorpe and Robert Hardy; Coriolanus, Laurence Olivier; Volumnia, Edith Evans; Menenius, Harry Andrews; (*above*) Cominius, Paul Hardwick

49 CORIOLANUS
A design for the open-
ing scene: backcloth
and wings

From a set of ten,
published by W.
West's Theatrical
Print Warehouse
in 1824